VIRGINIA WOOLF

Other Books by Bernard Blackstone

VIRGINIA WOOLF

A COMMENTARY

by

BERNARD BLACKSTONE

A Harvest Book

HBJ

HARCOURT BRACE JOVANOVICH, INC.

NEW YORK

for
BRUIN

CONTENTS

INTRODUCTION

IN the following pages I have aimed at presenting Virginia Woolf as an explorer of different worlds of experience—different, but intricately related, as they are all the creations of a human mind working upon the phenomena which veil reality. This kind of exploration was, it seems to me, her main preoccupation; and the result was her supreme contribution to the English novel. I might have described these worlds—the world of lovers, the world of marriage, the world of the intellectuals, the world of things, the world of society, the world of childhood, the world of vision—individually, assigning a single chapter of the book to each; and there was a temptation to do this, as my finished study would have been much tidier and clearer. If I had chosen this plan, I could have shown the mind of Virginia Woolf as an intellectual unity; and I should have drawn on the novels and the essays for illustrations without regard to sequence or development. In doing so, I should have avoided a great deal of repetition and discursiveness. But I should have falsified the picture and made no more than an academic study. For the repetition and discursiveness are essential to the pattern. There is nothing final and rounded-off about Virginia Woolf's vision of reality. Her interests blended into one another and the impression she produces is cumulative. It is true that there, in the early novels *The Voyage Out* and *Night and Day*, are all the seeds of her later development; but we do not know into what kind of soil—sandy, stony, dry or moist?—these seeds are to be blown, or by what winds. That is the fascination of her art: to see what possibilities come to fruition, according as the external climate is favourable or unfavourable. The Russian novel; the war; the growth of fascism; the feminist movement; friendships in London and Cambridge—these external factors affected her more perhaps than they have affected other novelists who have drawn primarily on active personal experiences. She was forced back by ill-health on the inner world, and on an activity of thought concentrated on reported experience. She was led to give great stress to books, to music and to art. Restricted along the lines of direct action, her interest delved all the deeper

9

into the subtle world where the springs of action lie, and into the life of things which stand still to be gazed at and enjoyed. Thus she attained understanding.

This remoteness from the life of action had its obvious effect on her writing. Her novels are not novels of action, or even of character in the ordinary sense. They are evocations of moods: of experiences which, though fleeting, have about them an eternal quality and seem to point to a meaning underlying them all. This underlying meaning is never made plain; Virginia Woolf tells us honestly that she never grasped it herself; yet what but it gives her work its extraordinary quality of unity? She achieves the impressive feat of building up a structure of incident and perceptions on a foundation which is invisible even to herself. It is a great act of faith. It is also an act of courage, that quality which certainly appealed to Virginia Woolf as much as any. Without attempting to construct a 'philosophy of life', not accepting the religious view, she yet weaves her frail dew-spangled web across the void. And in doing so she gives us, her readers, new glimpses into life—and death. For life and death form the inexhaustible counterpoint of her work. Not death coming as the ending to a completed story, but death inexplicable, torturing, making life meaningless; yet also mysterious, fascinating, giving depth to life. From these two strands —a feeling for the richness and beauty of life, and a patient recognition of the sovereignty and cruelty of death—her supreme themes are woven.

Her characters, I have said, are not characters—as the ordinary novel gives them to us. Like her incidents and her intuitions, they are unfinished, spreading as the ripples of a lake spread in the sunlight. For personality is like that, she thought. Mrs Ramsay, Mrs Dalloway, Jacob Flanders: they live tenaciously in our memories, they are as real as (I should say, myself, realler than) Emma or Mrs Proudie or David Copperfield: but we don't grasp them. Their creator hasn't drawn a neat line round them. The life with which they live in our consciousness is an organic life, spreading and growing, and merging indeed with our own perceptions until the moments come when we find, to our surprise, that in this instant and that we have been looking at the world through their eyes and not our own. They have become part of us. And this is because Virginia Woolf has left them with the power for growth, with potentialities which they have not completely realised in the limited world of the novel.

We are accustomed to this happening with 'abstract' ideas. Virginia Woolf's *dramatis personae* too are ideas, but not abstract. And because they are not abstract, they live all the more vividly. They are not single ideas, but organisations of intuitions, sensations, and emotions, projected into a semi-dramatic medium; and at the same time they are real human beings. In the novel, that is, we apprehend them as living persons. There is no philosophy jutting out of the frame. But in retrospect we apprehend them as persons plus an aura of consciousness in which we ourselves find it possible to participate. We share the lives, the points of view, the intuitions of these men and women and children: we look with their eyes, and feel with their emotions. In this way (and I have described it clumsily enough) Virginia Woolf produces in her readers an astonishing extension of sensibility. We are given some new windows into reality. We are treated to new sensations, new perceptions of truth. We are, in fact, educated into heightened and broadened perception. And thus, miraculously, we are freed from certain of our limitations.

The counterpoint of life and death lends itself in Virginia Woolf's novels to a number of patterns which embrace most of the basic interests of human life. She sees these patterns as involving the solitary mind, the mind in contact with things, or with another person (love and friendship), with predisposed patterns of ideas (religion, art and philosophy), or with predisposed arrangements of other individuals (the family, the social group, the nation). The relations of these patterns one with another evoke problems and conflicts, from which new patterns arise, and sometimes glimpses, very fleeting, of a vast underlying pattern in which they are all resolved. In this book I have considered her work on these patterns under the three divisions, Love and Freedom, Marriage and Truth, The World and Reality, which have suggested themselves as I have been reading through the novels. There is nothing rigid about them. In the two early novels, it is the dilemma of reconciling a free spirit's desire for independence with the longing for love and sympathy which is uppermost. In the novels of the middle period, Virginia Woolf presents us with situations in which various kinds of truth are examined in their relation to the compromises of married life. In the later books we see the vision of reality obscured by the claims of society and by the subterfuges which living in society entails. But the differences between the three periods are rather of emphasis. Freedom is the first necessity for the growing spirit; the early novels are about young people who are struggling for independence and need to think out their own attitudes to life. Truth is the second necessity: absolute honesty of purpose; *Mrs Dalloway* and *To the Lighthouse* are concerned with middle-aged people who in their various ways are experiencing the tension between family life and clear-sightedness. Freedom and truth, however, are simply the preconditions for the greatest gift of all: the vision of reality. This vision is never attained in its entirety; and in *The Waves*, *The Years* and *Between the Acts* we are shown elderly people, or people who grow up to be elderly during the course of the novel, wistfully realising that through some early taint, some injustice of society, some spirit of hatred, their vision has been clouded.

The wider implications of these three ideas, Freedom, Truth, Reality, as they appear in the novels, I have discussed at some length and with some repetitions, because without repetitions I should have been unable to present the peculiar spiral curve of Virginia Woolf's treatment of these themes. Thus, running through all the novels, but changing its slant in relation to whatever other two factors are being counterpointed at the moment, is her essential *sensationalism*: her belief that through a direct, immediate apprehension of the thing-in-itself we get our closest glimpses of reality. This sensationalism, this entranced attention to the forms, shapes, colours, feel, and scents of *things*, is for Virginia Woolf the one certain good in life. Sensation never lies. It provides a perfect pleasure, unsullied by thought, or emotion, unhindered by society, or religion: free to the solitary contemplative soul. Thus there is not one of the novels in which we do not find this binding thread of the spiral, related to the great opposites, or seeming opposites, of love and freedom, solitude and society, appearance and reality. These opposites I have also discussed at length, for it seemed to me that discussion of them rose naturally from the situations of Virginia Woolf's novels.

I
LOVE AND FREEDOM

CHAPTER I

The Voyage Out

[1915]

NINETEEN-FIFTEEN, when Virginia Woolf's first novel was published, was the second year of the war and marked a slump in English fiction. H. G. Wells had written his best books, and there is nothing between *The Wife of Sir Isaac Harman* (1914) and *Mr. Britling Sees It Through* (1916). Galsworthy's *The Dark Flower* had appeared as long ago as 1913, and his readers had to wait until 1918 for *Five Tales*. *The Forsyte Saga* did not make its appearance until 1922. Arnold Bennett had written nothing since *The Matador of the Five Towns* (1912) and his next novel, *The Pretty Lady*, appeared only in 1918. These, the Big Three of English respectable fiction, were either just nearing the peak of their achievement or just declining from it. A new star, however, is appearing on the horizon in this same year, with Somerset Maugham's *Of Human Bondage*.

Three new writers of a different order are also making their débuts around this time. James Joyce published *Dubliners* in 1914, and in 1916 *A Portrait of the Artist as a Young Man* was to appear. D. H. Lawrence had published his first four novels between 1911 and 1914; his fifth, *The Rainbow*, appeared in 1915 but was banned, and the next, *Women in Love*, was not to be published till 1919. Dorothy Richardson, the third of these new writers, brought out her first novel, *Pointed Roofs*, in this same year 1915. A fourth novelist, Mr E. M. Forster, had already given us some characteristic works.

The last four writers I have mentioned are important, and more interesting to us than the first four, because they were trying to do something different. Wells, Galsworthy, Bennett, Maugham, are all carrying on the settled tradition of the novel, which descends from Fielding and Smollett through Dickens, Trollope and Thackeray. They are very much concerned with plot, with telling a good story; and they want to create characters that will appear to be alive without being eccentric or out of the way. They don't want to upset or puzzle their

15

readers. And so they are unadventurous. Virginia Woolf herself criticises these writers because she thinks they are scratching at the surface of life, exploiting conventional situations and stock emotions. Their view of life is a commonplace one. Now this charge cannot be brought against the other writers I have mentioned. Lawrence was unconventional enough for his novels to be banned; and he has a philosophy of his own—too much of one, perhaps, for it is not fully absorbed into the stuff of fiction. Joyce also has a new scenario: life in an Irish city, and the problems of the creative mind therein. Forster had long ago shown his delicacy and originality of mind, his contempt for shams, his approval of the life of rightly adjusted personal relationships. But of the four Dorothy Richardson was the only one who had so far tackled the problem which we shall see occupying Virginia Woolf: the problem of a new mode of expression adequate to a new mode of experience.

The problem of expression is not a big issue in *The Voyage Out*. A writer has to convince himself that he has something new to say before he works out a means of saying it. In its technique Virginia Woolf's first novel is not startling. But it is a beginning. It is the first of her many attempts to explore different worlds of value; and she begins with the most conventional of all worlds of value for the novelist, the world of love. Look, she seems to say: so many novels have been written from the standpoint that love between a man and a woman is the most important thing in life, absorbing every moment, blotting out every other interest. I am not quite sure they are right, but I am going to start from that point of view; I am going to give you a young woman drawn as faithfully as I can, and a young man like the young men I know; we will bring them together, and see what happens. But in order that the balance of forces shall not be too much upset, I am going to put in another world, the world of the mind, and we shall see how it gets on with the world of the heart. And, running through it all, I shall show you the world of things like a scarlet thread, beautiful, strange, and self-sufficient.

There is a unity in Virginia Woolf's work that makes it possible for us to map it out and to travel backwards and forwards, sideways and crosswise about it, observing and tracing the course of ideas as an explorer may trace the course and confluence of rivers. Her main interests—the problems of freedom and love, of intellectual truth and intuitive grasp of reality, of family life and inner solitude—are treated strictly through the novelist's technique in characters and situations. We are spared the crude author's comments so dear to Hardy and Wells. Her results in the early novels are inevitably simpler and less assured than in the later; and it is interesting to look back from the great characters of the later books—Mrs Dalloway, Mrs Ramsay, Bart Oliver—to their prototypes in *The Voyage Out*: Mr and Mrs Ambrose, Rachel Vinrace, Mr Pepper, and note the process of development. These first novels, too, have a freshness and charm all their own; after *Orlando*, the music takes on a sombre intensity, and we are conscious, sometimes, that *saeva indignatio* is lacerating the heart and troubling the purity of motives and technique.

What kind of a novel is *The Voyage Out* to be? Perhaps some of Terence Hewlet's remarks about the novel, the conventional novel and his own attempt at originality, may be taken as representing Mrs Woolf's ideas. Writers usually put a good deal of themselves into their first books. Hewlet is telling Rachel about the novel he is writing: a novel about Silence: 'the things people don't say'. Nobody cares for such a subject, he says.

> Nobody cares. All you read a novel for is to see what sort of a person the writer is, and, if you know him, which of his friends he's put in. As for the novel itself, the whole conception, the way one's seen the thing, felt about it, made it stand in relation to other things, not one in a million cares for that. And yet I sometimes wonder whether there's anything else in the whole world worth doing.

Yes, that is precisely what we feel about Virginia Woolf's work. It is full of intense interest and excitement, not only about the characters and incidents, but about the way of seeing and feeling those characters and incidents; and that is why I am inclined to call her a *philosophical* writer, for what is this interest but the old metaphysical concern with the *how* of knowing, which has to be resolved before the forward step can be taken to *what* is known? And then there is the relation of one thing to other things, the power of seeing that relation, the ability to connect. From this comes insight. "What I want to do in writing novels", says Terence a little later, "is very much what you want to do when you play the piano, I expect. We want to find out what's behind things, don't we? Look at the lights down there, scattered

about anyhow. Things I feel come to me like lights . . . I want
to combine them . . . Have you ever seen fireworks that make
figures? . . . I want to make figures."

Figures—ciphers—deciphering: we see what Mrs Woolf is
getting at. The novel is no longer to be just an entertainment,
or propaganda, or the vehicle for some *idée fixe*, or a social
document: it is to be a voyage of discovery. By looking closely
at things, and at men and women, by making all sorts of combinations, but never falsifying one's vision (and by drawing
back immediately there is the slightest possibility of falsification)
one may construct a new road into the world of truth. The
philosophers have erred, perhaps, by over-abstraction; the
writers of fiction by over-particularisation; now let us, the new
writers, try to see and to show the eternal in the particular.

The technique would be clinical were it not for Virginia
Woolf's intense human sympathy. *Fiat experimentum in anima
nobili*. Rachel Vinrace, a girl of twenty-four who is much
younger than her years, is making the voyage out: out from the
security of her aunts' home in Richmond to all sorts of new
experiences. She is immature, but she is honest and eager. Her
immaturity is subjected to a series of shocks. On the voyage—a
real voyage on her father's steamer to South America—she
meets the fashionable, conventional world in Richard and
Clarissa Dalloway; Richard kisses her; she has sex explained to
her by her aunt, Helen Ambrose; she meets the world of
masculine thinking and arrogance in the shape of a Cambridge
don, St John Hirst; she falls in love with a young man, Terence
Hewlet; she prepares for marriage; she catches a tropical fever,
and dies. That is the bare outline of the plot. But round that
central strand many a pattern of thought and emotion is woven:
we are invited to note the relations of things.

ii

The Voyage Out has a real plot with a wealth of incidents and
characters. The scene moves from London to the steamer
Euphrosyne, then to the Villa San Gervasio in Santa Marina,
a South American seaboard town. The picture of London, with
fine rain falling along the Embankment, is a momentary one;
Ridley Ambrose and his wife are about to embark for a trip to

South America. We see them go on board the *Euphrosyne*, which is captained by Willoughby Vinrace, Helen's brother-in-law. There they meet his daughter Rachel, and Mr Pepper, a somewhat dusty old scholar.

Virginia Woolf cannot think in terms of crowds, as Fielding and Dickens can; living, for her, is a matter either of solitude or of personal relationships within small homogeneous groups. She likes to isolate her characters: on a ship, as an English colony in a South American hotel, on an island, in the self-contained world of childhood. Cambridge is attractive for her because it is a small but perfectly self-sufficient world. Her peculiarly concentrated way of presenting her *dramatis personae* requires a frame: and here Ridley and Helen Ambrose, Rachel, Mr Pepper, Willoughby Vinrace, are seen in the frame of a life at sea. Mr and Mrs Ambrose form Virginia Woolf's first sketch, one might say, of the Ramsays in *To the Lighthouse*. Like Ramsay, Ridley Ambrose is a scholar, an eccentric given to reciting poetry aloud, jealous of his fame. We don't see much of him in the course of the story because he is always shut up in his study, writing. Helen Ambrose is younger than Mrs Ramsay; she is only forty, but she also is beautiful, kind, and fond of her children; she hates to leave them behind. Like Mrs Ramsay, again, she is anti-religious.

William Pepper gets on well with Ridley; they can talk about the old days at Cambridge, discussing Jenkinson of Peterhouse, whose introduction to Jellaby still holds its own, and Jenkinson of Cats who never published his book because he was too busy putting Norman arches on his pigsties. Pepper is a little dried-up man, a scholar like Ridley, faddy about draughts and food, intensely egocentric.

> He had not married himself for the sufficient reason that he had never met a woman who commanded his respect . . . his ideal was a woman who could read Greek, if not Persian, was irreproachably fair in the face, and able to understand the small things he let fall while undressing. As it was he had contracted habits of which he was not in the least ashamed. Certain odd minutes every day went to learning things by heart; he never took a ticket without noting the number; he devoted January to Petronius, February to Catullus, March to the Etruscan vases perhaps . . .

A clever and humorous portrait of an old bachelor, suggesting a fusion of William Bankes and Augustus Carmichael in *To the*

Lighthouse; the wit is delightful, and we expect Mr Pepper to play an important rôle in the story. To our surprise, however, he vanishes from the stage: Virginia Woolf found she could not use him after all, and lets him go. It is one of the signs of immaturity in the book.

Rachel Vinrace herself is of course the central figure. She is quite an ordinary young woman, not beautiful, not well-read; bashful and *gauche*. She loves music, and spends most of her time playing the piano extremely well. She has the great quality of honesty. She says what she thinks, and she wants to find out the truth about the things that interest her. Terence Hewlet, much later in the story, finds that 'the great gift she had was that she understood what was said to her; there had never been anyone like her for talking to. You could say any-thing—you could say everything, and yet she was never servile.' But this, one must add, is a result of development, almost of forcing: I don't think this could have been said about Rachel at the beginning of the novel. She changes and grows very much. And the whole point of the story is to show Rachel subjected to various experiences.

The first experience is simply this of 'the voyage out'. The mere fact of being on a boat, of sailing out into the unknown, operates a subtle change. The process of discovery has begun. From time to time Virginia Woolf recalls our attention from the steamer and its inhabitants to the land which we have left: we see it under a new aspect, in strange proportions. There is the exhilaration of freedom.

> All the smoke and the houses had disappeared, and the ship was out in a wide space of sea very fresh and clear though pale in the early light. They had left London sitting on its mud. A very thin line of shadow tapered on the horizon, scarcely thick enough to stand the burden of Paris, which nevertheless rested upon it. They were free of roads, free of mankind, and the same exhilara-tion at their freedom ran through all.

This shifting of values and change of proportion is a device that Virginia Woolf praises in the writers she likes—Sterne, Defoe, the Russians—and employs constantly in her own work. She will take her characters up a mountain, and show them the vastness of the earth, or set them on the sea, and show them the insignificance of the land, or set them under the sea, and show them another world altogether; in their moments of greatest anguish or ecstasy, she will direct her readers' attention away from them and show how, surrounding all human passion, the quiet indifferent seasons continue and the wind blows a little dust about the floor.

In the exploration of reality that is to be Virginia Woolf's work as a novelist the first thing is to get the proportions right; we mustn't see human beings as more prominent than they really are in the scheme of things. Surrounding the human synthesis we have this great mystery of nature. Perhaps it is a chaos, perhaps it will reveal a pattern. We don't know. And the danger is this: that pattern-making, 'one-making' as she calls it in her last novel *Between the Acts*, is so inveterate a habit of the human mind that it makes clear vision very difficult. We want to see a pattern, and the pattern obediently appears. Lily Briscoe in *To the Lighthouse* painting her picture; Mrs Ambrose, here, at her embroidery frame: both illustrate this tendency. Mrs Woolf leaves us in no doubt of the significance of Mrs Ambrose's embroidery: she shows us the metaphysics being woven into the very stuff of the pattern.

> She had her embroidery frame set up on deck, with a little table by her side on which lay open a black volume of philosophy. She chose a thread from the varicoloured tangle that lay in her lap, and sewed red into the bark of a tree, or yellow into a river torrent. She was working at a great design of a tropical river running through a tropical forest, where spotted deer would eventually browse upon masses of fruit, bananas, oranges, and giant pomegranates, while a troop of naked natives whirled darts into the air. Between the stitches she looked to one side and read a sentence about the Reality of Matter, or the Nature of Good. Round her men in blue jerseys knelt and scrubbed the boards, or leant over the rails and whistled, and not far off Mr. Pepper sat cutting up roots with a penknife.

There is an entire adequacy about Mrs Woolf's technique here. That black volume of philosophy—it appears again in a key moment of *The Years*—is being incorporated in the web; all unknowing, Mrs Ambrose is anticipating the future happenings at Santa Marina. She is weaving the tropical river up which, on a happy excursion, Rachel is to catch her fever; she is weaving the deer they are to see ("so like an English park!"); she is weaving the anguish of futility, the problem of good and evil and pain and death. And thus, by a sudden shifting of the proportions, the figure of Mrs Ambrose looms gigantic. She is a

Fate, with the threads of life and death in her hands. The frame of the novel has been momentarily broken, and becomes an image of human destiny.

iii

When the *Euphrosyne* drops anchor in the mouth of the Tagus, and Mr and Mrs Dalloway come aboard, the curtain rises on a new act. In its episodic structure *The Voyage Out* differs from the rest of the novels. In *Jacob's Room*, indeed, Jacob is shown passing through a series of different environments and experiences. But these scenes and incidents serve only to illustrate in more ample detail aspects of the hero's personality that we have already noted in the small boy playing on the beach. The other novels are not episodic at all. 'Time stand still here' is the keynote of *To the Lighthouse*, 'Memory hither come' is the motto of *Mrs Dalloway*; Katherine and Ralph in *Night and Day* move from London to Lincolnshire and back but remain the same persons; and so on. But *The Voyage Out* is episodic in a real sense; it shows a series of shocks profoundly modifying the personality of a young woman. The Dalloways represent the impact of the fashionable world. They manage to get aboard the *Euphrosyne* as passengers because they are important people, can pull the right strings; Mr Dalloway is a Member of Parliament, his wife the daughter of a peer. They are slick and conventional, holding all the right opinions about life and art and literature; conventionally kind, conventionally charming; intensely critical of those who do not belong to their world, and especially of the eccentric intellectual.

It is hard to connect the picture of these two in *The Voyage Out* with the much firmer, rounder, and richer picture we get in *Mrs Dalloway*. But if we do compare the two pictures we have an excellent measuring-rod by which we can gauge the progress of Mrs Woolf's art, and her widening sympathy. The Dalloways in this first novel are not very pleasant people. They are narrow, intolerant under their mask of bonhomie; contemptuous of suffragettes, of scholars, of artists; immensely pleased with themselves and the Imperial destinies for which they believe they stand. The man is more agreeable than his wife. He is not very intelligent, and his self-control is of the slightest; but he is genuinely concerned for the welfare of the downtrodden classes, he is simpler and more honest than Clarissa. In *Mrs Dalloway* there is a great advance. Virginia Woolf has not changed her point of view, the life of the mind still seems to her preferable to the life of society and politics; but she can present Richard Dalloway as someone lovable; his Imperialism has sunk out of view, his labours for the poor have come to the fore. And Clarissa Dalloway has improved out of all recognition.

The Dalloways talk about the artist and his position in society; a problem which was very much in Virginia Woolf's mind at this time, for it is the period of suffragette revolt, and a writer of her preoccupations cannot stand above the battle. The question was, of course, how the cause of justice could best be served: by walking in processions and addressing meetings, or by exercising the peculiar gift of the artist, and writing about a world in which this problem can be seen among a number of others, forming a pattern. Virginia Woolf decided, fortunately, for the second alternative. It is not a retreat. And Richard Dalloway's presentation of the artist's attitude is a caricature, though it convinces the impressionable Rachel.

> We politicians doubtless seem to you a gross commonplace set of people; but we see both sides; we may be clumsy, but we do our best to get a grasp of things. Now your artists *find* things in a mess, shrug their shoulders, turn aside to their visions—which I grant may be very beautiful—and *leave* things in a mess. Now that seems to me evading one's responsibilities.

When Dalloway kisses Rachel it is completely unexpected; she hardly realises what has happened and does not understand at all the nature of her own emotions. She is upset for a long time after. But let us see what Mrs Woolf makes of the immediate moment. This is the first of the series of crises that Rachel has to undergo.

> "You tempt me," he said. The tone of his voice was terrifying. He seemed choked in fight. They were both trembling. Rachel stood up and went. Her head was cold, her knees shaking, and the physical pain of the emotion was so great that she could only keep herself moving above the great leaps of her heart. She leant upon the rail of the ship, and gradually ceased to feel, for a chill of body and mind crept over her. Far out between the waves little black and white sea-birds were riding. Rising and falling with smooth and graceful movements in the hollows of the waves they seemed singularly detached and unconcerned.

"You're peaceful," she said. She became peaceful too, at the same time possessed with a strange exultation. Life seemed to hold infinite possibilities she had never guessed at. She leant upon the rail and looked at the troubled grey waters, where the sunlight was fitfully scattered upon the crests of the waves, until she was cold and absolutely calm again. Nevertheless something wonderful had happened.

Thus we have thesis and antithesis: human passion and turmoil, and the detachment from passion. There is a standing-aside, a removal to another plane. Two worlds, equally significant; but do they combine? That is the basic question for Virginia Woolf, and it can never really find an answer.

The consequences of Richard Dalloway's action do not stay there; nor do they simply fulfil themselves in the remote future. That night, Rachel has a dream, a very significant dream.

She dreamt that she was walking down a long tunnel, which grew so narrow by degrees that she could touch the damp bricks on either side. At length the tunnel opened and became a vault: she found herself trapped in it, bricks meeting her wherever she turned, alone with a little deformed man who squatted on the floor gibbering, with long nails. His face was pitted and like the face of an animal. The wall behind him oozed with damp, which collected into drops and slid down. Still and cold as death she lay, not daring to move, until she broke the agony by tossing herself across the bed, and woke crying "Oh!"

Light showed her the familiar things: her clothes, fallen off the chair; the water jug gleaming white . . .

Rachel has the same nightmare again, at the end of the story, in her fever. It is the dark obverse of her longing for freedom; it is the image of imprisonment and frustration to which life will deliver her. And right at the end of Virginia Woolf's writings, in *The Years*, the same images are used for the same effect. Little Rose Pargiter dreams of the dreadful face: Sara Pargiter reads in the *Antigone* of the girl who was shut up in a brick vault.

iv

The Voyage Out is remarkable among Virginia Woolf's novels for its lack of those 'spots of time' which illuminate the other books, from *Night and Day* to *The Waves*. Moments of ecstasy there are, but they exist on the emotional plane, and embody the happiness of the ego. In the real moments of vision the personality is dropped altogether. It may be that these moments cannot occur for Rachel because she is not yet a person: she is becoming one. The personality can only be dropped when there is a personality. Rachel is in a chrysalis stage. A child can be a complete personality, a man can be a complete personality; but there is a stage in between, as Keats saw, where the 'imagination' is not 'healthy', or where the self is not whole. Hence the anguish and the struggles of adolescence, the quest for wholeness. Now this personality has to grow slowly and in conformity with its own laws; and what we are seeing in *The Voyage Out* is a not entirely natural growth of Rachel's personality. She is being forced, like a plant in a hot-house; forced by the insistence of time, by the special circumstances, first of the ship and then of the little English community at Santa Marina.

Willoughby Vinrace continues his voyage (he is going up the Amazon), Rachel stays with the Ambroses at the Villa San Gervasio; Mr Pepper decides to live in the hotel close by, for quiet. In the hotel we find a number of English people: the kind of specialised group Virginia Woolf loves to deal with. There are Hughling Elliot, an Oxford don, and his wife; Miss Allen, a spinster, who is writing a short history of English literature; Susan Warrington, a young woman on the look-out for a husband; Arthur Venning, a not very intelligent young man who falls in love with Susan; Terence Hewlet, a would-be novelist, and his friend St John Hirst.

St John Hirst is an E. M. Forster character. He reminds us irresistibly of Ansell in *The Longest Journey*. He is a fellow of King's, physically ugly, with an excellent brain (he considers himself one of the three most distinguished men in England), ill-mannered, yet craving affection. Like Dalloway, he is rather too simply drawn: his arrogance is too childish to be convincing. He is a misogynist, but finds in Helen Ambrose an intelligent woman and a good listener. With all his faults he is honest and his ideal is truth; and for this Virginia Woolf likes him, and puts her liking into the mouth of Terence Hewlet:

> Dwelling upon his [Hirst's] good qualities he became seriously convinced of them; he had a mind like a torpedo, he declared, aimed at falsehood. Where should we all be without him and his like? Choked in weeds; Christians, bigots—why, Rachel herself

would be a slave with a fan to sing songs to men when they felt drowsy.

"But you'll never see it!" he exclaimed; "because with all your virtues you don't, and you never will, care with every fibre of your being for the pursuit of truth! You've no respect for facts, Rachel; you're essentially feminine."

Hewlet is not right, of course; we know that Rachel has the desire for truth; the point about women which Virginia Woolf's novels emphasise is not that they despise truth but that they see something beyond truth, which we may call reality; and they see other roads of approach to this reality than the path of verbal logic. If verbal logic (which is what men generally mean by 'truth') gets in the way of kindness, or vision, it has to be given up; the human values are worth more than the merely intellectual. In the collocation of Rachel and St John Hirst we see the beginning of that antithesis which is to have so big a rôle in Mrs Woolf's novels: Clarissa Dalloway and Peter Walsh, Mr and Mrs Ramsay, Katherine Hilbery and Ralph Denham: the antithesis of intuition and reason, to put it in its simplest and crudest form. In *The Voyage Out* we have a plethora of intellect, four scholars, Ambrose, Pepper, Hirst and Elliot, set against two intuitives, Rachel and Helen. Intuition has not much of a chance.

Hirst and Hewlet are first shown talking in Hirst's bedroom at one o'clock in the morning. Hirst has been reading Gibbon, but is interrupted by his friend, who has something to discuss. It is the first of those scenes of intellectual young men talking, usually in Cambridge rooms and in London, which Virginia Woolf likes to give us. The conversation ranges over the characters of women, the cliques of English people in the hotel, the essential separateness of the self from all other selves, the beauty of the landscape, and the organisation of an expedition. Then Hewlet goes, and soon Hirst is fast asleep. And now Mrs Woolf uses her favourite device of showing the natural scene without the distraction of human presences, a device which is to be the groundwork of the technique of *The Waves*.

> Red and yellow omnibuses were crowding each other in Piccadilly; sumptuous women were rocking at a standstill; but here in the darkness an owl flitted from tree to tree, and when the breeze lifted the branches the moon flashed as if it were a torch. Until all people should awake again the houseless animals were

abroad, the tigers and the stags, and the elephants coming down in the darkness to drink at pools. The wind at night blowing over the hills and woods was purer and fresher than the wind by day, and the earth, robbed of detail, more mysterious than the earth coloured and divided by roads and fields. For six hours this profound beauty existed, and then as the east grew whiter and whiter the ground swam to the surface, the roads were revealed, the smoke rose and the people stirred, and the sun shone upon the windows of the hotel at Santa Marina until they were uncurtained, and the gong blaring all through the house gave notice of breakfast.

Rachel, at the villa, has been granted by Mrs Ambrose's wisdom a room of her own: 'a room cut off from the rest of the house, large, private—a room in which she could play, read, think, defy the world, a fortress as well as a sanctuary'. And there, music momentarily deserted, Rachel thinks about truth. 'What I want to know is this: What is the truth? What's the truth of it all?' She is overcome by the queerness of the world, the fact of things existing, of herself being there. 'And life, what was that? It was a light passing over the surface and vanishing, as in time she would vanish, though the furniture in the room would remain.' Rachel, we perceive, is not quite an ordinary young woman; she asks the ultimate questions. And indeed Virginia Woolf does not write about ordinary people; her characters have to be intelligent, and if they are odd and eccentric too, so much the better.

Upon her meditations there bursts the outside world in the shape of a letter from Terence Hewlet. Will Mrs Ambrose and Miss Vinrace join the hotel party for the picnic next Friday, and make the ascent of Monte Rosa? They decide to go, and on the expedition a number of things happen. Rachel and Terence get to know each other; Susan Warrington and Arthur Venning wander off by themselves, discover they are in love, and get engaged. Rachel's second shock of sex-experience comes when she, in Hewlet's company, finds the lovers embracing.

"Here's shade," began Hewlet, when Rachel suddenly stopped dead. They saw a man and woman lying on the ground beneath them, rolling slightly this way and that as the embrace tightened and slackened. The man then sat upright and the woman, who now appeared to be Susan Warrington, lay back upon the ground, with her eyes shut and an absorbed look upon her face, as though she were not altogether conscious. Nor could you tell from her expression whether she was happy, or had suffered something. When Arthur again turned to her, butting her as a lamb butts a ewe, Hewlet and Rachel retreated without a word. Hewlet felt uncomfortably shy.

"I don't like that," said Rachel after a moment.

Thus love, which had first turned on Rachel its frightening aspect, now is made to look ridiculous and sub-human. Mrs Woolf is turning the concept over and over, displaying now one facet, now another.

The days pass, there is a dance at the hotel, Rachel and Terence come to know each other better, and are insensibly falling in love. The world assumes a different aspect for Rachel; and this transformation is linked up, as so often in Mrs Woolf's writings, with trees. 'Life is full of trees and changing leaves' is the refrain of *To the Lighthouse*; here, in *The Voyage Out*, Rachel goes for a walk and sees a tree which appears so strange to her that 'it might have been the only tree in the world'. Not that it is at all remarkable in itself—simply, for a moment, it becomes the image of some half-sensed reality. She reads some sentences of Gibbon (as Mr Hirst has recommended) and the formal eighteenth-century periods take on a vivid beauty. Then the breeze blows and closes the leaves of the book.

"What is it to be in love?" she demanded, after a long silence; each word as it came into being seemed to shove itself out into an unknown sea. Hypnotised by the wings of the butterfly, and awed by the discovery of a terrible possibility in life, she sat for some time longer.

The terrible possibility is that of being bound to another person by emotional and physical ties. What Rachel has enjoyed in life up to now is the sensation, the blissful sensation of solitude, of being herself by herself. She explains to Hewlet.

"I like walking in Richmond Park singing to myself and knowing it doesn't matter a damn to anybody. I like seeing things go on—as we saw you that night when you didn't see us—I love the freedom of it—it's like being the wind or the sea." She turned with a curious fling of her hands and looked at the sea.

It's like being the wind or the sea! That freedom, that impersonality, is we find the breath of life to all Virginia Woolf's most deeply realised characters. To lose oneself in things, to *be* things, to slough off the ego: that is the secret. And how can marriage be reconciled with that? Rachel and Terence go on to discuss, tentatively, the whole problem of communication between human beings; they discover that they like each other more and more, but don't feel any nearer to each other. When they are separated for a time, they miss each other; but Rachel does not realise this is being in love.

Terence has a better idea of the situation but he is not happy about it. He doesn't want to marry. He wants to work at his own ideas, on his own. When he thinks about marriage certain very unpleasant pictures come into his mind: two people sitting over a fire, two people together with a friend, two people with their children around them.

> He tried all sorts of pictures, taking them from the lives of friends of his, for he knew many different married couples; but he saw them always, walled up in a warm firelit room. When, on the other hand, he began to think of unmarried people, he saw them active in an unlimited world; above all, standing on the same ground as the rest, without shelter or advantage. All the most individual and humane of his friends were bachelors and spinsters; indeed he was surprised to find that the women he most admired and knew best were unmarried women. Marriage seemed to be worse for them than it was for men.

This is Terence's feeling, before he is engaged to Rachel; but after the engagement it is the same, and Rachel agrees with him.

> "Perhaps I ask too much," he went on. "Perhaps it isn't really possible to have what I want. Men and women are too different. You can't understand—you don't understand——"
> He came up to where she stood looking at him in silence.
> It seemed to her now that what he was saying was perfectly true, and that she wanted many more things than the love of one human being—the sea, the sky. She turned again and looked at the distant blue, which was so smooth and serene where the sky met the sea; she could not possibly want only one human being.

Terence's difficulty is that women are so different from men; he wants them to be the same, and then, he thinks, they will be able to get on together. In her later novels Virginia Woolf shows that the solution is not so simple or so poor as that. Man and woman form a counterpoint: it is precisely in their differences that the possibilities of co-operation lie. This problem of two lives fitting together, and of the courage and faith required by intelligent people before they can decide on marriage, is the great theme of the novel which follows *The Voyage Out*. People who want freedom rather than security must always have this problem. One feels so often that people marry because they are afraid of the complexity of life and want to get inside a shell— 'Me this unchartered freedom tires'—not being able to bear very much liberty, and requiring constant reassurance and consolation. Mr Ramsay, in *To the Lighthouse*, uses marriage in this way, to the dismay of his wife who with all her domesticity is an infinitely freer and more adventurous spirit than he. It is a tragedy if getting married means losing all the real things of life, closing the avenues to more and more knowledge, slowing down one's progress or stopping it altogether.

v

Terence and Rachel join in a second expedition, this time up the river on a steamer. It is the river Mrs Ambrose wove into her pattern. It is now that they get engaged. Helen approves, but has some forebodings of disaster. How frail human bodies are, she thinks, compared with the great trees and deep waters. But Rachel and Terence are completely happy. For the time, their doubts have disappeared. They talk of all the things they are going to do together, in England; the dramatic irony becomes painful for the reader.

"We shall be doing that together in six weeks' time, and it'll be the middle of June then—and June in London—my God! how pleasant it all is!"
"And we're certain to have it too," she said. "It isn't as if we were expecting a great deal—only to walk about and look at things."

The Greeks would have told them that it is not wise for mortals to talk too much about their happiness; the gods may overhear and be jealous. In Rachel's bloodstream all this while a microorganism is proliferating. The moment comes when she feels a severe headache and retires to bed. The local doctor is inefficient (another Forster character): the illness is not serious, he says, the fever must run its course. When Helen at last realises that Rachel is seriously ill, it is too late. There is a strong sense of climax, a deep pathos, but no hysterics. Terence's despair is most convincingly drawn. And over it all there hangs the shadow of waste, of questioning. Life continues, the hotel guests resume their normal activities and try to read a purpose into it all. But for Helen and Hirst and Terence, who value truth above comfort of mind, there is no solution. Something malign and senseless behind the veil of things, the creature with the club who strikes down Percival in *The Waves*, has trampled on their lives: that is all.

CHAPTER II

Night and Day

[1919]

VIRGINIA WOOLF'S second novel continues the discussion initiated in *The Voyage Out*. The scene is London; the time, just before the war; the theme, love, marriage and the family. There is a touch of Jane Austen in the setting, a hint of Meredith in the interplay of characters, a flavour of E. M. Forster in the light conversational style. It is remarkably unlike *The Voyage Out* in tone. She seems resolved to keep adventure, and eccentricity, and the life of things, in the background. It is a comedy of drawing-rooms and tea-parties. She brings in her characters with straightforward descriptions and direct comment, and we don't expect them to develop much in the course of the story. There *is* a story, though not a very exciting one, and it's about love and marriage and their relations to a man's work and a woman's intellectual life. Katharine Hilbery and Ralph Denham are persons drawn in the round, but they are not so vital as Mrs Ambrose or Rachel Vinrace. And this is because Virginia Woolf denies them the attraction of lovable eccentricities and because she gives them a setting where they are debarred from linking up their beings with the world of things and escaping from their personalities into that world.

Night and Day starts off, like many comedies of manners, with a tea-party. Katharine and Denham have met before, we gather, but hardly know each other. Katharine is beautiful, practical, serene, and 'inclined to be silent'. Her secret passion is mathematics. Ralph Denham is a bony young man, nervous in society, with 'a face built for swiftness and decision rather than for massive contemplation'. His soul, we are told, is 'angular and acrid'. His rival, William Rodney, admits that he probably 'cares, naturally, for the right sort of things', which include Elizabethan drama and the theory of truth. There is a strong antagonism and a strong attraction between Ralph and Katharine. The antagonism comes from Denham; he is ferociously insistent on his family's poverty, his own unfitness for social contacts, and the artificiality of Katharine's life as the daughter of a well-to-do upper middle class household, with a famous poet for an ancestor. Katharine, for her part, does not lose her temper; but she knows that she has to work as hard in her own sphere as Ralph does in his.

> Katharine was a member of a very great profession which has, as yet, no title and very little recognition, although the labour of mill and factory is, perhaps, no more severe and the results of less benefit to the world. She lived at home. She did it very well, too. Anyone coming to the house in Cheyne Walk felt that here was an orderly place, shapely, controlled—a place where life had been trained to show to the best advantage, and, though composed of different elements, made to appear harmonious and with a character of its own.

The attraction, like that between Terence and Rachel, comes from the fact that they both are, and feel each other to be, sincere young people liking the same things. They meet again in Mary Datchet's rooms. Mary is twenty-five, a very efficient young woman who runs an office for the Women's Suffrage movement yet finds time to read Webster and Ben Jonson. William Rodney is reading a paper on the Elizabethan use of metaphor. It's a good paper but Rodney is nervous and makes a fool of himself. After the reading Denham goes up to Katharine and takes the opportunity of being disagreeable to her.

> "You know the names of the stars, I suppose?" Denham remarked, and from the tone of his voice one might have thought that he grudged Katharine the knowledge he attributed to her.
> She kept her voice steady with some difficulty.
> "I know how to find the Pole star if I'm lost."
> "I don't suppose that often happens to you."
> "No. Nothing interesting ever happens to me," she said.
> "I think you make a system of saying disagreeable things, Miss Hilbery," he broke out, again going further than he meant to. "I suppose it's one of the characteristics of your class. They never talk seriously to their inferiors."

It looks as if *Night and Day* were going to be one of those dreary books about class antagonism. But no: as the conversation proceeds, we see that it is to deal with the more interesting theme of the incompatibility of individuals. Denham has fallen in love with Katharine; he doesn't want to admit this to himself, so he makes himself unpleasant. Katharine is not upset because without formulating the thing to herself she knows what has happened. And Denham is jealous of William Rodney who, for all his ridiculousness of voice and figure, seems to be of the same world as Katharine.

Denham's family live shabbily in Highgate; and this picture is set against the elegance of the Hilbery home in Cheyne Walk. There is a widowed mother, seven brothers and sisters, and usually an aunt or uncle, to greet Denham when he returns from the office in the evening. The contrast with Cheyne Walk is carefully stressed. Yet we are made aware that the problem which afflicts him is Katharine's problem too—how to reconcile his claims as an individual with his duties as the member of a family. Katharine has to run the house in Cheyne Walk—her mother, a delightful and original person, has no practical sense for housekeeping—and snatch odd moments for her mathematics. Ralph has to retire to an attic for solitude. The family system, the patriarchal system of which Virginia Woolf was to write at length in *The Years* and *Three Guineas*, cramps them both. By sheer force of family pressure Denham is developing into a solitary and misanthropist.

This problem, as we shall see, is to occupy Virginia Woolf's mind a good deal. How can one live the free life, the good life of the mind if one has no solitude? One is either swamped, or one grows bitter and unsocial. It is the problem which affects the artist especially, and crops up whenever two people of original quality are thinking of getting married. Mary Datchet too has had to face it.

"I think you must be very clever," Katharine observed.

"Why? Because I run an office?"

"I wasn't thinking of that. I was thinking of how you live alone in this room, and have parties."

Mary reflected for a second.

"It means, chiefly, a power of being disagreeable to one's own family, I think. I have that, perhaps. I didn't want to live at home, and I told my father. He didn't like it . . . But then I have a sister, and you haven't, have you?"

Does mental independence necessarily involve the power of being unpleasant? Can one combine it with family life or with love? These are the questions Mrs Woolf is posing in *Night and Day*. This novel, we see, is not concerned simply with the fortunes of two young people in pre-war London. It is concerned with freedom, the life of the mind, the problem of value. The writer is carrying a step further the enquiry which she began in *The Voyage Out*. There, she tackled the question of love as a value, and the particular world which love creates—but in isolation; she isolated Rachel and Terence as a scientist might isolate two elements for examination. Here, in *Night and Day*, she adds London, tea-parties, discussion groups, the family, the suffragettes. And she complicates the plot by making triangles: Ralph, William, Katharine; Katharine, Mary, Ralph; Katharine, Cassandra, William.

The disadvantages of family life are seen under two different aspects in Ralph Denham and his sister Joan. In Joan, it is an obvious narrowing of interests. She has become incapable of detachment. 'Why, [Ralph] wondered, could Joan never for one moment detach her mind from the details of domestic life? It seemed to him that she was getting more and more enmeshed in them, and capable of shorter and less frequent flights into the outer world.' But Ralph, too, is enmeshed in a different way. He is incapable of disinterested judgment. He has taken sides, in spite of his irritation, or perhaps because of it, with his family against the outside world. He has given himself up to a false loyalty, and renounced the pure light of reason. He does not see things as they are, but as he wishes them to be. He has 'a fundamental belief that, as a family, they were somehow remarkable'. He sets them in his mind against the Hilberys and thus uses his family to bolster up his own sense of inferiority. This is the sort of false loyalty which makes a man prefer his own country, his own literature, his own university or his own class to any other on the grounds that, being his own, it must be superior. It is an error to be explicitly condemned in *Three Guineas*.

Through this feeling of the superiority of his own family, of the superiority of his class and the more honest quality of his mind, Ralph Denham seeks to dominate his relationship with Katharine. He doesn't want a perfect give-and-take. And this masculine need to dominate is found in William Rodney too. It is generally believed that Katharine will marry Rodney, 'by profession a clerk in a Government office, one of those martyred spirits to whom literature is at once a source of divine joy and of almost intolerable irritation' because 'not content to rest in their love of it, they must attempt to practise it themselves'. He is not a very sympathetic figure; he is weak, emotional, and selfish, but he is intelligent, and therefore his creator does not condemn him. He believes in the things of the mind. But his opinions on women are unenlightened. They are the kind of opinions that Virginia Woolf was to spend an unfortunately large part of her time in combating. He pesters Katharine to marry him, simply because he does not feel self-sufficient.

> ". . . Perhaps if you married me—I'm half a poet, you see, and I can't pretend not to feel what I do feel [he has just promised to drop the subject]. If I could write—ah, that would be another matter. I shouldn't bother you to marry me then, Katharine."
> He spoke these disconnected sentences rather abruptly, with his eyes alternately upon the moon and upon the stream.
> "But for me I suppose you would recommend marriage?" asked Katharine, with her eyes fixed on the moon.
> "Certainly I should. Not for you only, but for all women. Why, you're nothing at all without it; you're only half alive; using only half your faculties; you must feel that for yourself."

The irony is direct: Rodney ascribes to Katharine just the lack of self-sufficiency he feels in himself. Romantic love, certainly, does not enter into the matter. He wants a prop, a compensation.

A merciless dissection of Rodney follows the conversation with Katharine. Denham walks back with him to his rooms, which are tastefully decorated with oval Venetian mirrors and yellow and crimson tulips: a dilettante's *tour d'ivoire*. Quivering with 'vanity unrequited and urgent', Rodney gives Denham the manuscript of an unfinished play to read. The action is a compensation for his rejection by Katharine.

From the dilettante we are carried straight to the worker in a scene where Mary Datchet is busy in her women's suffrage office in Russell Square. She works hard, but she finds it a necessity to get away from her fellow-workers in the lunch hour. She goes to the British Museum and looks at the Elgin marbles; and the thought of Ralph Denham comes into her mind. She is betrayed to a momentary self-revelation. 'So secure did she feel with those silent shapes that she almost yielded to an impulse to say, "I am in love with you," aloud.' Later she is ashamed of this impulse.

> For, as she walked along the street to her office, the force of all her customary objections to being in love with anyone overcame

her. She did not want to marry at all. It seemed to her that there was something amateurish in bringing love into touch with a perfectly straightforward friendship, such as hers was with Ralph, which, for two years now, had based itself upon common interests in impersonal topics, such as the housing of the poor, or the taxation of land values.

Ralph, Katharine, Mary and William are all thinking very much the same thoughts, and there is little action to break the monotony. Mrs Woolf does give some variety, however, by introducing three subsidiary characters sketched rather in the flat than in the round. Mrs Hilbery, Katharine's mother, is a remarkable person, well advanced in the sixties; 'her face was shrunken and aquiline, but any hint of sharpness was dispelled by the large blue eyes, at once sagacious and innocent, which seemed to regard the world with an enormous desire that it should behave itself nobly, and an entire confidence that it could do so, if it would only take the pains'. Mrs Hilbery, with all her vagueness, has like Mrs Dalloway and Mrs Ramsay and Mrs Swithin the gift of insight, and this enables her, in the end, to act as the *dea ex machina* to the bewildered young people. Mr Hilbery is the type of Mr Ramsay, without his lovable eccentricities. He is elderly, bright-eyed, corpulent, and a scholar. 'He seemed to be providing himself incessantly with food for amusement and reflection with the least possible expenditure of energy. One might suppose that he had passed the time of life when his ambitions were personal, or that he had gratified them as far as he was likely to do, and now employed his considerable acuteness rather to observe and reflect than to attain any result.' The third character is frankly humorous in both the Jonsonian and the Dickensian sense. Mrs Seal, 'dressed in plum-coloured velveteen, with short, grey hair, and a face that seemed permanently flushed with philanthropic enthusiasm, was always in a hurry and always in some disorder. She wore two crucifixes, which got themselves entangled in a heavy gold chain upon her breast, and seemed to Mary expressive of her mental ambiguity.' She is given a characteristic phrase to pin her down in our minds: "The bare branches against the sky do one so much *good*": this she trots out on appropriate occasions, as she bustles about the Women's Suffrage office with good-natured incompetence. It is noteworthy that this use of 'flat' characters (to borrow Forster's useful term) is a device which Virginia Woolf jettisoned later together with plot and set descriptions and link passages—all of which are found in *Night and Day*.

Home life at Cheyne Walk is shown as something warm, gracious and charming, as Mr and Mrs Hilbery sit together over the fire. But Terence's comment from *The Voyage Out* is still in our ears. That is the kind of domestic scene he didn't like to think about. Katharine comes in and joins them at dinner, and then, with her mother, leaves Mr Hilbery to his port and cigar. It is very warm and secure; but the girl is conscious of something missing. There is a lack, a restriction. (Virginia Woolf was to paint this scene again, with sharper satire, in the pageant of *Between the Acts*.) Her father and mother always seem to 'fall short of her vision'. She likes to hear her mother talking about her grandfather, Richard Allardyce, the great poet, and is interested in the secret of his separation from his wife; but that secret is never disclosed, the presumably disreputable facts are hidden. Yet the mere mention of this domestic problem serves to link up past and present, and to give Virginia Woolf's treatment of the contemporary situation both solidity and a sort of locus in time. Was marriage *then*, or is marriage *now*, the more difficult? And thus the talk between mother and daughter comes round to William Rodney; Mrs Hilbery makes it plain that she wishes Katharine to marry him. There is no coercion, of course. But there is a slight, insidious pressure. Katharine remarks sharply that she doesn't want to marry anyone.

ii

What is it to be in love? This question also arises. Mrs Hilbery believes that William is deeply in love with Katharine; but we have seen that his emotion is made up of possessiveness and a desire for reassurance. Mary Datchet is certainly in love with Ralph Denham; but in what sense? It is not a devouring passion; it takes up only part of her mind. Ralph is in love with Katharine; his knees shake when he passes her in the street; but the emotion irritates at least as much as it stimulates. And Katharine—it is a long time before we get to know what she feels. Mrs Woolf, then, is again exploring the nature of love, this passion which is the theme of the vast majority of novels;

she is not disposed to reject it out of hand as material for her writing, but evidently she suspects that it does not take quite the place in life that it does in fiction, and that the place it does take is not quite so simple as is supposed. Like everything else, it is mixed. And the more intelligent the people concerned are, the more mixed it will be. Conventional novels are full of pure emotions: heroines capable of deathless devotion, heroes out of whom love has burnt every baser passion, wives dominated by jealousy. Life is certainly not like that, Virginia Woolf says. At the same time, love clearly is important, and it is worth while trying to find out just what it is and what place it takes in the pattern of life. So she continues to turn the idea over and over.

A good deal of the charm of reading Virginia Woolf's novels comes from this eminently reasonable tone. It is really very flattering. She addresses her readers as equals, she believes that we don't want to be led up the garden path or regaled with nursery tales, that we are interested in reality and want to see human beings as they are. Her own mind is intensely reflective and exploratory. "It's life that matters, nothing but life—the process of discovering, the everlasting and perpetual process," Katharine Hilbery says to herself as she passes Ralph without noticing him (and he, with trembling knees, does not dare to stop her). This is Mrs Woolf's own point of view. She is fascinated by the variety of human motives and the oddness of human actions. In all her novels there is a problem; but they are not 'problem novels'. The reasoning is absorbed fully into the stuff of fiction; there are no bits and bobs of philosophy hanging about which we can detach and piece into an abstract whole. And her characters develop with the best kind of development; that is to say, new qualities are not added as the plot proceeds, but qualities already shown are allowed to evolve according to their own life.

The plot doesn't matter so much, though in *Night and Day* it matters more than in the later books. There is even an element of chance allowed to step in to help the destinies of the chief characters. If Ralph *had* stopped Katharine, we reflect, she would not have gone on to William Rodney's rooms in the same frame of mind or promised to marry him. For certainly her engagement is a mistake. She is seeking freedom from her family but entering a worse servitude. And Ralph Denham, realising too late that he loves Katharine, is thrown headlong into a meaningless world. Mary Datchet, sensing Ralph's pain, seeks refuge in her Women's Suffrage work. There she feels convinced of right and wrong and cherishes the conviction that she can strike out for the one and against the other. But the sense of power, illusory as it is, also has its dangers, bringing the desire to dominate her fellow-workers and indulge in a 'lustful arrogance'. Everywhere there are pitfalls for that real life, the life of the spirit, which dwells in solitude.

iii

After fourteen chapters of London we are ready for a change and it is the village of Disham, near Lincoln, that we are transported to. Not a very picturesque locality, but giving scope for those collocations of persons and natural forms which we have seen in *The Voyage Out* but have missed, so far, in *Night and Day*. It is from these unions that Virginia Woolf's novels derive much of their peculiar force and flavour. We are given, too, an old house and garden, 'in which the Rector [Mary Datchet's father] took considerable pride'. The large house and garden are to appear again in *To the Lighthouse* as indispensable elements in the story; and the Rev. Wyndham Datchet is in some ways an anticipation of Mr Ramsay. He likes to pace up and down in his garden and declaim Horace. But he has 'more strength of purpose and power of self-sacrifice than of intellect or originality'. Virginia Woolf must not allow her clergymen to be too charming!

Ralph Denham has come to Disham to stay with the Datchets over Christmas. Katharine is staying at Stogdon House, Lampsher, not far away. Ralph is introduced to the freshness and simplicities of country life, and to another kind of family, with its special liberties and imprisonments for the spirit. Katharine is finding out her mistake in getting engaged to William, and is making him suffer for it by an attitude of contempt. Removed from her family and normal environment, she is coming to know herself better, to understand that she doesn't really care about people; she wants mathematics. 'If I could calculate things, and use a telescope, and have to work out figures, and know to a fraction where I am wrong, I should be perfectly happy.' Figures are so much pleasanter to deal with than human beings, especially human beings like Rodney, who fidgets about clothes, and suit-cases, and objects to her silences.

Ralph and Mary take a walk to Lincoln over the fields. They discuss the problems of government, and the meaning that state organisations have for the life of the individual. 'What they saw were the Houses of Parliament and the Government Offices in Whitehall. They both belonged to the class which is conscious of having lost its birthright in these great structures and is seeking to build another kind of lodging for its own notions of law and government.' Ralph tells Mary that he has made up his mind to escape from it all—to give up his work in the solicitor's office and live in Lincolnshire, in a little cottage, and write a book on the English village. He has come to understand that it is utter destruction for the spirit to work away, day after day, 'at stuff that doesn't matter a damn to anyone'. In his selfishness he does not consider Mary; but when she says that she wants to get away too, she wants to go to America, he cries out that she is not to go. Then he realises that he is always asking from her and never giving. For a moment he feels his selfishness and her goodness. But soon the sight of trees against a blue sky sends his thoughts and emotions off in another direction: he thinks of Katharine, and his old dream of life shared with her returns.

"Katharine, Katharine," he repeated, and seemed to himself to be with her. He lost his sense of all that surrounded him; all substantial things—the hour of the day, what we have done or are about to do, the presence of other people and the support we derive from seeing their belief in a common reality—all this slipped from him. So he might have felt if the earth had dropped from his feet, and the empty blue had hung all round him, and the air had been steeped in the presence of one woman.

Later, after they have lunched at an inn in Lincoln, Ralph realises that Mary is in love with him. He is filled with a mixture of feelings, gladness and repulsion, the wish to marry her and the wish never to see her again. He looks out of the window, and there he sees Katharine Hilbery walking along the street. At this moment Mary comes to the realisation that Ralph is in love with Katharine. Thus the complete knowledge comes to both at the same moment.

She noticed everything about him; if there had been other signs of his utter alienation she would have sought them out too, for she felt that it was only by heaping one truth upon another that she could keep herself sitting there, upright. The truth seemed to support her; it struck her, even as she looked at his face, that the light of truth was shining far away beyond him; the light of truth, she seemed to frame the words as she rose to go, shines on a world not to be shaken by our personal calamities.

iv

The light of truth! That is the consolation which is left to Mary after Ralph's stay in Lincolnshire. He asks her to marry him, but knowing the truth she refuses. The rest of the story works out a series of very complicated situations between Katharine, William and Ralph, which are only resolved when a new actor enters the scene, Cassandra Otway, a young cousin of Katharine's who plays the flute and cultivates silkworms. In her William finds the unquestioning adoration his ego requires. Ralph and Katharine, after much hesitation, decide to get married. First they meet for a talk in Kew Gardens. He tells her of his plans to live in a cottage and write a book; and she confesses her own passion for solitude. She develops a theory about knowing people without having relations with them: a theory of detachment from personal relationships.

"Don't you see that if you have no relations with people it's easier to be honest with them?" she enquired. "That is what I meant. One needn't cajole them; one's under no obligation to them. Surely you must have found with your own family that it's impossible to discuss what matters to you most because you're all herded together, because you're in a conspiracy, because the position is false——"

Ralph puts forward a counter-theory: that one *can* live with another person in perfect sincerity—'cases where there's no relationship, though the people live together, if you like, where each is free, where there's no obligation upon either side'. It sounds like the household of William Godwin. But Katharine thinks that obligations always grow up. Ralph maintains that this occurs only when the conditions are not made plain at the beginning; and he gives the rules for such a partnership. It must be unemotional. 'Neither is under any obligation to the other. They must be at liberty to break or to alter at any

moment. They must be able to say whatever they wish to say.'
These are the terms he offers Katharine.

She is ready to accept.

Why, she reflected, should there be this perpetual disparity
between the thought and the action, between the life of solitude
and the life of society, this astonishing precipice on the one side
of which the soul was active and in broad daylight, on the
other side of which it was contemplative and dark as night?
Was it not possible to step from one to the other, erect, and
without essential change? Was this not the chance he offered
her—the rare and wonderful chance of friendship? At any rate,
she told Denham, with a sigh in which he heard both impatience
and relief, that she agreed; she thought him right; she would
accept his terms of friendship.

But later on Ralph discovers it is not friendship, it is love
that he feels for Katharine; and the strange ballet of their lives
has to take another turn before the climax is reached with their
engagement.

And now, having glanced at the highlights of the plot of
Night and Day, we can answer the question, What is it about? It
is about the nature of freedom and the nature of love. People
want to be free to work as they wish, to live their own lives, to
fall in love and to marry whom they choose. But are these
different kinds of freedom compatible? Freedom, one would
think, means detachment; marriage means attachment, and so,
in another sense, does work. Lovers and husbands are notoriously jealous; jealousy confines the human spirit. Katharine
Hilbery, looking out of her window, knows that William
Rodney is thinking of her and wishes that he wouldn't. She
doesn't want anybody in the whole world to be thinking of her.
'She cast her mind out to imagine an empty land where all
this petty intercourse of men and women, this life made up of
the dense crossings and entanglements of men and women, had
no existence whatever.' But she has to conclude that there is no
way of escaping from one's fellow-beings.

Ralph Denham concludes that there is no way of escaping
from his work. He is a clerk in a solicitor's office, hard-working
and intelligent, and sure to rise finally to the head of his profession. Meantime life, the strange and beautiful order of the
world, is passing him by.

He prided himself upon being well broken in to a life of hard work, about which he had no sort of illusions. His vision of his own future, unlike many such forecasts, could have been made public at any moment without a blush; he attributed to himself a strong brain, and conferred on himself a seat in the House of Commons at the age of fifty, a moderate fortune, and, with luck, an unimportant office in a Liberal Government.

But it needs all Ralph's strength of will to keep him toeing the line. He has to go on telling himself that he is no worse off than anyone else. And he has to have other people's approval of his way of life; for this is not a genuine ideal that he has constructed, and it will not live in solitude. In solitude, indeed, strange images of freedom arise, and Ralph sees himself in romantic rôles.

Night and Day is a study of human complexity. One wonders how close it is to ordinary human experience. That men and women entertain doubts of their compatibility we know; but these doubts commonly come after marriage and not before it. To the ordinary novel reader in 1919, *Night and Day* must have seemed a queer sort of love story. Who is the hero and who is the heroine? There is nothing heroic about Ralph Denham, and still less about William Rodney; Mary Datchet is a more noble but a less prominent figure than Katharine Hilbery. Love, we are made to believe, may call forth the better qualities, but it does, also, evoke less admirable ones. It disturbs Katharine's detachment, makes her jealous and irritable; it makes Ralph behave like a cad to Mary, and puts him in a maudlin condition about Katharine; it increases William's capacity for insincerity, and leads him to make a fool of himself over a young girl. It is pre-eminently a bringer of confusion into tidy lives. Yet, it is suggested, it has also the power to illuminate, to make ordinary people something more than ordinary. It is an adventure requiring faith and tenacity and tolerance. If victorious, it holds out the hope that two minds may henceforward share the vision of reality which hitherto had seemed open only to the solitary mind.

Can it really do this? The novel ends on a question mark. Will Katharine's and Ralph's faith in marriage be justified? Is it possible for two original minds, each seeking truth, to live together, or must marriage be a life of compromise and insincerity? In *Mrs Dalloway* and *To the Lighthouse* Virginia Woolf is to investigate this problem also.

Meantime, in *Night and Day* she has touched on various other themes that are to occupy her through the length of her writing career. There is the great problem of society, masculine professional society, that she is to subject to detailed examination in *The Years* and *Three Guineas* right at the close of her life's work. There is the question of the co-operation of man and woman, which is to find its solution in *A Room of One's Own*. But the life of things, much more to the fore in *The Voyage Out*, is here kept in the background. *Night and Day* is an indoors novel of a kind she was not to attempt again until *The Years*. Mary Datchet is perhaps the most shut-in of the *dramatis personae*, with her Women's Suffrage office and her work after office hours, though we see her in her real element in Lincolnshire. It is in *Night and Day* and *The Years*, too, that the suffragette idea is most prominent; though we have it of course running through the essays and propagandist writings. In this early novel she is able to treat the idea lightly and wittily, while paying tribute to the spirit of self-sacrifice behind it; later she loses this sense of proportion and her work, when it touches this theme, ceases to be art.

The great motif of *Night and Day* is the exaltation of truth, 'shining far away beyond' human values and human striving. Truth can, however, be translated into human values as the reward of seeing clearly. Katharine and Ralph both seek it; Mary alone, we feel, fully achieves it. But it is this devotion to truth, this refusal to be put off with shams and conventions, which causes the difficulties that confront the lovers, and these difficulties can only be overcome by an act of faith. While clinging to truth, but uplifted by faith, they hope to be able to attain reality. Truth is not reality: it bears almost the same relation to it as logic bears to metaphysics. In the novel both Katharine and Ralph have momentary glimpses of reality, but these are not insisted on. Reality is to be the motif of the succeeding novels, and especially of those which follow *Jacob's Room*. Here we are occupied with its indispensable precursors, freedom and truth. It is the motif we have seen embodied, in *The Voyage Out*, in St John Hirst. Love, we are shown now, is a mixture of truth and illusion. The truth consists in the possibility that human beings can understand each other and live together. The illusion lies in the tendency of the mind, under the influence of passion, or insufficiency, to see other human

beings in a fictitious light. Human beings need each other, that
is certain. There must be communication, and communication
on the highest level. Can we share our visions of reality or are
they, as both Ralph and Katharine suspect, available only to
the solitary mind?

There are no masterpieces of character-drawing in *Night and
Day*. Katharine and Ralph are indeed less real to us than
Rachel and Terence. The concern for ideas has obscured the
outlines, and prevented the development, of individuality.
Katharine does not grow and change and blossom, as Rachel
did, in the course of the action. More than in any other of
Virginia Woolf's novels, we feel the characters to be mouth-
pieces. To some extent this failure to individualise is due to the
milieu which Mrs Woolf has chosen. Katharine and Ralph
cannot be wholly themselves because they are hemmed in and
frustrated by an unsympathetic environment. A person, in
Virginia Woolf's novels, commonly finds himself as a person
through his relation to the world of things; and in *Night and
Day* the world of things is almost wholly absent. Hence the lack
of depth, the failure to resonate. The same shallowness of
characterisation is found again in the later but in many ways
similar novel, *The Years*; and for the same reasons.

CHAPTER III

Monday or Tuesday

[1921]

*N*IGHT AND DAY was a not wholly successful amalgam of the comedy of manners and the comedy of ideas. It tried to pin a particular problem down to a particular time and place, and discuss it very much in the way it might have been discussed by Jane Austen or Meredith, or even by Shaw or Galsworthy. By doing so, it left hardly a loophole through which the gleam of reality as Virginia Woolf was coming to see it might enter. The moments of vision which are found here and there in the book don't seem to fit: they are not assimilated into the texture of the whole, they stand out as purple passages. In a way, it is a retrogression from *The Voyage Out.* Virginia Woolf has not yet found her technique.

The volume of short stories which appeared in 1921 shows her in search of it. *Monday or Tuesday* is an altogether experimental collection. She is trying to find a form and a style adequate to convey her individual vision of life: and not only of life on the objective plane, but also of that 'taste of eternity' which keeps breaking through at odd moments and seems to give her vision all its value. To convey that taste certain barriers of prose fiction have to be broken down; that is now obvious to her. The current form of the novel, in which she has been working up to now, will not do. She was hampered by the convention of an intricate continuous plot; by set descriptions of people and scenes from without; by the necessity to provide link passages. But when she examined the technique of poetry, she found that these mechanical devices were not essential; verse could achieve an economy and a directness which were lacking in prose. Moreover, by rapid transitions, by allusions and imagery, poetry could give precisely that complexity of impressions, that sense of the eternal glowing through the momentary, which was of the essence of her experience. She was interested more in the life of the mind—in sensations, thoughts, feelings, intuitions—than in the life of surface action. How do thoughts follow upon one another? What kind of a pattern do they build up? What happens if I just allow my thoughts, my mind-impressions, to flow of their own accord, without attempting to organise them or control them in any way? She is prepared, in short, to explore the 'stream of consciousness'.

But before embarking on a new novel she is going to experiment in the shorter form. The title story, *Monday or Tuesday*, gives the flow of ideas direct, without interposition of plot and characters. Here are the opening paragraphs.

> Lazy and indifferent, shaking space easily from his wings, knowing his way, the heron passes over the church beneath the sky. White and distant, absorbed in itself, endlessly the sky covers and uncovers, moves and remains. A lake? Blot the shores of it out! A mountain? Oh, perfect—the sun gold on its slopes. Down that falls. Ferns then, or white feathers, for ever and ever——
>
> Desiring truth, awaiting it, laboriously distilling a few words, for ever desiring—(a cry starts to the left, another to the right. Wheels strike divergently. Omnibuses conglomerate in conflict) —for ever desiring—(the clock asseverates with twelve distinct strokes that it is midday; light sheds gold scales; children swarm) —for ever desiring truth. Red is the dome; coins hang on the trees; smoke trails from the chimneys; bark, shout, cry "Iron for sale"—and truth?

It isn't very successful. She makes it more a series of bumps than a flow with her questions and exclamations. Her inversions, too, seem not quite right: 'red is the dome'—she is seeking to achieve a certain effect illegitimately, by employing the devices of bad verse. But she does, all the same, get the feeling of a mind trying to follow a certain train of thought while against that effort there runs ceaselessly the stream of sense-impressions.

Musical technique interests her. Can the novelist interweave themes somewhat in the musician's manner? Virginia Woolf will try, at any rate. She does it in *The Mark on the Wall*, first hypnotising herself by staring at the mark, then letting ideas arise, but relating them more closely than in *Monday or Tuesday*. The mark (it turns out in the end to be a snail) is not only a starting-point, it is also a nexus. Every time she finds herself being carried away by one stream of thoughts the mark pokes itself up and interrupts; but by interrupting connects with a new stream. And the stream flows through the fire into which she is gazing as she meditates. It is the glow of the fire and the shapes of the coals which give her the pictures: a cavalcade of red knights riding up the side of a black rock, 'spaces of light and dark intersected by thick stalks, and rather higher up perhaps, rose-shaped blots of an indistinct colour—dim pinks and blues' (these are flowers), and even inspiration falling like a shower of sparks in Shakespeare's brain. In those rose-shaped blots she is giving us the pure data of perception: the naked sensation which looms so large in all her later writing, which has its own peculiar value, and which gives an extraordinary happiness, perhaps the reallest we can know in this world.

In another sketch, *The String Quartet*, she tries to convey the effect of an early Mozart by means of a chain of images. From the pure sensation, that is, she goes on to the sensation as interpretative of something else. First we see the audience arriving— a picture of confusion and conventional greetings. Life is like that, full of loose ends and futilities. Then come the musicians to create the first semblance of order; then the music itself. Her mind overflows with images, favourite images of water and wavering fishes.

> Flourish, spring, burgeon, burst! The pear tree on the top of the mountain. Fountains jet; drops descend. But the waters of the Rhône flow swift and deep, race under the arches, and sweep the trailing water leaves, washing shadows over the silver fish, the spotted fish rushed down by the swift waters, now swept into an eddy where—it's difficult this—conglomeration of fish all in a pool; leaping, splashing, scraping sharp fins; and such a boil of current that the yellow pebbles are churned round and round, round and round—free now, rushing downwards, or even somehow ascending in exquisite spirals into the air; curled like thin shavings from under a plane; up and up . . .

The first movement, we gather, is a brisk allegro; then comes an adagio ('the melancholy river bears us on'); the minuet is translated into terms of eighteenth-century gallantry ('if, madam, you will take my hand——'); and the final allegro is a salute of silver horns.

The opening paragraphs of *The String Quartet*, with their tone of futility and indecision, are curiously paralleled in texture and rhythm by the early poems of T. S. Eliot. Here are two passages for comparison, the second being from *The Love Song of J. Alfred Prufrock*.

> . . . Yet I begin to have my doubts——
> If indeed it's true, as they're saying, that Regent Street is up, and the Treaty signed, and the weather not cold for the time of

year, and even at that rent not a flat to be had, and the worst of influenza its after-effects; if I bethink me of having forgotten to write about the leak in the larder, and left my glove in the train; if the ties of blood require me, leaning forward, to accept cordially the hand which is perhaps offered hesitatingly——

"Seven years since we met!"

"The last time in Venice."

"And where are you living now?"

"Well, the late afternoon suits me the best, though, if it weren't asking too much——"

"But I knew you at once!"

"Still, the war made a break——"

> *. . . There will be time, there will be time*
> *To prepare a face to meet the faces that you meet . . .*
> *And indeed there will be time*
> *To wonder, 'Do I dare?' and, 'Do I dare?'*
> *Time to turn back and descend the stair,*
> *With a bald spot in the middle of my hair—*
> *[They will say: 'How his hair is growing thin!']*
> *My morning coat, my collar mounting firmly to the chin,*
> *My necktie rich and modest, but asserted by a simple pin—*
> *[They will say: 'But how his arms and legs are thin!']*
> *Do I dare*
> *Disturb the universe?*
> *In a minute there is time*
> *For decisions and revisions which a minute will reverse.*

Both passages are marked by one plain characteristic: hesitancy. We feel no break in tone when passing from the first to the second. The rhythm is wavering, without assurance, infected by the banality of the people concerned and the insipidity of their conversation. Both writers are moved by the collapse of values which followed the first world war. Both use music as a pattern of order against which to set their purposeless human beings. Indeed, the frequency with which the post-war writers —Virginia Woolf, Eliot, Huxley, Forster, Joyce—turn to music to provide them with stabilising patterns for their works is a point of considerable interest. Music seems to take, for 'the sensitive modern mind', something of the place which religion had for earlier writers. A religion without dogmas, yet exquisitely ordered and giving all the consolations of faith. 'Through the long sarabande Bach meditated his lovely and consoling certitude', Huxley writes in *Point Counter Point* of the

Suite for Flute and Strings. What is this certitude? We don't know, it can't be put into words. And that is the point; being inexpressible, it is also invulnerable. We have no need to defend or attack it.

What exactly are we to call these experiments of *Monday or Tuesday*? They are not short stories in any recognisable sense. Mr Leonard Woolf, in his foreword to the reprint included in *A Haunted House* (1943), suggests the name 'sketches'. They have no plot; they have no characters. They have a certain very interesting interdependence of images: the red and blue flowers with long green stalks of *Kew Gardens*, shedding their coloured light, are present too in *The Mark on the Wall*, the swirl and waving water-weeds of *An Unwritten Novel* reappear in *The String Quartet*. *An Unwritten Novel* gives us our nearest approach to character and plot; but when she has carefully built the story up (showing us how she is doing it, revealing her tricks) Virginia Woolf throws it down again. The truth wasn't like that at all, she says. And this rejection of a conventional, carefully worked-out plot is in the nature of a manifesto. Virginia Woolf isn't going to write in that way, isn't going to tread in the footsteps of Bennett and Galsworthy. She has her own technique to work out; and these first sketches are *really* sketches.

They give one, sometimes, the impression of being passages from larger works. I don't think Virginia Woolf was ever very successful in the short-story form. She needed space to develop her impressionistic technique and her analysis of character, to build up her special atmosphere, and she didn't find this in the short story. Of course she grew more skilful later on. She dropped the stream of consciousness idea for a framework of fantasy, and she added character and even plot. Some of her later things are short stories in the accepted sense—*The Legacy* for example, which has characters, plot, mystery, suspense and climax.

These early experiments are interesting not merely from the point of view of technique but also from the thematic angle. They carry on many of the concepts of the two novels: e.g. the concern for truth, as illustrated by the above passage from *Monday or Tuesday*. And they anticipate other ideas which are to play a large part in the novels of Mrs Woolf's prime. In *A Haunted House* she gives us the notion of a house's atmosphere living on from one set of occupants to another and imposing its spirit; the house itself is a character in the story; and this idea is found again in *To the Lighthouse*, in *Orlando*, and in *Between the Acts*. In *An Unwritten Novel* we have one in the series of unattractive spinsters, twisted frustrated lives, which began with the hospital nurse in *The Voyage Out* and include Doris Kilman in *Mrs Dalloway*. *Kew Gardens* gives us already (published separately in 1919) all the brilliance and sensitiveness of her observation of natural objects. It also prepares us for her creation of a world or worlds in which conventional values will be upset and proportions modified. It suggests that she is going to write a good deal about memory and the passing of time. The fundamental questions are already being asked. Here, too, we have her first portrait of a lunatic or eccentric type: a portrait to be split later into Mr Ramsay and Septimus Warren Smith. She is feeling her way across the border of normal consciousness. And there are portraits too, in this extraordinarily rich little sketch, of the sound, healthy, elderly lower-class women that she likes for their humour and pluck.

CHAPTER IV

Jacob's Room

[1922]

REALITY, vision, understanding—whatever you like to call it—is certainly a difficult and confusing concept. There are as many attempts to describe the ultimate as there are religions and philosophies. Sages have squabbled for two or three thousand years and are no nearer an agreement; although the more positive among them, the mystics, appear to have a considerable body of doctrine in common. Whatever the truth may be, however, we can be sure that it will not be very like any of the current guesses. These all-too-human constructions have little relation to the extraordinary world of things in which we live, and they are likely to have still less relation to the reality behind the things. Religions and philosophies either miss too much out or put too much in. Idealism misses out matter, materialism misses out value, Christianity puts in a personal benevolent Creator, Buddhism and Hinduism introduce reincarnation. All of them omit (Virginia Woolf would say) the sandy cat filching the fish and stealing off round the corner.

There is good reason to think that 'reality' is not something that can be even adumbrated in general terms which will appeal to a majority of people. Unless we consider the ground behind appearances to be a magnified man, unless we believe that it is a personal God with ways of thinking very much the same as our own (though at a greater intensity and purity), we cannot expect that ground to be susceptible of expression in human terms at all. But this way of thinking leads to a very provincial view of the universe. Almost certainly reality is no more human than it is animal, vegetable or mineral. The greatest thinkers have held it to be impersonal; and so would it seem to all of us, I think, if we had not very pressing reasons to think it otherwise. We call Buddha and Lao-Tzu great simply because we recognise in them a detachment and realism of which the majority of men are lamentably incapable. "Things are what they are," wrote Bishop Butler, "and the consequences of them

53

will be what they will be; why then should we wish to be deceived?" Alas, most of us do wish to be deceived. Not to believe that the force behind the universe is personal and concerned with our welfare would rob us of delicious moments of self-congratulation, as well as more sober moods of quiet confidence. Such a negation might even, if seriously entertained, cause us to revise some of our most cherished attitudes.

The human mind has a strong bent towards unreality. For this reason, if for no other, we should be well advised not to seek for the absolute exclusively within ourselves. Our reasoning is too often rationalisation; we should beware of relying solely, or even chiefly, on the intellect. Intuition and the imagination, exercised upon exterior objects, will form an excellent corrective to logic, metaphysics and introverted meditation. The world of things is beautiful, varied and extraordinary. It seems to be expressing something, but we don't know what. Certainly nothing human. Therein lies its disappointment for the theologically minded, and its fascination, its perennial fascination, for the pure in heart—by which term I understand, somewhat arbitrarily perhaps, those who want to learn and refuse to teach.

But why not something human, it may be objected. Is not man as much an expression of reality as rocks and trees are— and more so, if we take the long view and see him as a product of evolution? Is his power of reasoning given him for nothing? Any answer one might try to make to these questions would involve all the complexity of human destiny. Yet one thing we can say. Man's development has been progressively away from unity with his non-human environment, towards the creation of an artificial human society. He has subdued his animal characteristics, dominated instincts, passions and intuitions, and cultivated conventions, reasonings and laws. The result has been an incredible advance in the mechanism of living. We have triumphantly asserted our autonomy against nature. But at the same time that we have cut ourselves off from a world of things which we felt was cramping our free development, we seem unfortunately to have cut ourselves off too from the reality that is behind nature.

This dilemma has been felt by sages of all times and expressed most cogently by the Chinese quietists. Lao-Tzu and Chuang-Tzu urge us to relinquish our human reason, to give up our strivings and ambitions and betake us to the woods and rocks. Loitering around a tree, they assert, with our minds emptied of thoughts and worries, we shall discover the secret happiness which is hidden in the life of things. We shall regain our child's heart. Calmly, unregretfully, these ancient sages throw away the civilisation of which most of us are so proud, and confidently assert that it has all been a mistake—all the religion and the morality, all the laws and codes of behaviour, all the arts and sciences. The cost we have paid for these things is too great. We have bought domination over things at the price of no longer understanding them. For understanding is not a matter of the intellect only. We have lost the happiness that comes from being one with Tao. We are cut off from the spirit of life.

All mystics stress the importance of a return to simplicity of living but I know of no others who put the emphasis quite where the Taoists do—on intuitive understanding of nature conse-quent on close observation, and on cultivation of the child heart. The child is not cut off from his environment as the adult is. There is not for him the same separation of the self from the not-self. Until he is taught by his parents or his nurse, he does not take up an attitude of fear or repulsion towards insects, reptiles and animals. Everything is new and delightful. Adults, however, soon rob the child of this communion which causes them intense annoyance. They impress upon him that earth is dirty, insects are horrid and reptiles are dangerous. It is more appropriate to throw stones at snakes and stamp on beetles than to watch them. Schools, later, try feebly to undo some of this mischief by teaching botany and 'nature-study'. But (quite apart from the consummate wrongness of their methods) they are unsuccessful because their pupils are now firmly convinced that plants and animals are contemptible. And the pre-eminence allowed to history, mathematics and the dead languages does nothing to persuade them to the contrary.

Jacob's Room is about a boy who does not allow the adult viewpoint to impose itself completely. His life is a clinging to reality, a rebellion against conventional standards. The rebel-lion is not violent or theatrical, it is rather a quiet obstinacy. Jacob's room, the many rooms he constructs throughout his short life, is a refuge against shams. This novel is about reality, as *The Voyage Out* and *Night and Day* were about freedom. The first passage in which the word reality is mentioned is significant. Jacob is at Cambridge, the city of Light. But even there shams and conventions are to be found. There is a dreary lunch party given by Mr Plumer, a science don. "Oh God, oh God, oh God!" exclaims Jacob as he leaves the house on the Girton Road, with his friend Timmy Durrant. Jacob is disturbed by the vision of unreality.

> The extent to which he was disturbed proves that he was already agog. Insolent he was and inexperienced, but sure enough the cities which the elderly of the race have built upon the skyline showed like brick suburbs, barracks, and places of discipline against a red and yellow flame. He was impressionable; but the word is contradicted by the composure with which he hollowed his hand to screen a match. He was a young man of substance.
>
> Anyhow, whether undergraduate or shop-boy, man or woman, it must come as a shock about the age of twenty—the world of the elderly, thrown up in such black outline upon what we are; upon the reality; the moors and Byron; the sea and the lighthouse; the sheep's jaw with the yellow teeth in it; upon the obstinate irrepressible conviction which makes youth so intolerably disagreeable —"I am what I am, and intend to be it", for which there will be no form in the world unless Jacob makes one for himself. The Plumers will try to prevent him from making it. Wells and Shaw and the serious sixpenny weeklies will sit on its head. Every time he lunches out on Sunday—at dinner parties and tea-parties— there will be this same shock—horror—discomfort—then pleasure, for he draws into him at every step as he walks by the river such steady certainty, such reassurance from all sides, the trees bowing, the grey spires soft in the blue, voices blowing and seeming suspended in the air, the springy air of May, the elastic air with its particles—chestnut bloom, pollen, whatever it is that gives the May air its potency, blurring the trees, gumming the buds, daubing the green. And the river too runs past, not at flood, nor swiftly, but cloying the oar that dips in it and drops white drops from the blade, swimming green and deep over the bowed rushes, as if lavishly caressing them.

And so the counterpoint is stated: unreality, the world of elderly men, dinner-parties and tea-parties with uninteresting people, conventional society in short; reality, the river flowing, the trees bowing, friendship. Beauty in the present and in memory comes to Jacob's aid. 'The reality: the moors and Byron, the sea and the lighthouse, the sheep's jaw with the yellow teeth in it', these are images from the past, from a childhood which was also a time of struggle. 'Thus build we up the being that we are.' It is by the sea that we have our first glimpse of Jacob. It is Cornwall, in the last decade of the nineteenth century. While his mother, Betty Flanders, is writing a letter, Jacob is investigating the wonderful world of the seashore. He doesn't want to play with his elder brother Archer. His passion, already, is for reality. He is living in his own world.

> The rock was one of those tremendously solid brown, or rather black, rocks which emerge from the sand like something primitive. Rough with crinkled limpet shells and sparsely strewn with locks of dry seaweed, a small boy has to stretch his legs far apart, and indeed to feel rather heroic, before he gets to the top.
> But there, on the very top, is a hollow full of water, with a sandy bottom; with a blob of jelly stuck to the side, and some mussels. A fish darts across. The fringe of yellow-brown seaweed flutters, and out pushes an opal-shelled crab——
> "Oh, a huge crab," Jacob murmured—and begins his journey on weakly legs on the sandy bottom. Now! Jacob plunged his hand. The crab was cool and very light. But the water was thick with sand, and so, scrambling down, Jacob was about to jump, holding his bucket in front of him, when he saw, stretched entirely rigid, side by side, their faces very red, an enormous man and woman.
> An enormous man and woman (it was early-closing day) were stretched motionless, with their heads on pocket-handkerchiefs, side by side, within a few feet of the sea, while two or three gulls gracefully skirted the incoming waves, and settled near their boots.

The same contrast, then, that was drawn so many years later, at Cambridge.

What a variety of worlds we have already in the short opening section! The maternal world of Mrs Flanders, writing her letter with the tears filling her eyes and thus making the external world wobble—but this world of emotion, so real to Betty Flanders, does not exist for Charles Steele in the Panama hat who is painting her into his landscape and is furious when she changes position. For him, Mrs Flanders the sorrowful widow is a mere brush-stroke. Then Archer's world, playing and wanting his brother to join him. Jacob's world, which for the moment is the world also of the rock and the sand, the pool and the blob of jelly and the crab. Jacob is the only one who really makes contact with something outside himself. He feels the immense solidity of the rock, its roughness; he establishes a satisfactory relationship with it. He feels the coolness and crystal texture of the water. The crab has colour and lightness. Reality. And then, thrust into this world of marvellous shapes and impressions, in which he can run and leap, dance and sing, alone, there comes the rigid, heavy, meaningless, ugly world of the adult.

It is disturbing, this world. He runs away, frightened after a while by the waves racing up to him. He thinks he sees his nurse, but when he comes nearer there is nothing but a rock, covered with seaweed. He is lost, cut off.

> There he stood. His face composed itself. He was about to roar when, lying among the black sticks and straw under the cliff, he saw a whole skull—perhaps a cow's skull, a skull, perhaps, with the teeth in it. Sobbing, but absent-mindedly, he ran farther and farther away until he held the skull in his arms.

The skull, the solid object again, bare and self-sufficient, has saved him; but to his mother, when she finds him, it is only something horrid which he must throw away at once. "Something horrid, I know. Why didn't you stay with us? Naughty little boy!" But Jacob surreptitiously detaches the sheep's jaw. He is obstinate, refractory to the herd, making his own world out of sheeps' skulls and rocks and sea. That night he sleeps with the jaw kicked down against the foot of his bed. Outside the rain beats on the garden, the world of things detached now from the lives of men. The crab struggles for its own life.

> Outside the rain poured down more directly and powerfully as the wind fell in the early hours of the morning. The aster was beaten to the earth. The child's bucket was half-full of rain-water; and the opal-shelled crab slowly circled round the bottom, trying with its weakly legs to climb the steep side; trying again and falling back, and trying again and again.

Thus, as in *The Voyage Out*, Virginia Woolf takes us outside the house at night-time, and shows us a life alien to the human. And now the first act is concluded; Jacob's childhood is over.

ii

Jacob's Room proceeds with something of the technique of the drama; intermediate stages are not filled in, time jumps forward and, if need be, backwards. Jacob's boyhood is spent in

Scarborough; there is Mr Floyd, a clergyman who teaches him Latin and wants to marry Mrs Flanders, and allows him to choose a parting present from his study before leaving to work in a parish in Sheffield. Jacob chooses the works of Byron. His interest in things continues; he collects moths and butterflies, and goes out at night into the wood with a lantern. One night when he is watching the insects and an old toad trying to butt their way into the light, a rotten tree falls. The noise of its falling is like pistol-shots.

iii

Jacob goes up to Cambridge in October 1906. We see Cambridge first as light—an intensely blue sky burning over the pinnacles of King's College Chapel by day, and the lamps of Cambridge burning into the night. But the light sometimes is coloured by human dreams. Inside King's College Chapel, for instance, as the great windows shed their red, yellow and purple on the stone: what dignity and authority of elderly people! The white-robed figures cross from side to side, now mounting steps, now descending, and the organ booms; there is the impression of order and illumination. The Chapel is like a great lantern in the night. But then, suddenly, Jacob's thought switches back to the lantern under the tree, with the old toad and the beetles and the moths crossing from side to side in the light, senselessly. "Now there was a scraping and murmuring. He caught Timmy Durrant's eye; looked very sternly at him; and then, very solemnly, winked."

From a boat on the Cam there is another sort of beauty to be seen. There are buttercups gilding the meadows, and cows munching, and the legs of children deep in the grass. Jacob looks at all these things and becomes absorbed. ' "Jacob's off," thought Durrant, looking up from his novel.' But there are other boats on the river, there is Lady Miller's picnic party. Jacob is recalled to the world of others.

"Oh-h-h-h," groaned Jacob, as the boat rocked, and the trees rocked, and the white dresses and the white flannel trousers drew out long and wavering up the bank.

"Oh-h-h-h!" He sat up, and felt as if a piece of elastic had snapped in his face.

Jacob has rooms in Neville's Court in Trinity. Yellow flags in a jar; his mother's photograph; cards from university societies, with their little raised crests; pipes; books—all the Elizabethans; Spinoza and *The Faerie Queene*; a Greek dictionary; shabby old slippers. One of many such rooms. In rather more commodious rooms there are dons: not wholly splendid, for there may be jealousy and even narrowness in commodious and learned rooms. But the light of Cambridge burns on into the night. Human beings, each seeking his own refuge from reality, are the lanterns through which the light must shine if it is to shine at all. Elderly dons, out of contact with the world of things— 'such is the fabric through which the light must shine . . . the light of all those languages, Chinese and Russian, Persian and Arabic, of symbols and figures, of history, of things that are known and things that are about to be known. So that if at night, far out at sea over the tumbling waves, one saw a haze on the waters, a city illuminated, a whiteness even in the sky, such as that now over the Hall of Trinity where they're still dining, or washing up plates, that would be the light burning there—the light of Cambridge'.

And reality? The boats have now left the river. But 'the feathery white moon never let the sky grow dark; all night the chestnut blossoms were white in the green; dim was the cow-parsley in the meadows'. The world of things, again, detached from the world of men.

The life of Cambridge, then, has not quite the same sacro-sanct quality for Virginia Woolf that it has for Leslie Stephen or for E. M. Forster. She loves Cambridge, but she is a woman, an outsider; she can compare and criticise. The great court of Trinity is beautiful, but is there not too much brick and mortar for a May night? In Turkey (another of her swift transitions) the bare harsh lines of the hills stretch far, with coloured flowers and women beating out their linen bare-legged in the streams. There is a gift from the past in Cambridge; but what of the present? These young men arguing in college rooms— admirable the pursuit of truth, the intellectual quest; but reality—is it not pressing in on all sides? Too intent on the one, they forget the many. Yet truth is good, it is splendid that young men should marshall their thoughts and sweep away lies and loose thinking. Jacob derives from the exercise of the mind an extraordinary pleasure. Cambridge has given him its gift.

iv

Of plot, we notice, there is nothing in *Jacob's Room*. There are no set descriptions. There is no clumsy articulation of episodes. The moments are picked out in spots of light, as the lamp in Betty Flanders' room picked out the objects in the garden, the tossing aster, the child's bucket with the crab. We have been freed from some of the tyrannies of the novel, and allowed to enjoy some of the privileges of poetry. It is exhilarating and refreshing. Now that we see it can be done, we wonder why it has not been done before. And then we remember Sterne—yes, he did it, but found himself without an imitator. We know from *The Common Reader* how much Mrs Woolf admired Sterne, not only for his 'philosophy of pleasure', but also for his technical innovations, his daring to write in a different way. Sterne had the art of varying the proportions of his creations, of getting at life from a new slant. He had, too, the secret of silence. 'In this interest in silence rather than in speech,' she says, 'Sterne is the forerunner of the moderns.'

Silence plays a big part in *Jacob's Room*, and particularly in the fourth act. Jacob is back by the sea; on the sea in fact, for he is in Timmy Durrant's boat sailing to the Scilly islands. He is trying to read Shakespeare. But the sea is very blue, the sun strong. He dives. Shakespeare is knocked overboard, floats away with his leaves ruffling, then goes under. Reality has conquered. And we are given a view of the distant shore.

> The mainland, not so very far off—you could see clefts in the cliffs, white cottages, smoke going up—wore an extraordinary look of calm, of sunny peace, as if wisdom and piety had descended upon the dwellers there. Now a cry sounded, as of a man calling pilchards in a main street. It wore an extraordinary look of piety and peace, as if old men smoked by the door, and girls stood, hands on hips, at the well, and horses stood; as if the end of the world had come, and cabbage fields and stone walls, and coast-guard stations, and, above all, the white sand bays with the waves breaking unseen by anyone, rose to heaven in a kind of ecstasy.

'The waves breaking unseen by anyone'—it is this exultation in the thought of nature *alone*, leading her own tranquil existence (we have noted it already in *The Voyage Out*, and in an earlier section of *Jacob's Room*), which refreshes the spirit worn by human contacts.

61

The mood cannot last, of course; there follows a philosophical argument with Timmy Durrant, and the pleasure in argument; then golden beams of light fall from clouds upon the sea, like the fingers of God. The colour fades from the sky; the light-house casts its beams. 'Infinite millions of miles away powdered stars twinkled; but the waves slapped the boat, and crashed, with regular and appalling solemnity, against the rocks.'

Jacob is 'the silent young man' at Timmy Durrant's home, where he pays a visit after six days at sea. They have dinner—what a contrast to gnawing a ham-bone on a boat! They all go out and look at the stars through a telescope. They make him act in their play. He almost falls in love with Clara Durrant, beautiful among the vine leaves. He escapes to London.

V

'If there is such a thing as a shell secreted by man to fit man himself here we find it, on the banks of the Thames, where the great streets join and St Paul's Cathedral, like the volute on the top of the snail shell, finishes it off.' There are two places where, we feel, Mrs Woolf is most comfortably herself: by the sea and in London. She is not a country novelist, though she can write persuasively about fields and gardens. She belongs to the great tradition of London novelists, and shakes hands with Dr Johnson and Dickens in her love for the metropolis. She loves the streets, the crowded life, the shops; she loves the sense of history and the tide of life. 'In these rooms lived . . .' she murmurs, and goes off into a day-dream of eighteenth-century beauties or Elizabethan swashbucklers. London is a city of the present, but it is also literary London, a pleasant place to read in, or to have long pedantic conversations.

Or to write. Jacob, still crusading against shams and 'bald heads forgetful of their sins', writes an essay against Professor Bulteel, of Leeds, who has published an expurgated edition of Wycherley.

An outrage, Jacob said; a breach of faith; sheer prudery; token of a lewd mind and a disgusting nature. Aristophanes and Shakespeare were cited. Modern life was repudiated. Great play was made with the professorial title, and Leeds as a seat of learning was laughed to scorn. And the extraordinary thing was that these young men were perfectly right—extraordinary, because, even as Jacob copied his pages, he knew that no one would ever print them; and sure enough back they came from the *Fortnightly*, the *Contemporary*, the *Nineteenth Century*—when Jacob threw them into the black wooden box where he kept his mother's letters, his old flannel trousers, and a note or two with the Cornish postmark. The lid shut upon the truth.

London means, plainly, a detachment from reality greater than Cambridge could inflict: Jacob is moving further and further away from the world of things. He is becoming more and more caught up in human society. The novel is developing into a commentary on Wordsworth's Ode. It is on Guy Fawkes Night that we meet Florinda, a pretty, brainless, fast girl who becomes Jacob's mistress. Again there is no direct description, no explanation. Jacob wanted her, we suppose, and took her. With his friends, with Timmy Durrant, he discusses the Greeks. 'The Greeks—yes, that was what they talked about—how when all's said and done, when one's rinsed one's mouth with every literature in the world, including Chinese and Russian (but these Slavs aren't civilised) it's the flavour of Greek that remains.' Truth, the spirit of Cambridge, still prevails above human passions. But human passion connects Florinda with the Greeks; she had sat on his knee as all good women did in the ancient days. Yet she hasn't a brain, and for a real companionship the brain is so necessary.

> The problem is insoluble. The body is harnessed to a brain. Beauty goes hand in hand with stupidity. There she sat staring at the fire as she had stared at the broken mustard-pot. In spite of defending indecency, Jacob doubted whether he liked it in the raw. He had a violent reversion towards male society, cloistered rooms, and the works of the classics; and was ready to turn with wrath upon whoever it was who had fashioned life thus.

The problem of love and sex, we note, is here given more cursory handling than in *Night and Day* and *The Voyage Out*. In her first novel Mrs Woolf was concerned with the nature of first love as it affected two fairly ordinary young people; in her second, with the problem of reconciling the life-patterns of two rather extraordinary young people. Here her treatment is lighter and more rapid. Is there a solution to be found in purely physical passion? There isn't, she decides. Companionship is necessary in love, and for companionship there must be intelligence on both sides or none. Jacob thinks that he can make do with Florinda's prettiness and fidelity until he sees her walking down the street on the arm of another man.

vi

A little action is introduced at last as Jacob rides to hounds over the Essex fields. Then we find him reading Marlowe in the British Museum. Does he never work for a living? we wonder. We know his mother is poor. But this detail, so important in most novels, is passed over. Jacob is intent on Marlowe, whom he conceives as a devouring fire in whose flames Mr Arnold Bennett and Mr John Masefield may be burnt to ashes. 'Don't palter with the second rate. Detest your own age. And to set that on foot read incredibly dull essays on Marlowe to your friends.' Back in his rooms, he reads Plato or Shakespeare, while out in the street a drunken woman batters at a door and shouts "Let me in!" The method of contrast yields Mrs Woolf some effective scenes. We have another glimpse of Jacob at a riotous and not too respectable party. 'He looked quiet, not indifferent, but like some one on a beach, watching.'

vii

In Paris, he discusses art; in Italy, he feels the bareness and fierceness of the country. He absorbs impressions. Undoubtedly travelling is the thing. He is alone. He visits Greece. He finds delight in solitude.

> To gallop intemperately; fall on the sand tired out; to feel the earth spin; to have—positively—a rush of friendship for stones and grasses, as if humanity were over, and as for men and women, let them go hang—there is no getting over the fact that this desire seizes us pretty often.

But at Olympia he meets Mrs Wentworth Williams, whose husband is insignificant, and falls in love with her. She thinks him a mere bumpkin. He gives her Donne's poems. They part, and do not meet again.

Jacob returns to England. He is killed in the war, and leaves his room in some confusion.

Jacob's Room ends then, not like *Night and Day* with a question mark, but like *The Voyage Out* with the page torn across. We do not know what the ending would have been if life had been allowed to go on to its normal close. Jacob's simplicity, his directness, his love for truth, his interest in things—here we have the material for a life out of the ordinary. Would he have gone into a bank and become respectable, as is suggested at one point? Would he have been very much hurt by women in middle life, as is also suggested? We do not know. Jacob has the making of many things in him: a poet, a thinker, a scholar. To follow the conjectural course of a deceased character in fiction is absurd, but Mrs Woolf does rouse our interest and liking for this young man, for she makes Jacob both highly individual and also an exemplar of all the other young men whose promise the war destroyed. In her first two novels it was the young women who were the most vivid characters; between *Night and Day* and *Jacob's Room*, we surmise, she has got to know young men better and can draw them with a firmer and less fantastic hand. St John Hirst owed too much to Forster's Stewart Ansell; Jacob Flanders is all her own. There are evident similarities between Jacob's career and that of Roger Fry as recorded in Virginia Woolf's biography: evident enough to make it a good guess that her pictures of Cambridge life, of travel in Greece and attic rooms in London owe a great deal to her conversations with him. Her Cambridge scenes are brilliant, appreciative with a touch of irony, perfectly creating an atmosphere.

Jacob's Room shows a great advance in technique. Mrs Woolf has come into her own in style and in construction. The novel proceeds not with mechanical regularity, but in a series of short pictures, sometimes linked together in time and place, sometimes detached. It is worth while at this point to compare the opening of *Jacob's Room* with that of *Night and Day*. The difference in style is enormous, and persists through the later novel.

It was a Sunday evening in October [*Night and Day* begins], and in common with many other young ladies of her class, Katharine Hilbery was pouring out tea. Perhaps a fifth part of her mind was thus occupied, and the remaining parts leapt over the little barrier of day which interposed between Monday morning and this rather subdued moment, and played with the things one does voluntarily and normally in the daylight. But although she was silent, she was evidently mistress of a situation which was familiar enough to her, and inclined to let it take its way for the sixth hundred time, perhaps, without bringing into play any of her unoccupied faculties. A single glance was enough to show that Mrs Hilbery was so rich in the gifts which make tea-parties of elderly distinguished people successful, that she scarcely needed any help from her daughter, provided that the tiresome business of teacups and bread and butter was discharged for her.

It is admirably limpid, pleasant, but self-conscious writing. What are the ingredients? Jane Austen, E. M. Forster, Henry James perhaps—a phrase here and a turn there recall these names. It is not quite alive yet, though it warms up in a page or two. But the opening of *Jacob's Room*, plunging into the stream of consciousness, is pulsating with life.

> "So of course," wrote Betty Flanders, pressing her heels rather deeper in the sand, "there was nothing for it but to leave."
> Slowly welling from the point of her gold nib, pale blue ink dissolved the full stop; for there her pen stuck; her eyes fixed, and tears slowly filled them. The entire bay quivered; the lighthouse wobbled; and she had the illusion that the mast of Mr Connor's little yacht was bending like a wax candle in the sun. She winked quickly. Accidents were awful things. She winked again. The mast was straight; the waves were regular; the lighthouse was upright; but the blot had spread.
> ". . . nothing for it but to leave," she read.
> "Well, if Jacob doesn't want to play" (the shadow of Archer, her eldest son, fell across the notepaper and looked blue on the sand, and she felt chilly—it was the third of September already), "if Jacob doesn't want to play"—what a horrid blot! It must be getting late.

We can see what has happened. In the first place, Virginia Woolf has found her style: free, conversational, musical, the short phrases following each other like waves of the sea. And she has devised a technique for communication more immediate than any that had gone before. She gets everything in, and without the sense of incongruity. She has assimilated what she learnt in the sketches of *Monday or Tuesday*. Her glance shifts without difficulty from Betty Flanders' heels to the gold nib oozing ink, and thence to the tears in Betty's eyes. And she doesn't have to say, 'Because her eyes were filled with tears it seemed to Betty

Flanders that the bay was quivering, an illusion natural enough';
no, she says directly, 'The entire bay quivered . . .' We are
invited to share Mrs Flanders' sensation direct, without the
interposition of the novelist's as if's or by reason of's. Then we
are carried straight on to the thought which arises in a simple
mind on seeing a boat's mast bending: 'Accidents were awful
things.' We are made aware (of what we know perfectly well
in life, but are rarely told in fiction) that the mind is a rag-
bag. Betty Flanders is thinking of her letter, of her dead
husband, of Mr Connor's little yacht, and of her eldest son
Archer, all at the same time. Four-fifths of Katharine Hilbery's
mind was concerned with what was going to happen the next
day, we are told, but we are not told what those things were;
and the very present considerations in Betty Flanders' mind
impress us much more. Then, too, the writer has here achieved
a most subtle counterpoint of movement and stillness; Betty
Flanders sits writing her letter, but her son Archer wanders
past shouting 'Ja—cob!', trailing his spade; Jacob clambers
over rocks in the middle distance; and in the background the
waves beat ceaselessly upon the sand. We hold all these varying
distances and movements in mind together, and a marvellous
feeling of depth, a three-dimensional quality, is achieved. We
note too the painter's direct vision: the pale blue ink at the
point of the gold nib, the yacht bending like a wax candle, the
cold blue shadow of Archer on the sand.

The things that occupy Jacob's mind in the beginning—the
sheep's jaw and the rock, the butterflies and the falling tree—
are not allowed to stiffen into symbols or dominate the action:
they recur now and then, in memory, but not with a fixed
rhythm. As Jacob moves into the world of men they occur less
frequently. The image of the crab trying to climb out of the
child's pail never comes again; and for that very reason, and
because it has been etched on our minds by the light which fell
from the cottage window, it seems the most significant of them
all. Virginia Woolf's imagination always delights in thoughts of
the sea, the cool green world of quiet currents and waving water-
weeds; and when we think of the crab, we think of this world
which it is desperately trying to get back to. Jacob's life, as it
exists fragmentarily in the novel, is a frustrated life; he has
moments of happiness, but no steady glow of achievement. And
this fragmentariness is admirably conveyed by the writer's

technique of flashing scene after scene at us, cinematographic-ally, scenes which almost but never quite unite to form a pattern. Yes, life is like that, we say; it is especially like that when one is young. Later life brings some conviction of a plan, a purpose. But it is open to doubt whether this conviction may not be a defence-mechanism, a delusion which enables us to carry on. Youth is critical and idealistic—it demands a great deal from life; but when we grow older we know better, and are ready to make do with the fragments we have. Custom takes the place of purpose, daily work does duty for a pattern; and as for meaning—there are the consolations of religion, or self-indulgence, or politics. We shall be interested to see what Virginia Woolf has to say, in her later books, of life as it presents itself to the middle-aged. So far she has focused her attention on the young. She has explored the possibilities of living for inexperienced young girls, for undergraduates, for daughters of well-to-do families. The report she has brought back is not very encouraging. The world of the elderly presses hard upon the young, inhibits their impulses, takes away their freedom, and bewilders their sense of value. Then there is death; death from disease and accident, and death in wars that the elderly men make. And still we are very far from being able to answer those questions which Virginia Woolf put at the very beginning: What is love? how many kinds are there? what position does it hold in a man's life and a woman's life? And that still more obscure group of questions: What is the relation of intellectual truth to reality? in what does reality consist? what is its meaning? what is the significance of momentary illuminations?

Her next novel is to deal with the problems of the middle-aged. It is to take up the theme of marriage where she left it at the close of *Night and Day*. *Mrs Dalloway* takes us into a new world.

II
MARRIAGE AND TRUTH

CHAPTER V

Mrs Dalloway

[1925]

IT is the world of middle age, but of middle age which has not lost its capacity for experience. Mrs Dalloway herself, over fifty and grown very white since her illness, is well aware of the danger.

> She feared time itself, and read on Lady Bruton's face, as if it had been a dial cut in impassive stone, the dwindling of life; how year by year her share was sliced; how little the margin that remained was capable any longer of stretching, of absorbing, as in the youthful years, the colours, salts, tones of existence . . .

Yes, that is the danger. Life consists in this capacity to absorb, to enjoy to the full, the strange and vivid experiences which time insists in pressing upon us. It is only too easy to reject these experiences. Professional men reject them, clergymen reject them, old men bury themselves in the brown leather armchairs of clubs to escape from them. And marriage? Is not that too an escape? May it not be, even, that one marries one man and not another because one is afraid of adventure? For to experience everything is to be hurt by many things, and sometimes the hurt appears greater than the ecstasy, and hardly to be borne. Yet the hurt itself may turn to a quiet sort of ecstasy, in memory.

ii

Mrs Dalloway is an experiment with time. It is a mingling of present experience and memory, for the most part in Mrs Dalloway's mind. The ostensible action of the novel is a single day, a June day leading up to a dinner-party. We follow Mrs Dalloway's activities through the course of this June day, we observe her reactions to her household in Westminster, to her husband Richard, to her daughter Elizabeth, and to Peter Walsh, an old suitor of hers, who is just back from India. But interwoven with these actualities is the still more real world of the past, more real because it exists not only in itself as the present does (and is there a present, or only the imaginary point between past and future?) but also in its consequences and its relations. The scene is London after the war; but the scene is also Bourton in the country thirty years ago. Experience is simultaneous.

Mrs Dalloway goes out to buy the flowers for her party herself, for Lucy has enough to do. Leaving the house on a bright morning—'fresh as if issued to children on a beach'—her mind goes back to Bourton. It is something in the feel of the air that takes her back. But at the same time she senses the living quality of everything that is going on around her—the public life of London.

> Such fools we are, she thought, crossing Victoria Street. For Heaven only knows why one loves it so, how one sees it so, making it up, building it round one, tumbling it, creating it every moment afresh; but the veriest frumps, the most dejected of miseries sitting on doorsteps (drink their down-fall) do the same; can't be dealt with, she felt positive, by Acts of Parliament for that very reason: they love life. In people's eyes, in the swing, tramp, and trudge; in the bellow and the uproar; the carriages, motor cars, omnibuses, vans, sandwich men shuffling and swinging; brass bands; barrel organs; in the triumph and the jingle and the strange high singing of some aeroplane overhead was what she loved; life; London; this moment of June.

With this life Mrs Dalloway is identified. Her husband is a Conservative M.P.; she is a hostess, she is going to give a party in the evening. Little by little Virginia Woolf builds up the impression of involvement. In the street Mrs Dalloway meets Hugh Whitbread, carrying a despatch-box stamped with the Royal Arms, a friend with 'a little job at Court'. Then the royal car passes down the street; everyone is agog; it is the symbol of England's greatness. A crowd collects outside Buckingham Palace. The aeroplane circles overhead, spelling out the word 'Toffee'. Now heads are raised to look at the white smoke-letters trailing past the clouds, now they are lowered to greet an oncoming car—the King's? the Queen's? The life of London is skilfully suggested.

Meanwhile the counterpoint of memory proceeds. Peter Walsh (whom she had rejected) used to be angry with her for liking Hugh; Peter was intolerant, Peter was intransigent; he had called her 'the perfect hostess' and said she would marry a Prime Minister and stand at the top of a staircase.

So she would still find herself arguing in St James's Park, still making out that she had been right—and she had too—not to marry him. For in marriage a little licence, a little independence there must be between people living together day in day out in the same house; which Richard gave her, and she him.

Is she selfish to be that independent?

So Mrs Dalloway persuades herself that she was right to reject Peter, 'though she had borne about with her for years like an arrow sticking in her heart the grief, the anguish'; she has decided on the life of pleasant compromise; Peter went off to India and married a woman he met on the boat. Now he is coming back any day. He has been a failure, of course. It makes her angry that Peter, with all his gifts, has been a failure and married another woman. *Is C a failure too for not marrying Peter? Or for marrying Richard*

She turns the critical searchlight on herself. She is not clever, not well-read (we remember Rachel Vinrace, Katharine Hilbery), but she has the gift 'for knowing people almost by instinct'. Sometimes she seems to slip out of her own existence; there is no division between herself and other people. Sometimes the body disappears altogether: 'she had the oddest sense of being herself invisible; unseen; unknown; there being no more marrying, no more having of children now . . .' Was she meant to marry, to have children? What about solitude? The question comes when she returns home with her flowers. She goes upstairs to her attic room. 'There was an emptiness about the heart of life; an attic room.' Here she can be more truly herself.

She could see what she lacked. It was not beauty; it was not mind. It was something central which permeated; something warm which broke up surfaces and rippled the cold contact of man and woman, or of women together. For *that* she could dimly perceive. She resented it, had a scruple picked up Heaven knows where, or, as she felt, sent by Nature (who is invariably wise); yet she could not resist sometimes yielding to the charm of a woman, not a girl, of a woman confessing, as to her they often did, some scrape, some folly. And whether it was pity, or their beauty, or that she was older, or some accident—like a faint scent, or a violin next door (so strange is the power of sounds at certain moments), she did undoubtedly then feel what men felt. Only for a moment; but it was enough. It was a sudden revelation, a tinge like a blush which one tried to check and then, as it spread, one yielded to its expansion, and rushed to the farthest verge and there quivered and felt the world come closer, swollen with some astonishing significance, some pressure of rapture, which split its thin skin and gushed and poured with an extraordinary alleviation over the cracks and sores. Then, for that moment, she had seen an illumination; a match burning in a crocus; an inner meaning almost expressed. But the close withdrew; the hard softened. It was over—the moment.

In this passage we have something familiar to us from the preceding novels, and something unfamiliar. The familiar thing is the 'moment'—the instant of illumination which brings happiness and suggests a meaning. The unfamiliar thing is the occasion of this illumination. Hitherto it has been *things* which have brought the illumination most strongly and clearly; then, more doubtfully, in *The Voyage Out* and *Night and Day*, the passion of love between man and woman. We have asked ourselves whether the illumination will survive the experience of marriage. But here, in *Mrs Dalloway*, we find the moment coming most strongly in an experience between women. It is an extension of the theme of the novels, and it embodies a conviction of Mrs Woolf's—first, that the novel as constructed by male writers is not a wholly satisfactory medium for the woman novelist, especially in its presuppositions about love; and, secondly, that there is something androgynous in the nature of the artist, and that this androgyny should be admitted into her work. It is the theme of Tiresias in Eliot's *The Waste Land*. The artist knows not only the emotion aroused in man by woman, but also that aroused in woman by man. Unless the artist has this knowledge, a large area of experience is closed to him.

Mrs Dalloway asks herself what love is, and remembers how she was in love at eighteen with Sally Seton, that astonishingly original girl who discussed everything and ran naked about the corridors. 'Then came the most exquisite moment of her whole life, passing a stone urn with flowers in it. Sally stopped; picked a flower; kissed her on the lips. The whole world might have turned upside down.' This, then, is love; not a love of possession, but something protective, conspiratorial against the world of pretence and fraud ('they spoke of marriage always as a catastrophe'), yet certainly bringing 'the revelation, the religious feeling'. Thus a new complexity is introduced into the ordinary human relations. How get along satisfactorily in the business of love, Mrs Woolf had asked in the three first novels, when there is this conflict between emotion and truth, between the desire for solitude and the longing to share experience, between physical passion and repulsion from stupidity? How reach an adequate solution, she now asks, when there is this further complication of a love between women and an understanding of what men feel for women—which one certainly cannot share with one's husband? For too intense an understanding is disruptive of spontaneity, utterly destructive. The leaves and flowers may twine and rustle together in the sunlight; but down below in the dark the roots must remain for ever separate.

iii

Sally Seton, Peter Walsh, Richard Dalloway—we see them first, before they enter in person, through Clarissa's eyes. We see them living again in memory; we become aware of their pasts before we know what they are in the present. Then, when they appear one by one, we have to make a slight readjustment. Memory is not an entirely impartial medium. Clarissa's mind is coloured by emotion. Now, as she sits mending her dress, Peter Walsh himself appears, back from India. He is embarrassed, he takes a large pocket-knife out and half opens the blade. The simple unconventional action makes him real to us. And we see Clarissa through the eyes of Peter Walsh.

> Here she is mending her dress; mending her dress as usual, he thought; here she's been sitting all the time I've been in India; mending her dress; playing about; going to parties; running to the House and back and all that, he thought, growing more and more irritated, more and more agitated, for there's nothing in the world so bad for some women as marriage, he thought; and politics; and having a Conservative husband, like the admirable Richard. So it is, so it is, he thought, shutting his knife with a snap.

That's a new view of Mrs Dalloway; coloured, no doubt, by passions—old resentments, jealousies and love; but adding something to our understanding of her. We have grasped by now that in this novel we are to be shown human beings, their

motives and actions, under very different lights and from varying angles. We are exploring points of view.

Now Peter's mind goes back to the past, remembers his love
for Clarissa, his rejection, the infernal anguish; goes back to
India, remembers that he is in love with Daisy, the wife of a
Major in the Indian Army; remembers that he is a failure 'in
the Dalloways sense'. (But what is failure, what is success, we
are impelled to ask? The attic room, and memories—are these
the sum of life for Clarissa Dalloway? Or receiving her guests
at a party?) But he has lived—'journeys; rides; quarrels; adventures; bridge parties; love affairs; work; work, work!' And he
makes Clarissa feel emptyheaded and useless, though he says
nothing, only fumbles with his knife; and she has to call up to
her mind her husband, her daughter Elizabeth, and the things
she likes, if she is not to feel defeated.

Then he tells her about Daisy; and she feels a pang that he
is still capable of that. Daisy has a husband, and two small
children, and Peter has come to London to see his lawyers about
the divorce. (His own wife is dead.) And he feels he is up against
Clarissa and Dalloway, and all the rest of them; and he bursts
into tears, and Clarissa kisses him.

> . . . and feeling as she sat back extraordinarily at her ease with
> him and light-hearted, all in a clap it came over her, If I had
> married him, this gaiety would have been mine all day!
> It was all over for her. The sheet was stretched and the bed
> narrow. She had gone up into the tower alone and left them black-
> berrying in the sun. The door had shut, and there among the dust
> of fallen plaster and the litter of birds' nests how distant the view
> had looked, and the sounds came thin and chill (once on Leith
> Hill, she remembered), and Richard, Richard! she cried, as a
> sleeper in the night starts and stretches a hand in the dark for
> help.

Then Elizabeth, Clarissa's daughter, comes in—"Here is my
Elizabeth"—and Peter leaves. He goes out into the streets of
London, as Clarissa had done that morning; and now we shall
see the past through Peter's eyes as we have seen it through
Mrs Dalloway's.

'There was always something cold about Clarissa,' he thinks.
He dislikes the artificiality of her saying, 'Here is my Elizabeth'
—why 'my'? He is a failure, he was sent down from Oxford.
'Still the future of civilisation lies, he thought, in the hands of

young men like that; of young men such as he was, thirty years ago; with their love of abstract principles; getting books sent out to them all the way from London to a peak in the Himalayas; reading science; reading philosophy.' Truth, we see, the ideal of disinterested intellection, is being set against the ideal of success; St John Hirst and Ralph Denham and Jacob Flanders rise to stand shoulder to shoulder by Peter Walsh against the world of politics, parties and despatch cases blazoned with the royal arms. Virginia Woolf does not intend us to forget this ideal of truth while we press on to reality I have not rejected truth, she says, I am still in love with intellectual integrity; it is the bones of reality, or at any rate the hard flinty path leading to it. We must keep our feet on that path. But we must look at politics and success, too, and see what truth and what reality may be concealed there. Mrs Dalloway now —is she an admirable character, or are we to pity her as one who has lost her way? Is the attic room all she has to show? We mustn't be prejudiced; we have heard what she has to say; we shall now listen to what Peter Walsh has to say; but in the end we shall draw our own conclusions.

Sitting in the sun in Regent's Park, his mind goes back over the past. He remembers how shocked Clarissa had been at Bourton with Sally Seton, because she had said after tea, 'Did it make any real difference to one's feelings to know that before they'd married [they are talking of a local squire and his housemaid] she had had a baby?' Clarissa did frighten people, it seemed; she had that streak of hardness and intolerance in her nature. And he thinks too of the dreadful moment when he realised that she was going to marry Dalloway, and the still more dreadful scene, by the fountain, when she had finally rejected him. Still, one got over things, Peter Walsh thought, as he sat in the sun in Regent's Park.

iv

'But Lucrezia Warren Smith was saying to herself, It's wicked; why should I suffer?' Lucrezia is also sitting in Regent's Park, with her husband. These are two characters we do not see through the mind of Mrs Dalloway or of Peter Walsh. Yet their lives, through this long summer day, run side by side with the other lives, touch lightly here and there, but never become involved. It is another order of reality. It is the world of insanity, cruelty and cowardice which exists within the texture of civilisation as firmly as the Dalloways' world exists. The two, indeed, are interdependent. Without the Dalloways there would be no Warren Smiths. Behind the Dalloways there rises the massive edifice of civilisation, the Houses of Parliament, St. Paul's Cathedral, the War Office, the Law Courts, the professional classes, Harley Street. The Dalloways feel these things as a support, and add their own brick to the structure. When the royal car sweeps down St James's Street,

> Tall men, men of robust physique, well-dressed men with their tail-coats and their white slips and their hair raked back who, for reasons difficult to discriminate, were standing in the bow window of White's with their hands behind the tails of their coats, looking out, perceived instinctively that greatness was passing, and the pale light of the immortal presence fell upon them as it had fallen upon Clarissa Dalloway. At once they stood even straighter, and removed their hands, and seemed ready to attend their Sovereign, if need be, to the cannon's mouth, as their ancestors had done before them.

Thus the relation: civilisation—Royalty—war: is satisfactorily established. The passage is satirical; *Three Guineas* is already adumbrated. The war is over, but not its anguish.

> The War was over, except for someone like Mrs Foxcroft at the Embassy last night eating her heart out because that nice boy was killed . . . or old Lady Bexborough who opened a bazaar, they said, with the telegram in her hand, John, her favourite, killed; but it was over; thank Heaven—over. It was June. The King and Queen were at the Palace.

The war is not over for Septimus Warren Smith, aged about thirty, with an apprehensive look in his eyes. 'The world has raised its whip; where will it descend?' Mrs Dalloway looks out of the flower-shop window (we are going back to the early morning now) as the royal car draws up outside; Septimus Warren Smith halts on the pavement, unable to pass. Lucrezia, his wife, a sallow-faced Italian girl with big eyes, tries to draw him on. 'I will kill myself,' he has said. The war, through which he has passed, has disturbed his brain. It has taken Septimus away from her and left her only a piece of bone to rest her hand on as they cross the street.

They sit down in Regent's Park. Lucrezia, who has been told by Dr Holmes to make her husband take an interest in things outside himself, draws his attention to the aeroplane writing 'Toffee' on the sky. It is a message, thinks Septimus, 'they' are signalling to him. Who are 'they'? He does not know. Tears roll down his cheeks. His malady has made him exquisitely, abnormally sensitive to sounds and colours. A nursemaid spells out the word—'K . . . R . . .'—and the roughness in her voice rasps his spine

> . . . and sent running up into his brain waves of sound which, concussing, broke. A marvellous discovery indeed—that the human voice in certain atmospheric conditions (for one must be scientific, above all scientific) can quicken trees into life! . . . they beckoned; leaves were alive; trees were alive. And the leaves being connected by millions of fibres with his own body, there on the seat, fanned it up and down; when the branch stretched he, too, made that statement. The sparrows fluttering, rising, and falling in jagged fountains were part of the pattern; the white and blue, barred with black branches. Sounds made harmonies with premeditation; the spaces between them were as significant as the sounds. A child cried. Rightly far away a horn sounded. All taken together meant the birth of a new religion—

It is a study in abnormal perception. It is the world seen through a mind so exquisitely sensitive that it has become unbalanced. But, we notice with something of a shock, it is Virginia Woolf's vision of *things* carried to an extreme point. Her sensitiveness is just of this quality, kept in check by humour and irony, by the historical sense, by an interest in human beings, in 'jolly old fishwives' and the discussions of undergraduates. But the basis is the same: the relation between people and things, the solitary mind finding a language in nature, the harmony of life in trees and sky. What she shows us is what happens to this vision when the checks have been removed. Septimus Warren Smith's confidence in the world of men, in civilisation, in human affection, has been shattered in the war.

Dr Holmes says there is nothing the matter with him. Dr Holmes feels the pulse, looks at the tongue; for him the soul does not exist; cannot, therefore, be sick. But Rezia, the poor little Italian girl Septimus married in Milan after the war, knows that he does not see her, he only looks at the sky and trees and 'makes everything terrible'. She loves him, she will protect him and will not let him kill himself. In a few strokes Rezia is made surprisingly real to us. These sections of the novel are full of compassion, a quality we have missed since *The Voyage Out*. Mrs Woolf shows us that Rezia and her mad husband are no less real in the texture of life than the Dalloways; perhaps more real, as they suffer more. Is that what is wrong with Clarissa, that she has not suffered enough? She has existed, buoyed up on the love of Peter, of Richard and Elizabeth, on the respectability of her social position. Has reality passed her by?

Rezia too goes back in memory. 'Far was Italy and the white houses and the room where her sisters sat making hats, and the streets crowded every evening with people walking, laughing out loud, not half alive like people here . . .' She is cut off from her own people, she feels alone; the spirit of Septimus has left her. She will never tell anyone that he is mad. She implores him to look at the boys playing cricket, at the sheep. But such common sights haven't much chance against the phantoms of the mind.

> He lay back in his chair, exhausted but upheld. He lay resting, waiting, before he again interpreted, with effort, with agony, to mankind. He lay very high, on the back of the world. The earth thrilled beneath him. Red flowers grew through his flesh; their stiff leaves rustled by his head. Music began clanging against the rocks up there. . . .

Thus his mind transmutes everything, connects the most disparate sounds and pictures. It is like a surrealist painting, or a photo-montage. He remembers he went under the sea and was drowned (the war). He opens his eyes and there is beauty all around him—leaves steeped in pure gold. But behind the leaves there is Evans, his friend, who was killed. To Peter Walsh, however, passing Rezia and Septimus fixed in this horror, they are only two young lovers having a scene.

V

Through Peter's mind as he walks there runs a pattern of impressions, memories, emotions. 'This susceptibility to impressions had been his undoing, no doubt.' His thoughts go back to Clarissa: how she admired Dalloway for his opinions about Shakespeare (the relationship suggested in the Sonnets was not one of which he could approve); how Sally Seton had begged him to save Clarissa from Richard and Whitbread and all the other perfect gentlemen who would make a mere hostess of her; how shrewd Clarissa was underneath, yet purely feminine, 'with that extraordinary gift, that woman's gift, of making a world of her own wherever she happened to be'. And he thinks that Clarissa is not striking, nor beautiful, not picturesque or clever; but 'there she was, however; there she was'. He hastens to assure himself that he is not in love with her any more. She is worldly, she cares for success, she admires stiff old Duchesses.

In all this there was a great deal of Dalloway, of course; a great deal of the public-spirited, British Empire, tariff-reform, governing-class spirit, which had grown on her, as it tends to do. With twice his wits, she had to see life through his eyes—one of the tragedies of married life.

She has an atheist's religion of doing good for the sake of goodness—to spite the Gods, who were furious if they saw you behaving decently without the inducement of immortality.

And of course she enjoyed life immensely. It was her nature to enjoy (though, goodness only knows, she had her reserves; it was a mere sketch, he often felt, that even he, after all these years, could make of Clarissa). Anyhow there was no bitterness in her; none of that sense of moral virtue which is so repulsive in good women. She enjoyed practically everything. If you walked with her in Hyde Park, now it was a bed of tulips, now a child in a perambulator, now some absurd little drama she made up on the spur of the moment. (Very likely she would have talked to those lovers, if she had thought them unhappy.) She had a sense of comedy that was really exquisite, but she needed people, always people, to bring it out, with the inevitable result that she frittered her time away, lunching, dining, giving those incessant parties of hers, talking nonsense, saying things she didn't mean, blunting the edge of her mind, losing her discrimination.

An admirable person this Peter Walsh, we perceive! He is critical, aware, detached, and holds to the supreme virtues of truth and reality. He is shedding a cool clear light on the frailties of Mrs Dalloway. No longer in love with her, he is doubtless able to see her, if not whole (he admits that) at least steadily. But then we remember the tears he shed in her room not long ago; we remember a certain irritation with the way she said, 'Here's my Elizabeth.' Tears, we know, blur the vision, make things wobble; irritation distorts. Perhaps a tear, not quite shed, remains in Peter Walsh's eye, a trace of irritation scratches a little like a grain of sand under the lid. We shall not quite accept Peter's portrait, we shall suspend our judgment a trifle longer, in case new light from another quarter should be shed on Mrs Dalloway.

vi

Rezia and her husband, meanwhile, are on their way to consult Sir William Bradshaw, the famous specialist in Harley Street. We cannot see Septimus through the eyes of Mrs Dalloway and Peter Walsh, for they never meet him. So the writer has to give us some direct description. To look at, he might have been a clerk, of the better sort; he left home and came to London because he could see no future for a poet in Stroud; he has had experiences 'such as change a face in two years from a pink innocent oval to a face lean, contracted, hostile'. He falls in love with Miss Isabel Pole, lecturing in the Waterloo Road about Shakespeare. He is one of the first to volunteer in the war. 'He went to France to save an England which consisted almost entirely of Shakespeare's plays and Miss Isabel Pole in a green dress walking in a square.' He develops manliness in the trenches, is promoted, becomes friendly with his officer, Evans. But Evans is killed, and Septimus feels nothing. He congratulates himself on this lack of feeling. 'When peace came he was in Milan, billeted in the house of an innkeeper with a courtyard, flowers in tubs, little tables in the open, daughters making hats, and to Lucrezia, the youngest daughter, he became engaged one evening when the panic was on him— that he could not feel.'

Again, we note, marriage to bolster up insufficiency. This fear, of not being able to feel, grows and grows. Septimus is shell-shocked. He marries to find security, he is sacrificing Lucrezia to his own fear. She is intelligent, artistic; at first she thinks only, 'The English are so silent'; she likes that. She wants to see London. At the office they give him a responsible post. He reads Shakespeare again; but the beauty of the language has vanished. All Septimus sees now is how Shakespeare loathed humanity—'the putting on of clothes, the getting of children, the sordidity of the mouth and belly'. Septimus refuses to have children, though they have now been married five years and Rezia wants a son. In the end he gives up the effort to live, and Rezia sends for Dr Holmes. Dr Holmes says there is nothing the matter with him, suggests a music-hall and two tablets of bromide at bedtime. It is no good. Dr Holmes sends them to Sir William Bradshaw, the great specialist. Sir William Bradshaw is Virginia Woolf's portrait, complete and of a certain magnitude, of the professional type. First, as is appropriate, we are introduced to his car, 'low, powerful, grey with plain initials interlocked on the panels, as if the pomps of heraldry were incongruous, this man being the ghostly helper, the priest of science'. Sir William is the son of a shopkeeper, he has risen by hard work, and now a wall of gold is mounting steadily every minute between him and all shifts and anxieties. There is a son at Eton. Sir William is himself no longer young, but he makes a fine figure-head at Ceremonies and speaks well—

. . . all of which had by the time he was knighted given him a heavy look, a weary look (the stream of patients being so incessant, the responsibilities and privileges of his profession so onerous), which weariness, together with his grey hairs, increased the extraordinary distinction of his presence and gave him the reputation (of the utmost importance in dealing with nerve cases) not merely of lightning skill and almost infallible accuracy in diagnosis, but of sympathy; tact; understanding of the human soul.

Sir William immediately diagnoses Septimus's case as grave—'complete physical and nervous breakdown, with every symptom in an advanced stage'. He gets from Rezia the confession that her husband has threatened to kill himself. Septimus, he decides, must go to a delightful 'home' in the country, away from Rezia. And if he does not wish to go, Rezia asks? Sir William explains, kindly, that it is a question of the law. Septimus has threatened to kill himself. That is enough. The machinery has been set in motion. 'Once you fall, Septimus repeated to himself, human nature is on you. Holmes and Bradshaw are on you. They scour the desert. They fly screaming into the wilderness. The rack and the thumbscrew are applied. Human nature is remorseless.' So the Warren Smiths leave Sir William, who gives three-quarters of an hour to each of his patients, and invokes for all of them silence and rest in one of his homes, away from friends. They must regain a sense of proportion, they must come to think like Sir William.

> Worshipping proportion, Sir William not only prospered himself, but made England prosper, secluded her lunatics, forbade childbirth, penalised despair, made it impossible for the unfit to propagate their views until they, too, shared his sense of proportion—his, if they were men, Lady Bradshaw's if they were women (she embroidered, knitted, spent four nights out of seven at home with her son), so that not only did his colleagues respect him, his subordinates fear him, but the friends and relations of his patients felt for him the keenest gratitude for insisting that these prophetic Christs and Christesses, who prophesied the end of the world, or the advent of God, should drink milk in bed, as Sir William ordered; Sir William with his thirty years' experience of these kinds of cases, and his infallible instinct, this is madness, this is sense, his sense of proportion.

Virginia Woolf gives us a brilliant and drastic picture of the professional man. The evil Sir William can do is rendered all the more horrible by the consideration that he is technically a healer; that society looks up to him, rewards him, and fails to look below the surface. He is the product, that is, of spiritual apathy, of ignorance, of the brute weight of non-awareness that afflicts our twentieth-century world. We live all the time in the realm of appearances. We worship power, and distrust pity and intuition. We send the Septimus Warren Smiths to the Sir William Bradshaws.

> And then stole out from her hiding-place and mounted her throne that Goddess whose lust is to override opposition, to stamp indelibly in the sanctuaries of others the image of herself. Naked, defenceless, the exhausted, the friendless received the impress of Sir William's will. He swooped; he devoured. He shut people up. It was this combination of decision and humanity that endeared Sir William so greatly to the relations of his victims.
>
> But Rezia Warren Smith cried, walking down Harley Street, that she did not like that man.

vii

Half-past one. Hugh Whitbread and Richard Dalloway are lunching with Lady Bruton. The life, the atmosphere of Mayfair hostesses are clearly delineated. The exquisite lunch gives the impression that it appears by magic, that no one has to pay for it. Old Lady Bruton, more interested in politics than in people, who does not like Clarissa's habit of discriminating between one perfect gentleman and another (for do we not all belong to the same side?) gives the information that Peter Walsh is in town. And they all remember Peter's hopeless passion for Clarissa, his rejection, his voyage to India, how he had 'come a cropper; made a mess of things; and Richard Dalloway had a very great liking for the dear old fellow too'. And Richard thinks that he will go home directly after lunch and tell Clarissa in so many words that he loves her.

Virginia Woolf puts a good deal of comedy into this lunch at Lady Bruton's; but it is comedy with a strong undercurrent of irony. Lady Bruton is a member, a more ineffectual member, of Sir William Bradshaw's clan of power-maniacs. She has called her two friends together to help her draft a letter to *The Times*. She wants to expound a 'project for emigrating young people of both sexes born of respectable parents and setting them up with a fair prospect of doing well in Canada. She exaggerated. She had perhaps lost her sense of proportion. Emigration was not to others the obvious remedy, the sublime conception'. Lady Bruton, we learn, cannot write this letter herself; there is a certain difficulty about marshalling her thoughts and getting them down on paper; in one from the lower orders, say a housemaid, it might be called stupidity, but in Lady Bruton, with her statesmanlike scheme of public welfare, it is rather a minor question of tactics, in which, it is said, great strategists are seldom successful. So she calls on Hugh Whitbread, who undoubtedly possesses the art of writing letters to *The Times*; she consults with Richard on what precisely is to be said, and with Hugh on how precisely to say it; and thus, miraculously, Lady Bruton's tangles are reduced to sense and her English to grammar.

It is a serious indictment of society that Virginia Woolf is building up, slowly, from the beginning, by cross-references and allusions—now directly, now ironically, now with the undertones of pity and terror. This solid structure of London—of what does it really consist? This parade of civilisation and culture, which can gladden the heart of Clarissa Dalloway because it is life and because she does not look below the surface, what does it hide? We are shown first all its colour and movement on a fine June day; then the great symbol of Royalty moves in a closed car across the woof; all is impressively knit together. Hugh Whitbread with his little job at Court, so happy and polite; the flower-shop; Clarissa's home, cool and dignified; the soldiers marching to the Cenotaph. But then in the smooth structure cracks appear, another order of reality thrusts itself forward. Peter Walsh comes home from India, critical, intransigent, loving truth; should I have married him? thinks Clarissa. There is the attic room, and loneliness. On the outskirts of her world, unseen by her but terribly real move the tragic figures of Rezia and Septimus. Under the genial mask of Sir William what harshness and cruelty! Overhead the aeroplane, that but lately has been raining down bombs, and will shortly do so again, traces the word 'Toffee'.

But, because she is fair, Mrs Woolf shows us the decencies of civilisation too: a man like Richard Dalloway, a product of the system but not so deeply involved in it that he cannot see some of its faults and want to cure them (as he tries his best to do, in the House)—not very wise, not very intelligent, but decent, simple and affectionate, with no illusions regarding the London police, about whose malpractices he is collecting information, 'and those costermongers, not allowed to stand their barrows in the streets; and prostitutes, good Lord, the fault wasn't in them, or in young men either, but in our detestable social system and so forth; all of which he considered, could be seen considering, as he walked across the Park to tell his wife that he loved her'. Richard Dalloway is good as an individual, yes; he is a product of the system; but Sir William is also a product, possibly more widespread; and isn't the price we pay for the Richard Dalloways rather too high?—war, snobbery, oppression, the trampling on imagination, and mighty poets in their misery dead.

viii

Three o'clock. Clarissa is sitting at her writing-table, worried, annoyed. Why should she invite Ellie Henderson if she doesn't want to? 'And there was Elizabeth closeted all this time with Doris Kilman. Anything more nauseating she could not conceive. Prayer at this hour with that woman.' Then in comes Richard with flowers. But he cannot bring himself to say that he loves her—not in so many words. They sit and talk. 'Happiness is this, he thought.' But he must go. He gets up, stands for a moment as though he is going to say something. What is it, she wonders? He is going to sit on a committee on the Armenians, or perhaps it was Albanians.

> And there is a dignity in people; a solitude; even between husband and wife a gulf; and that one must respect, thought Clarissa, watching him open the door; for one would not part with it oneself, or take it, against his will, from one's husband, without losing one's independence, one's self-respect—something, after all, priceless.

She is unhappy, though, when he goes. Something is missing, something hurts. Something that has happened earlier in the day. It is not the memory of Sally Seton saying that Richard will never be in the Cabinet because he has a second-class mind; it is not Elizabeth and Miss Kilman praying upstairs. Now she has it—it was Peter laughing at her parties. He thinks she is a snob, a lion-hunter. But she knows that it is life she loves—her parties give her the flavour of life. But if Peter asks her what is the sense of her parties, what is she to reply? Peter makes out that she complicates life, which is really perfectly simple; but who is Peter to say that, Peter who is always in love with the wrong woman?

> But to go deeper, beneath what people said (and these judgments, how superficial, how fragmentary they are!) in her own mind now, what did it mean to her, this thing she called life? Oh, it was very queer. Here was So-and-So in South Kensington; someone up in Bayswater; and somebody else, say, in Mayfair. And she felt quite continuously a sense of their existence; and she felt what a waste; and she felt what a pity; and she felt if only they could be brought together; so she did it. And it was an offering; to combine, to create; but to whom?

Oh, to whom?—that was the same question Katharine Hilbery asked herself, recalling a line of Shelley, in *Night and Day*; and it will be asked again in *The Years*. And the fact that neither Katharine nor Clarissa can answer this question is symptomatic of the lack of purpose in their lives: they are intelligent, energetic, capable of devotion and self-sacrifice, they rejoice in life—but they are without an aim. The question is posed once more: is it enough to love mathematics and solitude, like Katharine, to love making people happy and understanding their difficulties, like Clarissa—and all the time have one's own real existence in an attic room, which no one can enter, apart; or should there be something outside oneself, someone, some person or cause, to whom or which all one's life is directed? The crowds of London have such a cause, embodied in a person, the mystic person of the King passing in a closed car; Richard Dalloway has a cause, the rights of the poor and oppressed; Sir William Bradshaw has his two goddesses to serve, Proportion and Conversion. And Miss Kilman, who now enters the picture, has a cause, Religion. She serves God.

All Virginia Woolf's distaste for religion is poured into the mould of Doris Kilman. Distaste—but, also, pity. Miss Kilman belongs to that company of soured spinsters of whom Virginia Woolf gives us a considerable gallery—among others, Minnie Marsh, Miss Craddock, and the nameless 'hospital nurse' in *The Voyage Out*. She has been cheated of life, she feels, cheated by her unattractiveness, her poverty, her sincerity (which lost her her job during the war, for she could not honestly say all the right was on the English side). She has had to work hard for very small reward. Now she finds her reward in despising the others—people like Mrs Dalloway, who have never worked in their lives, fine ladies who ought to be in a factory, behind a counter. She has to make her living by giving lessons to the daughters of women like Mrs Dalloway. But she has her consolation—God.

> Bitter and burning, Miss Kilman had turned into a church two years three months ago. She had heard the Rev. Edward Whittaker preach; the boys sing; had seen the solemn lights descend, and whether it was the music, or the voices (she herself when alone in the evening found comfort in a violin; but the sound was excruciating, she had no ear); the hot and turbulent feelings which boiled and surged in her had been assuaged as she sat there, and she wept copiously, and had gone to call on Mr Whittaker at his private house in Kensington. It was the hand of God, he said. The Lord had shown her the way. So now, whenever the hot and painful feelings boiled within her, this hatred of Mrs Dalloway, this grudge against the world, she thought of God. She thought of Mr Whittaker. Rage was succeeded by calm. A sweet savour filled her veins, her lips parted, and, standing formidable upon the landing in her mackintosh, she looked with steady and sinister serenity at Mrs Dalloway, who came out with her daughter.

She feels the desire to dominate Mrs Dalloway, to overcome and unmask her. She would like to make her weep, to ruin and humiliate her and make her confess that she, Miss Kilman, is right. 'But this was God's will, not Miss Kilman's. It was to be a religious victory. So she glared; so she glowered.'

In Miss Kilman, Virginia Woolf is making her criticism of an all-too-common religious type; to which, she believes, not only frustrated women like Doris Kilman belong but also a good number of clergymen. It is a type in which the love of power is hidden under a religious cloak: a love of power mingled with invincible stupidity. These men would be worsted in the battles of the world: they would never rise to domination in the spheres of business, politics, medicine or law. They lack the ability to succeed in these professions. In the Church, however, their ambition is fulfilled. They have an assured spiritual position; they have the pulpit, an unassailable platform for the inflation of their egos; they have a flock, chiefly of women, over whom to rule undisturbed. In themselves insignificant, they are dangerous as a body, as a vested interest with a big say in the lives of the community. What kind of say this may be Virginia Woolf shows us in the person of Miss Kilman. Doris Kilman is in the Dalloways' house to teach history to Elizabeth, aged seventeen. Elizabeth is at an impressionable age. What a wonderful opportunity, thinks Miss Kilman, to get hold of Elizabeth's soul (her face and body, also, are beautiful) and bring it to God! To make her see her mother as she really is, to make her hate and despise her mother, and love and honour Miss Kilman. Elizabeth is young, beautiful, full of life, she loves the country; she does not like parties so much, and she thinks young men are silly, comparing her to poplar trees and hyacinths; but it is very exciting. Miss Kilman does not want her to love these things; she wants to capture her for God, and keep her with her in the cage she has constructed.

And Clarissa Dalloway, who has that gift of seeing into the heart, has seen into Miss Kilman and knows that she is evil. But she knows too that she must not try to separate Elizabeth from her by force, by giving an order. She lets Miss Kilman take Elizabeth shopping to the Stores.

Love and religion! thought Clarissa, going back into the drawing-room, tingling all over. How detestable, how detestable they are! For now that the body of Miss Kilman was not before her, it overwhelmed her—the idea. The cruellest things in the world, she thought, seeing them clumsy, hot, domineering, hypocritical, eavesdropping, jealous, infinitely cruel and unscrupulous, dressed in a mackintosh coat, on the landing; love and religion. Had she ever tried to convert anyone herself? Did she not wish everybody merely to be themselves? And she watched out of the window the old lady opposite climbing upstairs. Let her climb upstairs if she wanted to; let her stop; then let her, as Clarissa had often seen her, gain her bedroom, part her curtains, and disappear again into the background. Somehow one respected that—that old woman looking out of the window, quite unconscious that she was being watched. There was something solemn in it—but love and religion would destroy that, whatever it was, the privacy of the soul.

The supreme mystery, Clarissa thinks, is human isolation—'here was one room; there another. Did religion solve that, or love?' And the supreme virtue, the supreme social virtue, is tolerance: to let people go their own way, be themselves, do what they like, so long as they are not hurting other people. Not 'so long as they are not offending against a code of morality or social behaviour'—that doesn't matter. What matters is the freedom of the soul. Not to impose, not to wish to dominate, not to twist other people to one's own image. But religion and love are intolerant, both destructive of the human image and fatal to human freedom, as William Blake showed in a hundred pages. The thirst for possession and power is in them.

It is for possession and power that Miss Kilman thirsts as she has tea with Elizabeth in the Army and Navy Stores. Mrs Dalloway has laughed at her; she is ugly and clumsy; but at least she has got Elizabeth. Miss Kilman eats with intensity, and this puzzles Elizabeth, who does not realise that 'eating was almost the only pure pleasure left her'. (Pretensions to spirituality, we note, result in unrestrained animality. 'Seeking to be more than man, we become less,' says Blake.) Miss Kilman also indulges in self-pity: 'people don't ask me to parties . . . I'm plain, I'm unhappy'. She knows it's idiotic to go on like this to Elizabeth—it's the way to lose her; but go on she does, pushed by some ineluctable necessity. Then Elizabeth takes her leave, glad to escape from the stuffy stores and Miss Kilman. Off she goes, in her very well-cut clothes, boarding an omnibus, any omnibus, sailing down Whitehall.

Elizabeth is a breath of young life in the middle-aged world of *Mrs Dalloway*—an effective point of contrast. She is enchanted, like her mother, with the sheer movement of life. 'She liked those churches, like shapes of grey paper, breasting the stream of the Strand.' A puff of wind blows a thin black veil over the sun.

ix

Septimus Warren Smith is lying on the sitting-room sofa, watching the light and shadow pass over the wall. Has it a meaning? He is not afraid any more. He sits up, takes an interest in what Rezia is doing. She is making a hat for Mrs Filmer's married daughter. He asks the lady's name. He thinks the hat is too small. He says it is like an organ-grinder's monkey's hat, and makes Rezia laugh as she has not laughed for weeks. He laughs and jokes and is perfectly all right. Then Rezia leaves the room, and he becomes frightened again; she returns, and he is happy. But there is Sir William Bradshaw in the background, who has said they must be separated. Rezia is sure that no one can separate them against their will. Nobody can hurt them, now that Septimus has laughed again. But who is that coming up the stairs? Rezia runs down. It is Dr Holmes.

Septimus could hear her talking to Holmes on the staircase.
"My dear lady, I have come as a friend," Holmes was saying.
"No. I will not allow you to see my husband," she said.
He could see her, like a little hen, with her wings spread barring his passage. But Holmes persevered.
"My dear lady, allow me . . . ." Holmes said, putting her aside (Holmes was a powerfully-built man).

Holmes was coming upstairs. Holmes would burst open the door. Holmes would say, "In a funk, eh?" Holmes would get him. But no; not Holmes; not Bradshaw. Getting up rather unsteadily, hopping indeed from foot to foot, he considered Mrs Filmer's nice clean bread-knife with 'Bread' carved on the handle. Ah, but one mustn't spoil that. The gas fire? But it was too late now. Holmes was coming. Razors he might have got, but Rezia, who always did that sort of thing, had packed them. There remained only the window, the large Bloomsbury lodging-house window; the tiresome, the troublesome, and rather melodramatic business of opening the window and throwing himself out. It was their idea of tragedy, not his or Rezia's (for she was with him). Holmes and Bradshaw liked that sort of thing. (He sat on the sill.) But he

would wait till the very last moment. He did not want to die.
Life was good. The sun hot. Only human beings? Coming down
the staircase opposite an old man stopped and stared at him.
Holmes was at the door. "I'll give it you!" he cried, and flung
himself vigorously, violently down on to Mrs Filmer's area railings.
"The coward!" cried Dr Holmes, bursting the door open.
Rezia ran to the window; she saw, she understood . . .

The ambulance bearing Septimus's body passes Peter Walsh
on his way to his hotel. 'One of the triumphs of civilisation,'
he thinks, the speed and efficiency of the ambulance. Later we
shall see him going through London, observing, admiring,
noting the civilisation of it all, on his way to Clarissa's party.
And there we find them—all the threads of the day gathered
up, as Mrs Dalloway had gathered up the threads of her green
dress—at this party to which the several events of the day have
led. The Prime Minister himself is there, the symbol of the
majesty of England as the closed car had been its symbol in the
early morning. Peter Walsh is there, wishing he had not come
—how effusive Clarissa is, how insincere! ('She could see Peter
out of the tail of her eye, criticising her, there, in that corner.')
There is Lady Rosseter—who is Sally Seton, after all these years!
—come without an invitation. Old Lady Bruton, talking to the
Prime Minister; Hugh Whitbread, 'snuffing round the precincts
of the great'; Richard, looking very pleased. And there were
the Bradshaws, whom she disliked. Why did the sight of Sir
William, looking so distinguished, curl her up? He was a great
doctor, deciding questions of appalling difficulty. 'Yet—what
she felt was, one wouldn't like Sir William to see one unhappy.
No; not that man.' Sir William is talking to Richard about this
new Bill—something to do with the deferred effects of shell-
shock: they must get some provision in the Bill about that. Lady
Bradshaw tells Clarissa that a young man has killed himself. And
so Septimus Warren Smith, too, comes to Mrs Dalloway's party.

What business had the Bradshaws to talk of death at her party?
A young man had killed himself. And they talked of it at her party
—the Bradshaws talked of death. He had killed himself—but
how? Always her body went through it, when she was told, first,
suddenly, of an accident; her dress flamed, her body burnt. He
had thrown himself from a window. Up had flashed the ground;
through him, blundering, bruising, went the rusty spikes. There he
lay with a thud, thud, thud in his brain, and then a suffocation
of blackness. So she saw it. But why had he done it? . . .

Or there were the poets and thinkers. Suppose he had had that passion, and had gone to Sir William Bradshaw, a great doctor, yet to her obscurely evil, without sex or lust, extremely polite to women, but capable of some indescribable outrage—forcing your soul, that was it—if this young man had gone to him, and Sir William had impressed him, like that, with his power, might he not then have said (indeed she felt it now), Life is made intolerable; they make life intolerable, men like that?

Clarissa sees. This is her triumph, her justification for us in the book (and, Mrs Woolf would say, the justification for women like her in life) in spite of her love of parties, her shrinking from experience—that she sees, she knows, she pierces below the surface. It is a dramatic moment this, the unveiling of Sir William Bradshaw; for though the discovery is only in Clarissa's mind, though the great doctor will continue his smooth destructive course to the end, something has been completed, a tragic anagnorisis. And Clarissa is identified with Septimus. She feels that it is she who has failed. And then she feels glad he has done it—as we, the readers, felt glad (despite the waste of it) when we heard Dr Holmes burst the door open, and knew that Septimus had escaped.

Our last glimpse of Clarissa—pity and understanding. She has gone away from her party, stepped aside into a little room, to be alone with the thought of this young man who has killed himself. Peter Walsh wonders where she has got to—no doubt she is talking to one of her celebrities, he grumbles. He sits chatting with Sally, laughing at Clarissa and her parties, her snobbery. It is easy to find fault with her. And all the time he is wanting her to come. Sally rises to go.

"I will come," said Peter, but he sat on for a moment. What is this terror? what is this ecstasy? he thought to himself. What is it that fills me with extraordinary excitement?

It was Clarissa, he said.

For there she was.

Mrs Dalloway is a much bigger job than any of the novels that go before it. There is a double plot. There is a greater variety of well-realised characters. There is a subtler manipulation of time—the action exists in the past as much as in the present. And there is a *leit-motiv*—the song from *Cymbeline*—running through and occurring to both Mrs Dalloway and Septimus Warren Smith at critical moments. The personality of Clarissa

Dalloway is presented to us with a fullness and intricacy which we rarely get in a character in fiction. She dominates the book —she passes, as she herself feels, into other people's lives and environments, so that we see Peter Walsh and Doris Kilman as moths circling round her flame; and even Septimus Warren Smith, whom she never sees, finds his life illuminated by the thought which passes from her brain to his: 'Fear no more the heat o' the sun.' Then, in return, we know Mrs Dalloway through the minds of other people as much as through her own thoughts. The final clear picture is gained from the integration of a series of distortions, ranging from the subtle distortion of egotism in her own thinking about herself, to the gross distortion of hatred in Doris Kilman's mental picture. Richard, Peter Walsh, Lady Bruton, Sally Seton, all have their separate pictures, which are laid before us in turn; but we are not invited to choose. For each of these persons wishes to impose his own picture as the correct one; and what the story is about, we soon learn, is the crime of making or accepting any imposition. Mrs Dalloway is herself, above the power of any alien vision to change her into its likeness; but she is only secure because of her money and social position. If she were as defenceless as Septimus Warren Smith there would be many Sir William Bradshaws eager to teach her a sense of proportion, to drag her out of her attic room.

What then are we to think of Mrs Dalloway at the end? Not wholly admirable, certainly, this woman who preferred the 'safe' Richard to the unsteady Peter; who loves parties and Duchesses; who is annoyed at criticism. She does not try to penetrate deeply below the surface of society; Richard's Armenians (or is it Albanians?) mean nothing to her. Her life is intuitive, not ratiocinative. But where her instincts are concerned—how magnificently right! She sees through Sir William Bradshaw, she understands Richard and Peter, she pities and admires (while she detests) Miss Kilman. If only she could have met Rezia and Septimus in the Park, we tell ourselves regretfully, she would certainly have spoken to them (as Peter realised), she would have protected them and Sir William would not have got near them. And it is this instinctive rightness which attracted all hearts to her, which enslaved Peter in spite of himself, and sent Richard home with flowers and the words he could not bring himself to say. She does not pretend, she is

herself, and she wants everybody else to be themselves. She is
love with life, with its diversity and colour; and if there
something she has missed, she doesn't moan about it, she sit
down and mends her green dress. Yet this consciousness of
having missed something (something she might have had with
the failure Peter) brings a sadness into her eyes, a certain hardness into her manner, a little artificiality into her voice when
she is caught off her guard. In Virginia Woolf's next novel,
To the Lighthouse, we shall meet another character very like
Clarissa Dalloway; but Mrs Ramsay hasn't missed what
Clarissa has missed; the hardness isn't there, and there is a
new depth.

It isn't only a question of marriage, but of love too. Clarissa
comes to think love as detestable as religion; and the book gives
us many aspects of this passion. Her own love for Sally, the
protecting love of a woman for a woman; her love for Peter and
Richard, each different; Peter's love for her and his foolish loves
for the wrong women; Miss Kilman's love for Elizabeth: what
complications all these introduce into life! Is it possible to have
the clear vision of reality when such disturbing colours flash
in front of the eyes? Is to love always to go up into the tower
alone and leave the others blackberrying in the sun?

The sense of loneliness in marriage fills *Mrs Dalloway*. Has
she any friends—real friends? We certainly do not hear of them.
Peter leaves her, she has no time to visit Sally Seton, Lady
Bruton criticises her and asks Richard to lunch without her.
She has only acquaintances, people she asks to parties for her
husband's sake. Even Elizabeth is taken from her by Miss
Kilman. The novel is the portrait of a lonely woman, who is
yet indomitable, kindly, full of life. Peter admits it.

> She had felt a great deal; had for a moment, when she kissed
> his hand, regretted, envied him even, remembered possibly (for he
> saw her look it) something he had said—how they would change
> the world if she married him perhaps; whereas, it was this; it
> was middle age; it was mediocrity; then forced herself with her
> indomitable vitality to put all that aside, there being in her a
> thread of life which for toughness, endurance, power to overcome
> obstacles and carry her triumphantly through he had never
> known the like of.

It is these qualities of courage and obstinacy that Mrs Woolf
admires in men and women—not above all others, for there are

greater qualities of imagination, devotion to truth, wisdom, which belong to a higher order; but admires all the same, because they are the virtues of our common humanity without which the others become corrupt and vanish. We are shown them, in a little scene that appears to have nothing much to do with the rest of the novel, a picture of an old woman singing outside Regent's Park tube station; and in the portrait of Mrs McNab in *To the Lighthouse*; and again and again, in her descriptions of women whom fortune has tried to batter down in vain. That old woman outside the tube station, Rezia Warren Smith barring the passage of the burly Dr Holmes— these too are projections of Clarissa Dalloway.

The novel has a quality of pity and a dramatic intensity which Virginia Woolf has not given us since *The Voyage Out*. It is an extraordinary art which develops the abnormal episode of Septimus Warren Smith and keeps it going against the other strand of the Dalloways without its leaping out of the frame. It is analogous to the technique of musical counterpoint, even, perhaps, of writing music in two keys at once; but there is no suggestion of a *tour de force*. While the story of Mrs Dalloway mounts up slowly and unemphatically to its climax which is the party, the story of Septimus and Rezia proceeds with horrible and growing intensity to the suicide. This presentation is extremely moving, with something of the atmosphere of Greek drama. Holmes and Bradshaw are the Furies, Septimus has the rôle of Orestes. But the two doctors are unworthy of their parts, Mrs Woolf hates them with a kind of personal hatred; and sometimes the feeling of evil, of suffocation, becomes too poignant. The scenes of Septimus's hallucinations are beautifully done; it is the madness of a poet which is being portrayed, which only a little understanding, a little peace would be enough to bring back to sanity. And Rezia is one of the most moving characters in modern fiction. She is loyal without needing to understand; and that is the greatest kind of loyalty, for it depends on a right relation between persons and not on a community of ideas.

The idea of Time dominates *Mrs Dalloway*. A single day, Wednesday, unfolds the action of the story, and there are no artificial chapter divisions. The stages of the day itself are, however, clearly indicated. The early morning, when Clarissa steps out of her house in Westminster; eleven o'clock when

Peter bursts in; half-past eleven when Peter, in Trafalgar Square, receives a strange illumination; a quarter to twelve when Septimus smiles at the man in the grey suit who is dead; precisely twelve o'clock when Septimus and Rezia enter Sir William Bradshaw's house and Clarissa Dalloway lays her green dress on the bed; half-past one when Hugh Whitbread and Richard Dalloway meet for luncheon at Lady Bruton's in Brook Street; three o'clock when Richard comes home with his flowers; half-past three when Clarissa sees the old lady move away from the window; six when Septimus kills himself and Peter thinks with admiration of civilisation. Time is an inexorable stream knitting together the incongruous, separating friends, and making nonsense of emotions. In a single day, a lifetime may be lived through. Virginia Woolf is to take up this treatment of time again, and develop it along still more complex lines, in *To the Lighthouse*.

With its time-limit, and its sense of destiny, the insistent hours pressing on, the texture of *Mrs Dalloway* is closer-knit than that of the preceding novels. There is a sense of pressure, strain and (with London's buses and ambulances and the royal car and the aeroplane) of business, which never becomes confusion because Mrs Woolf holds all the strings perfectly distinguished. The moments of alleviation and escape are briefer and tinged with haste. Clarissa experiences one, Peter experiences one and so does Septimus; but they do not hold the place in *Mrs Dalloway* that they have in some of the other novels. They do not blossom, as it were; they die in the bud. They do not give even the sensation of meaning, though it is 'almost expressed' in Clarissa's attic room. These moments are smothered in the vast official life of London. Then, too, the narrative technique has become more *serré*. The gain in intensity is balanced by a corresponding loss in expansiveness and allusion. There is no time to pause and enjoy the sights. There are no fine imaginative descriptions as of the British Museum in *Jacob's Room*. Clarissa's house is dismissed in a paragraph. We spend quite a long time in Regent's Park, but we have no leisure to look about us. Septimus's delusions, Peter's memories, it is on these that we must fix our attention. There are boys playing cricket, there is little Elise Mitchell who runs full tilt into Rezia, there are trees, swallows, flies; but it is a poor collection when we think of *Kew Gardens* and *Jacob's Room*, with their brilliant evocation of the life of things. Things, in *Mrs Dalloway*, are swamped by the tangled lives of men.

The style, light and easy, an eminently civilised prose, lacks the overtones of *Jacob's Room*. It is as though the light of imagination had been stuffed altogether into poor Septimus's head, leaving the rest of the book a little pallid, as freckles draw colouring matter from the rest of the body. In *Jacob's Room* one feels Mrs Woolf is playing delightedly with a new instrument, weaving melody-patterns for the sheer beauty of them. Serious and indeed tragic as the theme of the book is, it does not hold the writer from feats of virtuosity. *Jacob's Room* is Mrs Woolf's *Songs of Innocence*, *Mrs Dalloway* her *Songs of Experience*. It is not the war that has intervened—*Jacob's Room* is post-war too, and is almost a sigh of relief that it is all over; it is the experience of the years following the war. Deferred shell-shock is Sir William Bradshaw's diagnosis of Septimus's malady; deferred war-shock might, perhaps, be our account of the total motif of *Mrs Dalloway*. The full weight of such a tremendous catastrophe cannot be felt all at once. Only in *To the Lighthouse* do we find her climbing again out of the trough and regaining the brilliance of *Jacob's Room*.

CHAPTER VI

To the Lighthouse

[1927]

TO THE LIGHTHOUSE, if not Mrs Woolf's greatest novel, is certainly a favourite with the general reader. It hasn't a plot, it's true; but it has everything else: a variety of interesting, well-rounded characters, great emotional force, a lovely style vibrating as it were with light, and a fascinating manipulation of time. The human intensity of *Mrs Dalloway* is joined to the visionary gleam of *Jacob's Room*. Mrs Ramsay, Mr Ramsay, the child James, Lily Briscoe—how real and living they are!

It isn't the busy society world of London this time. It is a remote corner of the Hebrides. Mrs Woolf hasn't finished with the theme of marriage; but this time she is going to show it in isolation, not pressed upon and crushed by society, and she is going to add to it a family, and friends, real friends, not Lady Brutons and Bradshaws. Mrs Ramsay is married to a man who is certainly not a successful politician—who often, indeed, does not feel himself a success at all; a man of brains rather than of character, as eccentric and wayward as Peter Walsh. One might almost think that Virginia Woolf had said to herself, "Well, supposing Clarissa Dalloway had married Peter Walsh —what would have been the outcome?" Of course, Mrs Ramsay is not Clarissa, and Mr Ramsay is not Peter; but the parallel is close enough.

Mrs Ramsay and Clarissa Dalloway are of an age—fifty; they have the same gift of charming people; but Mrs Ramsay has the warmth which Clarissa owned she lacked. She, her husband and eight children are at their home in the Hebrides. Mr Ramsay is a scholar, a philosopher honoured by several universities. They have a number of guests staying with them. Charles Tansley, a disagreeable young man with a good brain, is a protégé of her husband's. Minta Doyle and Paul Rayley, a young man and a girl destined to fall in love, resemble Arthur Venning and Susan Warrington in *The Voyage Out*. There is Augustus Carmichael, an old gentleman, a poet; and Lily

99

Briscoe, who paints, and (Mrs Ramsay is afraid) will never marry. William Bankes, finally, an old friend of Mr Ramsay's. There they all are; but William Bankes and Lily Briscoe have rooms in the village, for the Ramsays' house is not a big one.

The house itself is the structure which binds the story together. In no other of Mrs Woolf's books does the actual dwelling-place of her characters play so important a part. We feel that this house, windswept, bleak, remote, on the Isle of Skye, has a soul of its own, which exists through the three divisions of *To the Lighthouse*. In the first section, 'The Window', we find the house containing two worlds, separate but connected—the masculine and the feminine. Mrs Ramsay sits inside the drawing-room with her little boy James: a warm world of love and understanding; Mr Ramsay strides up and down the terrace outside the window with Charles Tansley: a chill world of abstraction and intolerance. In the second section, 'Time Passes', the house is alone, deserted by the human element; Mrs Ramsay is dead, Mr Ramsay and the children have gone away. In the third section, 'The Lighthouse', the masculine world of Mr Ramsay is sailing away from the house, and only Lily Briscoe remains to re-create the figure of Mrs Ramsay.

These, then, are the themes of the new novel: marriage, the family, the relation of the masculine and feminine worlds, and the recurrent theme of values. Marriage: Mrs Ramsay is what Clarissa might have become if she had married Peter Walsh; Mr Ramsay is what Peter Walsh might have become had he married Clarissa; Augustus Carmichael is what Peter Walsh may become, not having married Clarissa. The family: seen now from the mother's standpoint and not, as in *Night and Day*, from the children's. The relation of the masculine and feminine worlds: not now complicated with the interposition of indiscriminate social responsibilities, but isolated and prepared for minute analysis. The question of values: the passion for truth embodied in Mr Ramsay, the strong feeling for reality incarnate in his wife.

The special technique of *Mrs Dalloway* is repeated and carried a stage further in *To the Lighthouse*. In *Mrs Dalloway* we noted two main technical elements: the focusing of different points of view, different personal judgments, on the character of the chief personage; and the use of memory as a narrative medium.

These two elements existed together. In *To the Lighthouse* they recur, but separated. The first section gives us the personality of Mrs Ramsay, and the personality of Mr Ramsay, through the eyes of James, Lily Briscoe, Charles Tansley, William Bankes and the rest of the guests—they are there, isolated in Skye, to give us as full and as varied a view as possible of the principal characters. Then, in the second section, memory begins its task —memory curiously operative in the mind of old Mrs McNab the charwoman. We see Mrs Ramsay and the rest as reflected in a very simple mind which can give a detached if elementary judgment. Then, in the third section, memory again, chiefly in the recollections of Lily Briscoe. The resultant portrait is incomparably rich and living.

To put the point in a different way, we can consider the manipulation of time. In the first section, time stands still. It stands still because Mrs Ramsay wills it to. She wills it, in the first place, emotionally: because she wants the world of her children and her family never to pass away. The thing that she has created, the house that she fills with warmth and laughter, her husband's confidence in her and in himself—these things are too good to perish. We are shown that everything *outside* Mrs Ramsay—house, family, friends—has its real existence only *in* Mrs Ramsay. She is the unity in which they subsist. Then, again, she wills it mystically: that time shall stand still; for we are made aware that her own real existence is in none of these things, but in that silence and that darkness into which she sinks when she is alone. The moment becomes eternity. When she has sunk into her 'proper dark' she does not wish to be brought to the surface again by the insistence of time. In the second section, time passes; and there is nothing but the passing of time. The human agents have vanished. Life goes on, the life of Mr Ramsay and Mr Carmichael and the rest, but it goes on away from the house, which is left to itself. Finally, in the third section, time proceeds in contrary motion, like the two hands starting from middle C and playing the same scale, one hand rippling up to the highest note of the treble and the other thundering down to the lowest note of the bass. The house has the position of middle C: Mr Ramsay sails with Cam and James into the future, to the lighthouse; and Lily Briscoe, sitting on the lawn in front of the house, allows her thoughts to wander back into the past until the figure of Mrs Ramsay is re-created.

ii

The time extension of the first part of *To the Lighthouse* is even less than that of *Mrs Dalloway*: there, we had a single day; here, we have a single evening, the space between six o'clock and the dinner to which the action leads up. It is some years before the war, and the month is September.

Mrs Ramsay is sitting with her little boy James at the window. He is six, and belongs already 'to that great clan which cannot keep this feeling separate from that, but must let future prospects, with their joys and sorrows, cloud what is actually at hand'. What is occupying him at the moment is the prospect of going to the lighthouse in the morning—if it is fine. ' "But," said his father, stopping in front of the drawing-room window, "it won't be fine." ' At once we are presented with the contrast on which the book is based: the warm maternal love and care of Mrs Ramsay, promising pleasure and hoping to fulfil that promise; the cold truthfulness of Mr Ramsay, anxious to assert itself without thinking to temper the wind to the shorn lamb.

Little James hates his father for his brutality, and for disturbing the excellent common-sense relations which exist between himself and his mother by interposing emotions, claims for sympathy, rages. He almost feels that his father is responsible for the weather. The expedition to the lighthouse has been planned for some time. Mrs Ramsay is knitting stockings to take to the lighthouse keeper's little boy. And now Charles Tansley joins in to support Mr Ramsay: Charles Tansley, Mrs Woolf's portrait of the narrowest type of masculinity. He and her husband are outside the window, walking up and down the terrace, discussing other men of their stamp; living in a world of abstraction, yet needing from time to time to enter the world of warm reality which is Mrs Ramsay and her children. Charles Tansley is the dull academic type at its worst, rejecting the warm realities for 'the influence of something on somebody ... dissertation ... fellowship ... readership ... lectureship ...' Yet even for Charles Tansley Mrs Ramsay has affection, thinking of his struggles and his youth.

It would be difficult to find in modern literature a lovelier picture than Virginia Woolf gives us, in this first part of *To the Lighthouse*, of a mother with her children. She creates a world, compact and self-sufficient, suffused with emotion, yet without a trace of sentimentality. We didn't get this world in *Jacob's Room*, where Betty Flanders and her son are seen as emotionally separate. There is no real family life in *Mrs Dalloway*; and it is only hinted at in *The Voyage Out*. But in *To the Lighthouse* it is the dominant theme: the at-oneness of a mother with her children, the uneasy balance of a wife with her husband. We see Mrs Ramsay first with James, her youngest, comforting him after his disappointment.

> "Perhaps you will wake up and find the sun shining and the birds singing," she said compassionately, smoothing the little boy's hair, for her husband, with his caustic saying that it would not be fine, had dashed his spirits she could see . . .
> "Perhaps it will be fine tomorrow," she said, smoothing his hair.

Mrs Ramsay understands what her husband does not understand: that we do not live on truth, though we should live by truth, but on faith and hope and charity; she understands that mercifulness to the sensitive mind of a child ('This going to the Lighthouse was a passion of his, she saw') comes before loyalty to an abstraction (which is only too often our disguise for personal egotism and cruelty). Mrs Ramsay's is a reverence for the spirit in others, for the frail human personality, so easily wounded.

There are eight children; it is clearly not possible to make them all real to us, in the space of a short novel; but with a few rapid strokes Mrs Woolf does wonders. We see them quite sharply outlined—Cam the Wicked, James the Ruthless, Andrew the Just, Prue the Fair (as Mr Bankes calls them after the Kings and Queens of England), Nancy, Roger, Rose and Jasper. Mrs Ramsay does not wish them to grow a day older —Cam and James especially. She knows how much they will lose of sensitiveness and the faculty for wonder; and she thinks how they will be hurt by the world.

> They were happier now than they would ever be again. A tenpenny tea set made Cam happy for days. She heard them stamping and crowing on the floor above her head the moment they woke. They came bustling along the passage. Then the door sprang open and in they came, fresh as roses, staring, wide awake, as if this coming into the dining-room after breakfast, which they did every day of their lives, was a positive event to them; and so on, with one thing after another, all day long, until she went up to

say good-night to them, and found them netted in their cots like birds among cherries and raspberries still making up stories about some little bit of rubbish—something they had heard, something they had picked up in the garden.

Through this understanding Mrs Ramsay is constantly giving to her children; but she is also receiving something, something which keeps her alive and young at fifty. Through her immediate sympathy with the minds of her children she is able to live in their world of wonder and vivid perception; mother and children are all the time pointing things out to each other, sharing and stimulating contact with the world of reality. 'One's children,' she herself reflects, 'so often gave one's own perceptions a little push forward.'

Is not this, then, the ideal companionship? a companionship in the perception and enjoyment of reality, where neither party gets in the way of the other's vision, where there is a mutual stimulation, where love is not dependent on passion. The answer has already been given in Mrs Ramsay's sorrow that Cam and James cannot always remain children. This happy relationship is the most transitory of all, without an element of permanence. It is at the mercy of time, the destroyer.

This life lived in a perfect relationship is not possible between Mr and Mrs Ramsay because he is simply the demanding party, she simply the giving. But Mrs Ramsay has far more reality in her life than Clarissa Dalloway. With all his egotism, his brutality, his eccentricities, Mr Ramsay is spiritually a more wholesome man to live with than Richard Dalloway with all his kindness and courtesy, because he is more intelligent, more bent on truth. He is more lovable. His own weakness and inadequacies come from the fact that he has preferred the lonely pursuit of truth to any kind of worldly success. Which is not to say that he does not want success. But Richard Dalloway wants success in the first place, and he wants the kind of success which involves parties, social engagements and knowing the right people. Hence Clarissa is stifled, without quite knowing why or how; she has neither the fulfilment in her children, nor the wholehearted admiration for her husband's intellect, nor the resource of sinking completely into herself, that Mrs Ramsay has. We are never made to feel that Mrs Ramsay regrets her marriage, as we are made to feel that Clarissa wonders if she ought not, after all, to have married Peter Walsh; it is

Mr Ramsay who toys for a moment, traitorously, with the thought that he might be a better philosopher if he were unmarried. The Galloways seem, from the outside, more homogeneous than the Ramsays; but this is because Clarissa is moulding herself to Richard's image and of course stultifying something of herself in the process. The Ramsays are more obviously disparate, but in this very disparateness there lies the possibility of being complementary.

iii

If the house in Skye is the unifying element of the novel, serving to knit Mrs Ramsay and Mr Ramsay and the children into the whole which Mrs Ramsay has created, there is another element outside the house which brings Mrs Ramsay herself at times into a deeper unity from which the others are excluded: the sea. We have seen in the earlier novels how Virginia Woolf loves to set her characters by the sea when she wishes to show us their most intimate, their most real aspects; we first meet Jacob Flanders by the sea, and in *To the Lighthouse,* too, the laughter of children blends with the murmur of the waves. But in *To the Lighthouse* there is something more. The scene is set on an island. Human life, family life, real as it is, is something isolated in the midst of a greater reality. That reality may be forgotten for a while, human voices may drown the sea's voice; but moments come when the human voices are still. Such a moment occurs while Mrs Ramsay is looking with James through the Army and Navy Stores list to find something for him to cut out. The sound of her husband and Charles Tansley talking as they walk up and down the terrace has been forming a background to her thoughts.

But here, as she turned the page, suddenly her search for the picture of a rake or a mowing-machine was interrupted. The gruff murmur, irregularly broken by the taking out of pipes and the putting in of pipes which had kept on assuring her, though she could not hear what was said (as she sat in the window), that the men were happily talking; this sound, which had lasted now half an hour and had taken its place soothingly in the scale of sounds pressing on top of her, such as the tap of balls upon bats, the sharp, sudden bark now and then, "How's that? How's that?"

of the children playing cricket, had ceased; so that the monotonous fall of the waves on the beach, which for the most part beat a measured and soothing tattoo to her thoughts and seemed consolingly to repeat over and over again as she sat with the children the words of some old cradle song, murmured by nature, "I am guarding you—I am your support," but at other times suddenly and unexpectedly, especially when her mind raised itself slightly from the task actually in hand, had no such kindly meaning, but like a ghostly roll of drums remorselessly beat out the measure of life, made one think of the destruction of the island and its engulfment in the sea, and warned her whose days had slipped by in one quick doing after another that it was all ephemeral as a rainbow—this sound which had been obscured and concealed under the other sounds suddenly thundered hollow in her ears and made her look up with an impulse of terror.

They had ceased to talk; that was the explanation. . . . The island may sink into the sea . . . the reality of human life and human love may be engulfed in the greater reality. Engulfed —then the two cannot blend? This question, which we have seen Virginia Woolf posing in one way after another in all the novels so far, is still without a satisfactory answer. Real as her love for and companionship with her children are, Mrs Ramsay finds, as Clarissa Dalloway had found, that the deeper life opens itself only in solitude. That is the terror which the voice of the sea brings. Must reality always separate us from those we love? Is there no way of communion open?

When James is packed off to bed Mrs Ramsay has an interval of peace. She need not think about anything or anybody, she can just be herself. And now comes the moment of reality.

She could be herself, by herself. And that was what now she often felt the need of—to think; well, not even to think. To be silent; to be alone. All the being and the doing, expansive, glittering, vocal, evaporated; and one shrunk, with a sense of solemnity, to being oneself, a wedge-shaped core of darkness, something invisible to others. Although she continued to knit, and sat upright, it was thus that she felt herself; and this self having shed its attachments was free for the strangest adventures. When life sank down for a moment, the range of experience seemed limitless. And to everybody there was always this sense of unlimited resources, she supposed; one after another, she, Lily, Augustus Carmichael, must feel, our apparitions, the things you know us by, are simply childish. Beneath it is all dark, it is all spreading, it is unfathomably deep; but now and again we rise to the surface and that is what you see us by. Her horizon seemed to her limitless. There were all the places she had not seen; the Indian plains; she felt herself pushing aside the thick leather curtain of a church in Rome. This core of darkness could go anywhere, for no one saw it. They could not stop it, she thought, exulting. There was freedom, there was peace, there was, most welcome of all, a summoning together, a resting on a platform of stability. Not as oneself did one find rest ever, in her experience (she accomplished here something dexterous with her needles), but as a wedge of darkness. Losing personality, one lost the fret, the hurry, the stir; and there rose to her lips always some exclamation of triumph over life when things came together in this peace, this rest, this eternity; and pausing there she looked to meet that stroke of the Lighthouse, the long steady stroke, the last of the three, which was her stroke, for watching them in this mood always at this hour one could not help attaching oneself to one thing especially of the things one saw; and this thing, the long steady stroke, was her stroke. Often she found herself sitting and looking, sitting and looking, with her work in her hands until she became the thing she looked at—that light for example.

"We become what we behold"—Blake's saying sums up an experience common to mystics of all ages and all places. It is always some light shining from things, rocks or streams or trees, which transforms us so that we enter into the very life of those things and so lose ourselves.

It is worth while considering Mrs Ramsay's experience in some detail, for it brings us to the heart of the problem for Virginia Woolf, and is also in itself a remarkable mystical document. That 'wedge-shaped core of darkness'—the phrase has the visual definitiveness we expect from Mrs Woolf, but the idea is exactly that of the mystics of the *via negativa*: not light but darkness, not substance but nothingness, is the image by which alone we may attempt to convey the sensation of reality. There is a shrinking, a retraction of one's being from all the thoughts and actions in which it has been engaged. Attachments are shed, reality grows. And with reality, the sense of freedom, of unlimited possibilities. Life, in other words, consists not in doing but in being; and being means the sinking down into darkness. The personality that we present to the world, to our nearest friends, is unreal, for it is composed of the attachments, desires, fears and hopes which we have to shed in the rare moments when we can feel ourselves as ourselves.

It is natural that anyone who has realised this truth will find it easier to live with *things* than with human beings. Hence the attraction of inanimate things for Virginia Woolf. There is no pretence, no false personality, in a tree or a rock, and therefore a real communion, on the plane of 'darkness', is possible. Mrs Ramsay feels this without quite understanding it. 'It was odd, she thought, how if one was alone, one leant to things, inanimate things; trees, streams, flowers; felt they expressed one; felt they became one; felt they knew one, in a sense were one; felt an irrational tenderness thus (she looked at that long steady light) as for oneself.'

But Mrs Ramsay is not permitted to exist long as a wedge of darkness.

> *We have lingered in the chambers of the sea*
> *By sea-girls wreathed with seaweed red and brown*
> *Till human voices wake us, and we drown.*

Her husband, who is walking up and down, alone now, and chuckling to himself, suddenly notes the remoteness of her bearing; and this pains him. He must stand and watch her. And she feels she must come to the surface again. She looks again at the light.

> . . . the steady light, the pitiless, the remorseless, which was so much her, yet so little her, which had her at its beck and call (she woke in the night and saw it bent across their bed, stroking the floor), but for all that she thought, watching it with fascination, hypnotised, as if it were stroking with its silver fingers some sealed vessel in her brain whose bursting would flood her with delight, she had known happiness, exquisite happiness, intense happiness, and it silvered the rough waves a little more brightly, as daylight faded, and the blue went out of the sea and it rolled in waves of pure lemon which curled and swelled and broke upon the beach and the ecstasy burst in her eyes and waves of pure delight raced over the floor of her mind and she felt, It is enough! It is enough!

Mr Ramsay looks at her, recognises her beauty, feels that he should not interrupt her, though he feels urgently too the need to speak to her; and would have passed without a word 'had she not, at that very moment, given him of her own free will what she knew he would never ask, and called to him and taken the green shawl off the picture frame, and gone to him. For he wished, she knew, to protect her'.

And in those few words Virginia Woolf accomplishes an

extraordinary feat of art, the same feat that Shakespeare accomplishes with his "Master Shallow, I owe you a thousand pounds", the transmutation of comedy into high tragic irony.

iv

The element of comedy is indeed more to the fore in *To the Lighthouse* than in any of the preceding novels. In *Jacob's Room* and *Mrs Dalloway* it is almost entirely absent. But in *To the Lighthouse* a series of comic interludes, centring in the figure of Mr Ramsay, gives depth and variety to the action. The egocentricity of Mr Ramsay makes an admirable foil to his wife's gracious altruism. One of these episodes of selfish solitariness comes at the close of his conversation with Tansley, when the sudden silence makes Mrs Ramsay conscious of the menacing murmur of the sea. Mr Ramsay begins to stalk up and down the terrace, and about the lawn, reciting *The Charge of the Light Brigade*. He is dramatising himself. Tennyson's poem just expresses the feeling he has at the moment, of being the leader of a lost cause, worthy of pity but unflinchingly doing his duty. These moods come upon Mr Ramsay frequently, whenever something goes a little wrong; and it need not be anything external—a sudden thought will do it, the thought that he is not appreciated as he ought to be, or that his books are fated to be forgotten, or that he himself is not a first-rate intelligence, or that he ought not to have married. He makes no attempt to curb these impulses of dejection, either for his own sake or that of his family or his guests; he indulges them to the limit, keeping away from the others until the moment comes when he feels the overpowering need of comfort and runs to his wife.

But now he almost knocks Lily Briscoe's easel over, shouting 'Boldly we rode and well' and flinging his arms about. Lily is sitting on the lawn, painting the façade of the house, with the window at which Mrs Ramsay is sitting with James—a difficult subject. Lily Briscoe does and says little in the course of the novel, but she is a most important character. Together with William Bankes she constitutes a kind of Greek chorus, commenting on the personalities of the Ramsays. Lily gives us the feminine viewpoint, William the masculine. It is significant that Mrs Woolf makes her chief commentator a painter, even if a bad painter. It is the painter's eye and the painter's intuition which are required to get at the essence of Mrs Ramsay; and, in part at least, Lily Briscoe achieves this. For being a painter she is able to consider Mrs Ramsay dispassionately, as a *thing*, as it were, as still life; though with another part of her being she is passionately in love with Mrs Ramsay, with the house itself and the children. It is to Lily Briscoe that we have to come back, in the end, to get our last glimpse of Mrs Ramsay.

Mr Bankes is a botanist, a widower, 'smelling of soap, very scrupulous and clean', a bit of an old faddist, but kindhearted and sincere. He respects Lily Briscoe for her devotion to work, her poverty, her common sense. (Mrs Ramsay, who is a born matchmaker, hopes they will marry.) Both are embarrassed by Mr Ramsay's striding up and down reciting; so now they take a little walk. They come to a halt at a break in the hedge and look out over the sea. They stand and watch and muse. Both are thinking about the Ramsays.

First we have Mr Ramsay seen through the eyes of William Bankes.

> Looking at the far sand hills, William Bankes thought of Ramsay; thought of a road in Westmorland, thought of Ramsay striding along a road by himself hung round with that solitude which seemed to be his natural air. But this was suddenly interrupted, William Bankes remembered (and this must refer to some actual incident), by a hen, straddling her wings out in protection of a covey of little chicks, upon which Ramsay, stopping, pointed his stick and said "Pretty—pretty," an odd illumination into his heart, Bankes had thought it, which showed his simplicity, his sympathy with humble things; but it seemed to him as if their friendship had ceased, there, on that stretch of road. After that, Ramsay had married.

It is beautifully done, this figurative contrast between Mr Ramsay as a young man, solitary and whole, and Mr Ramsay as he is now, enmeshed by domestic happiness, his being scattered among his wife and children. The men's friendship had ended there, because William Bankes, though he too marries, preserves his identity inviolate (his marriage was not a happy one), while Ramsay's, he feels, is dissipated and lost. Yet he feels envy too.

In Lily Briscoe's mind the image of Mr Ramsay appears as a

scrubbed kitchen table, lodged at the moment in the fork of a pear tree. She had asked Andrew once what his father's books were about. "Think of a kitchen table when you're not there," he had replied (subject and object and the nature of reality). So she concentrates her mind on this table, its shape obliterating the leaves and bark of the tree, and thinks what a curious way of looking at the world this is. She compares Mr Ramsay with Mr Bankes: Mr Bankes, who is good, not vain, entirely impersonal, finer than Mr Ramsay, without wife or child, living entirely for science; but then she remembers he is also a crank, has brought a valet with him to the Hebrides, and proses for hours about salt in vegetables and the iniquities of English cooking. And so she finds it difficult to judge people. Mr Bankes has greatness, and Mr Ramsay hasn't. 'He is petty, selfish, vain, egotistical; he is spoilt; he is a tyrant; he wears Mrs Ramsay to death; but he has what you (she addressed Mr Bankes) have not; a fiery unworldliness; he knows nothing about trifles; he loves dogs and children. He has eight. You have none. Did he not come down in two coats the other night and let Mrs Ramsay trim his hair into a pudding basin?' Thus, by these little touches, given through the musings of William Bankes and Lily Briscoe as well as by overt actions, the personality of Mr Ramsay, complex and fascinating, is built up for us.

v

Mr Ramsay, disgruntled and a little ashamed at having barged into Lily and William like that, shivers and quivers as he walks. 'Someone had blundered.' His wife senses his uneasiness and wonders what has caused it. He pauses by the window, and tickles James's leg with a spray. Mrs Ramsay remarks absently that she is trying to get the stockings finished to send to the lighthouse the next day; and Mr Ramsay is infuriated by her refusal to accept the fact that it will be impossible to go to the lighthouse. He swears at her. "Damn you!" he says. It is a blow in the face to Mrs Ramsay sitting there with James on her knee. She does not know what she has done to deserve it. And again we have the contrast between the masculine mind and the feminine brought out with great insight.

To pursue truth with such astonishing lack of consideration for other people's feelings, to rend the thin veils of civilisation so wantonly, so brutally, was to her so horrible an outrage of human decency that, without replying, dazed and blinded, she bent her head as if to let the pelt of jagged hail, the drench of dirty water, bespatter her unrebuked. There was nothing to be said.

He stood by her in silence. Very humbly, at length, he said that he would step over and ask the Coastguards if she liked.

There was nobody whom she reverenced as she reverenced him. She was quite ready to take his word for it, she said. Only then they need not cut sandwiches—that was all. They came to her, naturally, since she was a woman, all day long with this and that; one wanting this, another that; the children were growing up; she often felt she was nothing but a sponge sopped full of human emotions. Then he said, Damn you. He said, It must rain. He said, It won't rain; and instantly a Heaven of security opened before her. There was nobody she reverenced more. She was not good enough to tie his shoe strings, she felt.

The portrayal of goodness—of sheer goodness for its own sake—has not been presented before in Virginia Woolf's books. There is goodness in Clarissa Dalloway, of course; her compassion for Septimus Warren Smith would be enough to demonstrate that; but there is also a certain harshness and narrowness —her sympathies have been stunted by a wrong environment. Her kindness, the way she speaks to her servants, for instance, has in it much of the desire to make things work smoothly for herself; Peter Walsh catches the overtone of insincerity. Katharine Hilbery is firmly bent on working out the solution of her own happiness, she wants to live her own life. But Mrs Ramsay finds her life by losing it; she is completely unselfish, and she is absorbedly interested in the lives of others, not through stupid curiosity, but through the desire that they shall be happy and the instinct to do all she can to bring this about. All the time she is spending herself. We are reminded again and again that she is remarkably beautiful; but it is only rarely that she herself remembers the fact. The physical beauty is simply the last inevitable touch given to the picture of a per-fectly balanced personality; and for this reason Mrs Ramsay can still, at fifty, move the heart of a Charles Tansley. Mrs Woolf has succeeded in making goodness interesting.

There is, of course, more in Mrs Ramsay than goodness; but goodness is the bright centre round which all the other qualities revolve. She 'has the whole of the other sex under her protection', we are told, 'for reasons she could not explain, for their chivalry and valour, for the fact that they negotiated treaties, ruled India, controlled finance; finally for an attitude towards herself which no woman could fail to feel or to find agreeable, something trustful, childlike, reverential . . .' She has intuition: 'she knew then—she knew without having learnt. Her simplicity fathomed what clever people falsified. Her singleness of mind made her drop plumb like a stone, alight exact as a bird, gave her, naturally, this swoop and fall of the spirit upon truth which delighted, eased, sustained—falsely perhaps'. She is full of energy, and with this energy she animates others. Her simplicity rids others of their tensions. 'Men, and women too, letting go the multiplicity of things, had allowed themselves with her the relief of simplicity.'

Love, then, married life, a family—the theme to whose complete discussion Mrs Woolf's novels have been leading up, to find their consummation in *To the Lighthouse*, the mature masterpiece—are in the end this: a weary woman happy in her children, torn and exhausted by her husband, spreading the mantle of charity around her friends. The second great quality which emerges from the presentation of Mrs Ramsay is courage. She is undaunted. Life has not conquered her, and though darkness is pressing in on every side, she throws out as from a focus of warmth and light great rays which push the darkness back. Love is useless without courage; it becomes the destroying thing which creates a hell in heaven's despite. But with courage love is triumphant; and for this reason, when Mrs Ramsay dies, the reader's emotion is that of the highest tragedy and not of pathos, because she has made of her life a complete whole, a structure of light, which in some sense still stands when she is gone.

vi

The comic interlude is now resumed. 'Someone had blundered'—Mr Ramsay repeats the line as he leaves his wife, but without the old conviction. He is restored to his privacy, and now he concentrates his mind on the metaphysical problem which is occupying it. Virginia Woolf gives us a very clever and amusing picture of Mr Ramsay trying to push his mind (we are told it is a splendid mind) forward to a point which he has hitherto been unable to reach. She sees the points on the metaphysical journey as letters of the alphabet: Mr Ramsay has succeeded, so far, in reaching the letter Q. R is the next stopping place: on, then, to R. Mr Ramsay braces himself.

> Qualities that would have saved a ship's company exposed on a broiling sea with six biscuits and a flask of water—endurance and justice, foresight, devotion, skill, came to his help. R is then —what is R?
>
> A shutter, like the leathern eyelid of a lizard, flickered over the intensity of his gaze and obscured the letter R. In that flash of darkness he heard people saying—he was a failure—that R was beyond him. He would never reach R. On to R, once more. R——
>
> Qualities that in a desolate expedition across the icy solitudes of the Polar region would have made him the leader, the guide, the counsellor, whose temper, neither sanguine nor despondent, surveys with equanimity what is to be and faces it, came to his help again. R——
>
> The lizard's eye flickered once more. The veins on his forehead bulged. The geranium in the urn became startlingly visible and, displayed among its leaves, he could see, without wishing it, that old, that obvious distinction between the two classes of men; on the one hand, the steady goers of superhuman strength who, plodding and persevering, repeat the whole alphabet in order, twenty-six letters in all, from start to finish; on the other the gifted, the inspired who, miraculously, lump all the letters together in one flash—the way of genius. He had not genius; he laid no claim to that: but he had, or might have had, the power to repeat every letter of the alphabet from A to Z accurately in order. Meanwhile, he stuck at Q. On, then, on to R.

In this miraculously poised and balanced prose, devoid of mannerism yet original and constructed to reflect every movement and glancing aside of the intelligence, Mrs Woolf achieves a texture of diverse moods and tones unparalleled, almost, since the seventeenth century. It is so supremely well done that we take in the effect without pausing to note the means. But it is good, sometimes, to pause and appreciate the skill of a great artist before giving up ourselves once again to the spell. Note here the wealth of suggestion (and the whole passage, of which the above is only a fragment, must be read to gain the full effect) and the complexity of motives. Ramsay is genuinely concerned for the truth; he really wants to know what he will find at R; but he is dramatising himself all the time. The two images of a Polar expedition and a shipwrecked crew, and a third image of a lost mountaineer, simply continue the histrionics of *The Light Brigade* in a minor key. Mr Ramsay's concern is not only for the truth: it is also for his own reputation, and the lizard's eyelid which flickers over the vision of the truth is only, perhaps, his own self-pity, though he fails to realise it.

The suggestion we are meant to take is to compare the activity of Mr Ramsay's mind in solitude and the activity of Mrs Ramsay's mind in solitude (the account of which comes later in the story, though I have talked about it first for purposes of exposition). We have seen Mrs Ramsay sinking to become a wedge of darkness, shedding her personality, and thus experiencing the emotion of unity. Mrs Ramsay's goal was reached because she did not set herself any goal. Now we see her husband setting himself a definite goal, and failing; failing for two possible reasons other than the one he himself supposes. He thinks that he fails to reach R because his brain is not good enough (and there is a glance aside at his marriage in the thought 'he had, *or might have had*, the power to repeat every letter'), but the reader is conscious of two other impediments: first, the mixture of self in his motives, and secondly, the possibility that R is to be reached, if at all, by another path than that of abstraction.

That issues so fundamental and so absorbingly interesting are woven into the texture of *To the Lighthouse* makes plain the seriousness of Virginia Woolf's conception of the novelist's task. Themes which hitherto have been treated, outside the manuals of metaphysics and devotion, only by a single poet in a generation—Shakespeare, Milton, Wordsworth—have now become the terrain of the novelist, and with the spread of the novel's appeal are opened to the consideration of a much vaster public. Mrs Woolf is of course not the first to use the novel for this purpose. Hardy, Meredith, Henry James, and, contemporary with Mrs Woolf, Dorothy Richardson—they are all discussing reality and appearance, truth and illusion, the relations of men and women, in the prose narrative form. But in none of these, unless in James, is the material so perfectly absorbed into its texture as in the later novels of Virginia Woolf. A great deal of Dorothy Richardson's sequence, *Pilgrimage*, for instance, is concerned with precisely the problems treated of in *To the Lighthouse*. But the latter's richness of texture is quite lacking;

the singleness of theme in *Pilgrimage*, the spotlight directed on a single character through four long volumes, becomes monotonous; and the indignation at masculine vanity and obtuseness, the praise of feminine intuition, have not been absorbed into an artistic whole.

The themes of intuition and ratiocination, of self-shedding and self-dramatisation, which run through *To the Lighthouse*, have not merely been grafted on to the alien organism of a story. The story is the mode of apprehension of these ideas, and so successful is this novel that one is led to ask if such themes can ever really be discussed with profit *in vacuo*—whether, in fact, metaphysical ideas have any relevance apart from a concrete situation, real or imagined, in which they may root themselves. The sterility of most abstract discussion is due to this rootlessness, and the abiding vitality of even absurd religious systems springs from their relation to the life of a founder, to legend and to tradition. In Mr Ramsay's presence the air is thin and dry; but the flickering of the lizard's eye, or the vivid glimpse of the geranium, which he waves aside as impediments to his quest, would have been seized upon by Mrs Ramsay as a help: she would have let herself be absorbed into the flower, and sunk her own personality in its petals and stalk. The difference of approach is fundamental.

vii

The dinner is the climax of the first part of *To the Lighthouse*, just as the party was the climax of *Mrs Dalloway*; but Mrs Ramsay is surrounded by real friends, and by her family. She has had a bœuf en daube specially made for William Bankes; she is interested in Paul and Minta who have been for a long walk by the sea shore and have come back (she guesses) engaged. But she is tired. She sees that her husband is grumpy and that Charles Tansley is going to be difficult; and she hardly feels able to cope with the situation. The dinner-party is not a whole yet, it is an assembly of separate individualities.

And the whole of the effort of merging and flowing and creating rested on her. Again, she felt, as a fact without hostility, the sterility of men, for if she did not do it nobody would do it, and so, giving herself the little shake that one gives a watch that has stopped, the old familiar pulse began beating, as the watch begins ticking—one, two, three, one, two, three. And so on and so on, she repeated, listening to it, sheltering and fostering the still feeble pulse as one might guard a weak flame with a newspaper.

All Mrs Woolf's narrative skill—a skill which has no aid from exciting incident, but depends on the subtle discerning of motives and temperaments—is laid out in the long, but never tedious course of this dinner-party. As Mrs Ramsay's pulse ticks steadier and steadier we see her spreading the radius of her light and warmth further and further until all the guests are included and moulded into a single unity: her husband's bad temper is assuaged, Charles Tansley's uncouthness is mitigated, William Bankes is won over by the perfection of the bœuf en daube. Mr Ramsay, at the further end of the long table, is reciting; and the words seem to sum up what has been the mood of the evening.

> *And all the lives we ever lived and all the lives to be*
> *Are full of trees and changing leaves.*

And then she gets up from the table and Augustus Carmichael opens the door for her to go out.

viii

Sitting with her husband later that night (he is reading Scott, for the men had been discussing Scott at dinner—is he still worth reading?) 'she grew still like a tree which has been tossing and quivering and now, when the breeze falls, settles, leaf by leaf, into quiet'. She too reads; but she sees that her husband is deeply affected by the humour and simplicity of Scott (he had maintained at dinner that Scott was still readable, and felt secretly that if Scott could be forgotten so could he) and the tears are running down his cheeks. He wants to complain to his wife that young men don't admire him. But she looks so peaceful reading that he will not disturb her again.

Mrs Ramsay raised her head and like a person in a light sleep seemed to say that if he wanted her to wake she would, she really would, but otherwise, might she go on sleeping, just a little longer, just a little longer? She was climbing up those branches, this way and that, laying hands on one flower and then another.

Nor praise the deep vermilion in the rose,

she read, and so reading she was ascending, she felt, on to the top, on to the summit. How satisfying! How restful! All the odds and ends of the day stuck to this magnet; her mind felt swept, felt clean. And then there it was, suddenly entire shaped in her hands, beautiful and reasonable, clear and complete, the essence sucked out of life and held rounded there—the sonnet.

But she becomes conscious of her husband smiling quizzically at her, and begins to knit. She tells him that Paul and Minta are engaged. 'So I guessed,' he says, and that is all. She wants him to say something—anything. And at last he speaks. ' "You won't finish that stocking tonight," he said, pointing to her stocking. That was what she had wanted—the asperity in his voice reproving her. . . . "No," she said, flattening the stocking out upon her knee, "I shan't finish it." ' Then she realises that he is waiting for her to say that she loves him; and she cannot do it. 'A heartless woman he called her; she never told him that she loved him. But it was not so—it was not so. It was only that she never could say what she felt. Was there no crumb on his coat? Nothing she could do for him?' She goes and stands by the window.

Then, knowing that he was watching her, instead of saying anything she turned, holding her stocking, and looked at him. And as she looked at him she began to smile, for though she had not said a word, he knew, of course he knew, that she loved him. He could not deny it. And smiling she looked out of the window and said (thinking to herself, Nothing on earth can equal this happiness)—
"Yes, you were right. It's going to be wet tomorrow." She had not said it, but he knew it. And she looked at him smiling. For she had triumphed again.

These images of completeness and incompleteness—the sonnet, the stocking—are brought in with such entire naturalness that we might miss their relevance to the action of the novel, were it not that that relevance is so vital that it calls for no more than a subconscious response: and towards that response these images, together with that of the window which separated Mrs

Ramsay and her husband at the beginning of the book and now unites them—

The curtains drawn upon unfriendly night

—make their small but definitive contribution.

ix

If we were to give the first part of *To the Lighthouse* a title which might indicate its scope, perhaps no better could be chosen than the word 'Integration': the integration of a family, of a community of friends, and of human personalities, through a woman's creative understanding, faith and courage. Then the second part would certainly have to be called 'Disintegration', for now Mrs Ramsay is removed and all falls apart; and the third part would be 'Reintegration', the piecing together of the past in Lily Briscoe's memory and imagination as she sits in her old position sketching on the lawn.

Mrs Woolf calls her second part 'Time Passes'. The space of time is ten years, and there are ten sections, but each does not represent a year. The first two simply continue the narrative of 'The Window'. Mr Bankes, Andrew, Prue, and Lily Briscoe come indoors, for it is growing dark, and put out the lights. Mr Carmichael is in bed, reading Virgil. Then we have an impression of the night settling down upon the house, the little winds creeping around the rooms. Mr Carmichael blows out his candle. It is past midnight.

Night succeeds to night, winter to autumn; and in this orderly progression of the seasons, and in their beauty, is there not some revelation of Divine goodness? It is interesting to see that 'Time Passes' raises in a very definite form the issues already touched on in Mrs Ramsay's mystical experience. How far can we take our apprehensions of beauty as apprehensions of significance, and consider them windows into reality? There is an overwhelming temptation to do so, and it is the best, the most sensitive minds which are faced with this temptation. But such minds are also faced most acutely with 'the misery of the world, which will not let them rest', and are torn between these two poles.

It seemed now as if, touched by human penitence and all its toil, divine goodness had parted the curtain and displayed behind it, single, distinct, the hare erect; the wave falling; the boat rocking, which, did we deserve them, should be ours always. But, alas, divine goodness, twitching the cord, draws the curtain; it does not please him; he covers his treasures in a drench of hail, and so breaks them, so confuses them that it seems impossible that their calm should ever return or that we should ever compose from their fragments a perfect whole or read in the littered pieces the clear words of truth. For our penitence deserves a glimpse only; our toil respite only.

More abstract, more generalised, we perceive; for the human figures have been removed from the stage in this part of the novel, and their fate recorded, telegrammatically, within brackets. The tempo and the texture of the novel have altered with the removal of these figures; man has receded into the background, and time and change and God (strangely resembling Hardy's President of the Immortals) have come to the fore.

Mrs Ramsay, we learn from one of these bracketed interpolations, has died rather suddenly one night. That is all we are told; the simple statement bears down upon us with all the weight of loss and regret that the first part has made inevitable. Any attempt at pathos is out of the question, and quite unnecessary. And the Ramsays do not return to the house on Skye. The winds and the damp and all the forces of decay have it their own way. It seems that the peace of the house will never be broken, until one day Mrs McNab comes to open all the windows and dust the bedrooms. Mrs McNab is the charlady, one of those witless, humorous, courageous old women we meet with so often in Virginia Woolf's novels. She cannot work very hard now, at close on seventy, but she does what she can.

And now we have another statement of the quest for certainty, sandwiched between the reports of Prue Ramsay's marriage and death. It is worth while giving this in full.

[Prue Ramsay, leaning on her father's arm, was given in marriage that May. What, people said, could have been more fitting? And, they added, how beautiful she looked!]

As summer neared, as the evenings lengthened, there came to the wakeful, the hopeful, walking the beach, stirring the pool, imaginations of the strangest kind—of flesh turned to atoms which drove before the wind, of stars flashing in their hearts, of cliff, sea, cloud, and sky brought purposely together to assemble outwardly the scattered parts of the vision within. In those mirrors, the minds of men, in those pools of uneasy water, in which clouds for ever turn and shadows form, dreams persisted, and it was impossible to resist the strange intimation which every gull, flower, tree, man and woman, and the white earth itself seemed to declare (but if questioned at once to withdraw) that good triumphs, happiness prevails, order rules; or to resist the extra-ordinary stimulus to range hither and thither in search of some absolute good, some crystal of intensity, remote from the known pleasures and familiar virtues, something alien to the processes of domestic life, single, hard, bright, like a diamond in the sand, which would render the possessor secure. Moreover, softened and acquiescent, the spring with her bees humming and gnats dancing threw her cloak about her, veiled her eyes, averted her head, and among passing shadows and flights of small rain seemed to have taken upon her a knowledge of the sorrows of mankind.

[Prue Ramsay died that summer in some illness connected with childbirth, which was indeed a tragedy, people said. They said nobody deserved happiness more.]

Nature, then, the external shows of things, is self-contradictory, rousing inescapable notions of meaningfulness in one's mind, only to shatter them the moment after. Mrs Ramsay's faith was unjustified. See what the world is doing to her children, for whom she sacrificed so much, prophesied so much! (Andrew Ramsay is killed in the war.) There is no meaning. And the temptation to find a meaning, it is suggested, had best be resisted. The war itself is sufficient to disprove all consoling philosophies. The blood-stain of a destroyed submarine, rising to the surface of the water, is enough to introduce irreconcilable discord into the sea-scape which ordinarily is 'calculated to stir the most sublime reflections and lead to the most comfortable conclusions'.

Did Nature supplement what man advanced? Did she complete what he began? With equal complacence she saw his misery, condoned his meanness, and acquiesced in his torture. That dream, then, of sharing, completing, finding in solitude on the beach an answer, was but a reflection in a mirror, and the mirror itself was but the surface glassiness which forms in quiescence when the nobler powers sleep beneath? Impatient, despairing yet loth to go (for beauty offers her lures, has her consolations), to pace the beach was impossible; contemplation was unendurable; the mirror was broken.

What has happened? Mrs Woolf has abandoned the point
of view (and it is the measure of her stature as an artist that she
can abandon it) implicitly adopted in the first part: that the
feminine approach, the way of intuition and faith and imagination is the right one, and that the masculine approach of
intellection, reasoning, logic, is unprofitable. For what are these
'nobler powers' which must fall asleep before the vision of faith
arises? Precisely the guardians, logic and reasoning, which must
try to take in *all* the facts and accept nothing on faith. As the
person of Mrs Ramsay has been withdrawn, so too the qualities
she stood for are withdrawn. The book has now another slant
and another tone. The rich texture of the first section, iri-
descent and vivid, has been abandoned for an austere control.
We are in a different world.

Time passes. It seems that, in spite of all Mrs McNab's efforts,
the house will topple over into ruin. But then comes a letter;
the house is to be got ready; the family may be coming for the
summer. Mrs McNab is joined by Mrs Bast; George, Mrs
Bast's son, catches the rats and cuts the grass. They have the
builders in. And Mrs McNab and Mrs Bast talk about the
family, about Mr Ramsay and Mrs Ramsay, the children and
the guests; and thus begin to create already a life within the
house. Late one evening in September Lily Briscoe and
Augustus Carmichael arrive; Mr Ramsay, Nancy, Cam, James,
and a Mrs Beckwith are there; James is sixteen now, Cam
seventeen. They wait for the morning. For tomorrow Mr
Ramsay and James and Cam are going to the lighthouse. The
wheel is come full circle.

X

Everything seems so strange, so different, to Lily Briscoe as
she sits by herself at the breakfast table that first morning.
Everything is in confusion. Cam and James are late—they
should have been ready long ago. Mr Ramsay, striding furiously
up and down the terrace, is declaiming Cowper's *The Castaway*,
dramatising his impatience. Nancy does not know what one
ought to send to the lighthouse. No one seems to know how to

set about anything. Disintegration. It is like a scene of long ago seen through a distorting medium.

Old Mr Carmichael came padding softly in, fetched his coffee, took his cup and made off to sit in the sun. The extraordinary unreality was frightening; but it was also exciting. Going to the Lighthouse. But what does one send to the Lighthouse? Perished. Alone. The grey-green light on the wall opposite. The empty places. Such were some of the parts, but how bring them together? she asked.

And Lily Briscoe remembers her picture, the picture she was painting all those years ago. That is the way to bring them together. Finish the picture; impose the unity of art. Art, not life, has unity; art has meaning. There is the secret. She pitches her easel on the lawn, near Mr Carmichael's deck-chair, for she feels she needs his protection against Mr Ramsay, who is bearing down on her, declaiming. 'Every time he approached—he was walking up and down the terrace—ruin approached, chaos approached.' For Mr Ramsay needs her sympathy and understanding.

Thus the situation of 'The Window' is reconstructed, but with the central figure, the uniting force, left out. Confusion reigns instead of order, resentment and bitterness (for James still hates his father) have got the upper hand of affection and understanding. The six children had sat dumb and resentful last night, raging inwardly under their father's tyranny. Cam and James don't want to go to the lighthouse, but dare not say so. 'It was a house full of unrelated passions—she had felt that all the evening.' And this is the real tragedy, she thinks: that the children should be coerced, their spirits subdued. And she looks round for Mrs Ramsay.

So, at forty-four, Lily Briscoe sits on the lawn trying to finish her picture. She can't do it, because there is Mr Ramsay bearing down upon her, demanding her sympathy. 'That man, she thought, her anger rising in her, never gave; that man took.' The intolerable man comes and stands over her, asks if there is anything she wants. She says no, and looks at the sea. Mr Ramsay wonders why she should look at the sea when he is there. He gives a groan, a terrible sigh, and waits. But Lily says nothing. She does not seem to see what he wants from her. And then, suddenly, she looks down at Mr Ramsay's boots—

remarkable boots, sculptured, colossal. "What beautiful boots!" she exclaims. And to her surprise this commendation of his boots is enough for Mr Ramsay. He smiles and recovers his gaiety. 'They had reached, she felt, a sunny island where peace dwelt, sanity reigned and the sun for ever shone, the blessed island of good boots.' And suddenly she feels a flood of affection for him, she feels his loneliness and his pathos and his goodness.

This element of humour—we recognise the touch of Sterne in the absurdity, the irrelevance of the boots—lightens and irradiates the wistful atmosphere of the closing scenes of *To the Lighthouse*. Mrs Woolf is ever on her guard against sentimentality, and at this point it would be particularly easy to topple over into mawkishness. And without this preliminary assurance of Mr Ramsay's good humour the expedition to the lighthouse would have been a dismal failure. Cam and James come up reluctantly; Mr Ramsay, with 'all the appearance of a leader making ready for an expedition' (another subtle flash-back to 'The Window') hands out parcels, sends Cam for a cloak, and leads the way to the beach. Lily feels curiously divided, as though part of her were accompanying the expedition, and part of her remained on the lawn in front of the house. The reader too is involved in this division of interest. For now two divergent but contemporary lines of action are in progress: a line towards the future, across the sea to the lighthouse, and a line into the past, as constructed inside Lily Briscoe's brain under the compulsion of art.

As she paints, adding blues and greens, she begins to lose consciousness of outer things. Her mind throws up images and scenes from the past which, in the moment of creation which is now upon her, are vitalised and unified. She thinks of Mrs Ramsay, how she spread happiness around her.

But what a power was in the human soul! she thought. That woman sitting there, writing under the rock, resolved everything into simplicity; made these angers, irritations fall off like old rags; she brought together this and that and then this, and so made out of that miserable silliness and spite (she and Charles squabbling, sparring, had been silly and spiteful) something—this scene on the beach for example, this moment of friendship and liking—
—which survived, after all these years, complete, so that she dipped into it to re-fashion her memory of him, and it stayed in the mind almost like a work of art.

' "Like a work of art," she repeated.' Yes, perhaps this is the secret: that there is no unity in life, no meaning to be found in the shows of earth and sea and sky; that man has to create what unity he can in his own limited sphere; and Mrs Ramsay was really an artist—an artist in life. Her creations were happiness and security, her materials men and women and children, her frame the house on Skye. The old question comes back to Lily—what is the meaning of life? Perhaps there is no vast inclusive meaning; the universe is chaos; but only little islands of meaning scattered here and there, created by persons like Mrs Ramsay, meaning valid only for one time and for one place, existing as music exists in the memory.

Lily Briscoe is left alone with her painting and her memories; Mr Ramsay and his two children sail away towards the lighthouse. Or rather, try to sail away, for there is no wind, and the boat is almost motionless. (Another vivid expression of the absence of Mrs Ramsay.) Cam and James are leagued together against their father; they sit in silence. It is an alliance against tyranny. They hope there will be no wind. But suddenly it comes, and their father, they know, is quite happy, for he has the power of being happy even while those about him are resenting him bitterly. He talks to Macalister, the boatman, about the wreck in the great storm last Christmas; and Cam, as she looks at him, cannot help feeling proud without knowing why: 'had he been there', she muses, 'he would have launched the lifeboat, he would have reached the wreck. He was so brave, so adventurous, Cam thought. But she remembered. There was, the compact; to resist tyranny to the death'.

The tie between her and James slackens a little; for she is like her mother, she cannot keep up resentment, something of the infinite beauty and pathos of life flashes across her vision and suddenly all is changed. Mr Ramsay begins to dramatise himself.

Sitting in the boat he bowed, he crouched himself, acting instantly his part—the part of a desolate man, widowed, bereft; and so called up before him in hosts people sympathising with him; staged for himself as he sat in the boat, a little drama; which required of him decrepitude and exhaustion and sorrow (he raised his hands and looked at the thinness of them, to confirm his dream) and then there was given him in abundance women's sympathy, and he imagined how they would soothe him and sympathise with him, and so getting in his dream some reflection of the exquisite pleasure women's sympathy was to him, he sighed and said gently and mournfully,

> *But I beneath a rougher sea*
> *Was whelmed in deeper gulfs than he,*

so that the mournful words were heard quite clearly by them all. Cam half started on her seat. It shocked her—it outraged her . . .

But Mr Ramsay wants to make Cam smile at him. He talks about her puppy; and James fears she will break their compact: to resist tyranny. Cam's mind is torn by the struggle, by the desire to be loyal to James, and the longing to respond to her father, who is now telling her about a dog he had when he was a little boy. And James's mind goes back to the past, he remembers how he stood at his mother's knee, and his father pausing and standing over them, and how his mother laughed and surrendered.

xi

On the lawn, Lily Briscoe lives in her memories and confronts the technical problems of her picture. 'As she dipped into the blue paint, she dipped too into the past there.' And suddenly there is an extraordinary anguish. She feels the want of Mrs Ramsay, and calls out to her. Her eyes fill with tears. On the distant sea she can see Mr Ramsay's boat sailing further and further away.

xii

Mr Ramsay is reading a little shiny book; James fears that at any moment he may look up and say something sharply to him. 'And if he does, James thought, then I shall take a knife and strike him to the heart.' It is the old symbol of his hatred which came to him as he stood by his mother long ago and felt his father destroying their calm. Yet it was not the old man reading that he wanted to kill, but the black harpy of egotism and coercion which descended upon him from time to time; it was that incubus which he must fight, not only in his father but in all its manifestations. Tyranny. For in his father there was also another spirit: the devotion to truth.

Yes, thought James, while the boat slapped and dawdled there in the hot sun; there was a waste of snow and rock very lonely and austere; and there he had come to feel, quite often lately, when his father said something which surprised the others, were two pairs of footsteps only; his own and his father's. They alone knew each other.

And Cam, looking at her father reading his little shiny book, loves him.

xiii

Lily Briscoe continues to think of Mrs Ramsay. She thinks of the multiplicity of her personality: her beauty, her aloofness and silence, her friendliness and interferingness and masterfulness, her kindness to the poor and the sick. 'One wanted fifty pairs of eyes to see with, she reflected. Fifty pairs of eyes were not enough to get round that one woman with, she thought.' And the relationship between her and her husband: one must be careful not to oversimplify that. 'It was no monotony of bliss —she with her impulses and quicknesses; he with his shudders and glooms.' Lily Briscoe focuses her attention again on her painting. She looks at the window, and then suddenly someone inside the house sits down by it—someone throws an odd-shaped triangular shadow over the step. Sit still, she prays. For the shadow is interesting; it alters the composition, gives it balance. Then the figure stirs.

Her heart leapt at her and seized her and tortured her. "Mrs Ramsay! Mrs Ramsay!" she cried, feeling the old horror come back—to want and want and not to have. Could she inflict that still? And then, quietly, as if she refrained, that too became part of ordinary experience, was on a level with the chair, with the table. Mrs Ramsay—it was part of her perfect goodness to Lily —sat there quite simply, in the chair, flicked her needles to and fro, knitted her reddish-brown stocking, cast her shadow on the step. There she sat.

xiv

The boat is very close to the lighthouse now. James looks at the thing which has held his imagination all these years. 'It was a stark tower on a bare rock. It satisfied him. It confirmed some obscure feeling of his about his own character.' He feels he is one with his father in understanding the loneliness which that gaunt tower represents. He speaks to himself exactly in his father's manner. Mr Ramsay shares out the sandwiches. He looks at his watch, makes some mathematical calculation, and says "Well done!" to James for his steering. James is very pleased and very silent. And they land on the lighthouse rock.

XV

Lily Briscoe thinks they must have landed. Suddenly she feels tired out. "It is finished," she says aloud. She turns to her picture. She sees it clearly at last—the whole problem, suddenly resolved. She draws a line with her brush in the centre. 'It was done; it was finished. Yes, she thought, laying down her brush in extreme fatigue, I have had my vision.'

The extreme fatigue of Lily Briscoe must have been Virginia Woolf's own fatigue at the close of this extraordinary novel. For such a work could only have been written at a pitch of intense spiritual excitement which must have been exhausting. The book is incredibly rich; it is packed with thought, with emotion, and with integrated and elaborate imagery. It is a living whole; and such a whole, though bearing upon it no mark of effort, could not have been brought forth without great labour. The analysis I have given is a mere skeleton, a summary of the principal theme; there are side-issues and adventitious characters about which I have said little or nothing. By cutting out almost entirely the element of plot Virginia Woolf has made possible for herself an unparalleled depth of psychological description. There is no more living character in fiction than Mrs Ramsay. Mr Ramsay, Lily Briscoe, Charles Tansley and the rest, down to Mrs McNab, are all given in the round; there are no two-dimensional characters. And with all this, there are the riches of thought, the exploration of points of view and the consideration of ultimate issues, which never get out of hand or detach themselves from the living framework of the book. To read any ordinary novel after reading *To the Lighthouse* is to feel oneself turning from the light of day into the world of puppets and paste-board. Yet all this weight of thought and complexity of emotion is balanced with an incomparable lightness; the thing seems as weightless as thistledown; there is no hanging fire, no tedium, no overbalancing at any point.

The ultimate impression of *To the Lighthouse* is of its *magnanimity*, in every sense of that word. The greatness of mind which could plan it all and carry it through, the great tolerance and clearsightedness of that mind, the refusal to take sides, the pity and the ecstasy interwoven. Mrs Woolf is not sustaining a thesis, she is describing or representing life as she catches it in a moment of time. There are no hard blacks or whites. It is not a feminist tract. Mr Ramsay wears down his wife's strength, we can see that; but Mrs Woolf does not condemn Mr Ramsay, she tries to understand him, and through James's thoughts in the boat suggests that he may sometimes be carried away by a force over which he has no control. Bitterness and partisanship are burnt out of the book by the fire of art. Mrs Ramsay's struggles and hopes come to nothing, she is proved wrong about the great future awaiting Prue, and Andrew, and Paul and Minta, and Lily Briscoe. She is defeated, just as when she turned from the window and said to her husband "Yes, you were right. It's going to be wet tomorrow," yet this moment of defeat is also, paradoxically, her moment of triumph. Why should this be so? It is difficult to say how Virginia Woolf achieves her effect, as difficult as to say why *Lear* or *Othello* leaves us with that odd exaltation. It seems, however, that goodness in defeat has a note of triumph utterly missing from evil victorious.

One thing is certain, that the writer does not achieve this triumph through dishonesty, through blinking the facts. There is no element of fantasy in *To the Lighthouse*. A lesser writer than Mrs Woolf might have left us on the heights reached by Mrs Ramsay in her vision of reality: surely that is a legitimate and noble happiness, one might say, the solitary moment of sinking into oneself when the day's work is done, and surely there one touches a genuine truth, a real fund of strength and wisdom? Surely on that basis a structure of faith may be raised? There are no dogmas there, no creeds or mythological figures. But no: we are shown the sea and the sky and the earth under another aspect than that mild one which led Mrs Ramsay down into her experience; we are shown the blood of drowned sailors staining the waves, and fragments of Andrew's body strewing the land. Mrs Ramsay can only say, 'Time stand still *here*': her experience is only for one time and for one place. There is no general solution. Nature contradicts herself; and the mind that seeks reality must still seek it along the narrow white road of truth. The great masculine virtue, to which Mrs Ramsay herself pays homage, still holds its place. *To the Lighthouse* throws a new and brilliant light on the problem, but gives no solution.

CHAPTER VII

Orlando

[1928]

ORLANDO is the watershed in the range of Virginia Woolf's writings. Hitherto there has been the one great problem, exhaustively treated: how to reconcile divergent personalities within marriage. To that problem there is, it seems, no final solution, and in *Orlando* she seeks to escape from it. This fantasy-biography is a *tour de force* and a retreat. The escape is provided by a whimsical accentuation of the Tiresias motif that we noted in *Mrs Dalloway*. Man and woman are united in a single person: not only Orlando, but the Archduke Harry and Marmaduke Bonthrop are androgynous. Marriage and understanding thus become possible. The fantasy is light and airy, there is an unaccustomed humour, yet we cannot overlook an undertone of defeat, even of self-mockery. This evasion is what I am brought to, is the confession written between the lines. This solution is no solution.

It is not only the Tiresias motif that is parodied here. Many of Mrs Woolf's favourite themes reappear in a lighter guise: the attic room of *Night and Day* and *Mrs Dalloway*, the Turkish hills sighed for amid all the civilisation of Cambridge in *Jacob's Room*, the house which is a main character in *To the Lighthouse*. All are woven together against a background of history—the pageant device which is to be used again, even more precisely, in *Between the Acts*. Through the metamorphoses of a single individual the changing spirit of English history and the English way of life is re-created. Orlando is masculine and violent in the dashing Elizabethan age, pensive and morbid in the early seventeenth century, presides at literary tea-parties in the Augustan period, and blushes and swoons in crinolines in the sentimental age of Victoria. The temperament of each age is conveyed in a series of brilliant vignettes: the boy Orlando kneeling with an ewer of rose-water before the aged Queen Elizabeth, the Great Frost of James I's reign, Pope unforgivably witty at a fashionable tea-party. The mastery of detail is admirable, and yet we miss the personal touch, the note of passion and pity which raised the novels to tragic heights.

ii

The ripe fruits of Virginia Woolf's reading appear in *Orlando*. Always fascinated by the colour and the violence, the dirt and the splendour of Shakespeare's age, it is over this period that she lingers. We see Orlando first as a handsome boy of sixteen, slashing away in his attic room at a Moor's head which swings from the rafters. And at once all the adventure and strangeness and danger of that romantic age are suggested.

> It was the colour of an old football, and more or less the shape of one, save for the sunken cheeks and a strand or two of coarse, dry hair, like the hair on a cocoanut. Orlando's father, or perhaps his grandfather, had struck it from the shoulders of a vast Pagan who had started up under the moon in the barbarian fields of Africa . . .

Behind the great ancestral house in which Orlando lives (a portrait, it seems, of Knole) there is this background of action and freedom. No wonder the thirst for greatness has entered his spirit, though with him it takes the form of literary ambition, the longing to write a great poem. (The mingled character of the Elizabethan age is suggested.) And with it goes the love of solitude. 'Orlando naturally loved solitary places, vast views, and to feel himself for ever and ever and ever alone.' It is this love of solitude and beauty which cuts him off from his kind, while his grace of body draws all hearts to him.

The old Queen is charmed on their first meeting; and two years later, when he comes to Court, she confers on him the Order of the Garter, and loves him for his innocence. But Orlando leads his own life, not so innocent. He is a true Elizabethan.

> The withered intricacies and ambiguities of our more gradual and doubtful age were unknown to them. Violence was all. The flower bloomed and faded. The sun rose and sank. The lover loved and went. And what poets said in rhyme, the young translated into practice. Girls were roses, and their seasons were as short as the flowers'. Plucked they must be before nightfall; for the day was brief and the day was all.

Orlando has a liking for low company. He listens to sailors' stories and lies with oyster-wenches as readily as with court ladies. He is feeding on the same sustenance of experience as provided matter for Shakespeare's plays and Dekker's satires.

iii

The scene changes, kaleidoscopically, to the Jacobean age. We see the Thames frozen over in the great frost of 1608; Orlando has a passionate affair with a Russian princess, who betrays him and almost breaks his heart. He falls into a seven-day trance. When he wakes, he is changed. The violent longings of the spacious days are passed, and now Orlando's temperament reflects the elegiac mood of the early seventeenth century.

Orlando now took a strange delight in thoughts of death and decay, and after pacing the long galleries and ballrooms with a taper in his hand, looking at picture after picture as if he sought the likeness of someone whom he could not find, would mount into the family pew and sit for hours watching the banners stir and the moonlight waver with a bat or death's head moth to keep him company. Even this was not enough for him, but he must descend into the crypt where his ancestors lay, coffin piled on coffin, for ten generations together. The place was so seldom visited that the rats had made free with the lead work, and now a thigh bone would catch at his cloak as he passed, or he would crack the skull of some old Sir Malise as it rolled beneath his foot.

No longer Shakespeare and Marlowe, but Donne and Sir Thomas Browne are behind this metamorphosis. But to one thing Orlando remains faithful: to poetry, and above all to his own practice of the art. He is writing a pastoral, 'The Oak Tree', and cannot decide 'whether he is the divinest genius or the greatest fool in the world'. To settle the question he invites Nick Greene, the hack writer, to pay him a visit. The episode is a humorous one: Nick Greene is entirely self-centred, hates the quiet of the countryside, will not allow Orlando to read him a tragedy, 'The Death of Hercules', and only consents to take it away and read it when he has been promised a yearly pension. When he gets home he at once sits down and writes a satiric poem, 'A Visit to a Nobleman in the Country', in which his benefactor is pilloried unmercifully and the unfortunate tragedy pulled to pieces. Orlando is cut to the heart by this ingratitude, burns all his manuscripts except 'The Oak Tree', and renounces the society of men.

Orlando is now thirty: and he plunges into a life of thought. His passion for solitude is accentuated. He ponders the nature of love, the virtues of obscurity, and the enjoyment of the present moment. Lying on the hillside, he looks down on his great house, and thinks of all the lives that have gone to building it and making it lovely through the centuries.

> There it lay in the early sunshine of spring. It looked like a town rather than a house, but a town built, not hither and thither, as this man wished or that, but circumspectly, by a single architect with one idea in his head. Courts and buildings, grey, red, plum colour, lay orderly and symmetrical; the courts were some of them oblong and some square; in this was a fountain; in that a statue; the buildings were some of them low, some pointed; here was a chapel, there a belfry; spaces of the greenest grass lay in between and clumps of cedar trees and beds of bright flowers; all were clasped—yet so well set out was it that it seemed that every part had room to spread itself fittingly—by the roll of a massive wall; while smoke from innumerable chimneys curled perpetually into the air.

The description is a detailed and a loving one. Virginia Woolf feels the personality of the house, and brings it to the forefront, for it is, with 'The Oak Tree', to be the unifying factor of her story. Its function now is to recall Orlando from his lethargy; he feels that he must do something to beautify it, and as there is no room for additions to the fabric, he refurnishes it throughout. And then, when it is all ready, there must be guests and revelry.

A farcical episode with the Archduchess Harriet Griselda of Finster-Aarhorn and Scand-op-Boom follows, and Orlando leaves the country. He is made British Ambassador to the Sublime Porte (it is now the reign of Charles II); and with Constantinople, and the vast arid spaces of Turkey, there comes a new freedom, a new enlargement of the spirit. The pretty, petty domesticities of England are driven out of his mind.

> Nothing, he reflected, gazing at the view that was now sparkling in the sun, could well be less like the counties of Surrey and Kent or the towns of London and Tunbridge Wells. To the right and left rose in bald and stony prominence the inhospitable Asian

mountains, to which the arid castle of a robber chief or two might hang; but parsonage there was none, nor manor house, nor cottage, nor oak, elm, violet, ivy, or wild eglantine. There were no hedges for ferns to grow on, and no fields for sheep to graze. The houses were white as egg-shells and as bald.

He rejoices in this wild panorama; something comes back to him of the spirit of the boy who slashed with his sword at a Moor's head in an attic room, and he breathes the air of adventure in reality. He is an excellent Ambassador, receives the Order of the Bath and a Dukedom; but at night he slips out into the crowded streets in disguise, and marries a gipsy girl.

Now comes the great metamorphosis. Immediately after his marriage, Orlando falls into a trance. It again lasts for seven days, during which there is a rising in Constantinople; foreigners are put to the sword, but the sleeping Orlando is presumed dead and so spared. When he awakes, in a deserted Embassy, it is to find he is a woman. His personality remains unchanged, his memory goes back through all the events of his (but now we must say *her*) life without a hesitation. She dresses in the Turkish fashion 'in those coats and trousers which can be worn indifferently by either sex', and rides off on a donkey to join the gipsies.

The gipsies welcome her, and for long enough she is happy with them. But then the accursed *cacoëthes scribendi*, inspired by the 'English disease, a love of Nature', seizes her, and cuts her off from harmony with the gipsies, who know Nature to be ruthless and cruel. Hating what they cannot understand, Orlando's uncanny silences and scribblings, they plan to murder her; but fortunately she decides in time to go back to England and so spares them the unpleasant necessity.

On the boat, returning to England, Orlando enters into possession of her feminine nature. As a woman she is cossetted and flattered by the captain, and finds it all strangely agreeable. She can enjoy the experience from the vantage of her double personality.

She remembered how, as a young man, she had insisted that women must be obedient, chaste, scented, and exquisitely apparelled. "Now I shall have to pay in my own person for those desires," she reflected; "for women are not (judging from my own short experience of the sex) obedient, chaste, scented, and

exquisitely apparelled by nature. They can only attain these
graces, without which they may enjoy none of the delights of life,
by the most tedious discipline. . . ."

And thus a constant double analysis proceeds, deliciously witty
and ironic and good-humoured. The balance comes down on
the side of women: for women desire a kind of power which is
not, at any rate, destructive or exclusive.

iv

It is eighteenth-century London to which she returns: Wren's
St. Paul's, and Greenwich Hospital, and 'broad and orderly
thoroughfares' in place of the dark, huddled streets of the old
mediaeval town. She returns too to a lawsuit. All her estates
are in Chancery and her titles are in abeyance until her sex,
and her claim to be alive are legally determined. Meanwhile
she is permitted to reside at her country seat.

The ridiculous episode of the Archduchess Harriet is now
resumed. The Archduchess turns out to be an Archduke after
all, he pesters Orlando with proposals of marriage, and she
only gets rid of him by cheating at Fly Loo and dropping a
toad between his shirt and his skin. Then she posts off to
London and joins the fashionable society of the day. All her
old reverence for writers returns; she meets Pope and Swift
and Addison, and finds it is the age of satire. Again she receives
a shock when Pope, suspecting an insult, turns on her 'with the
rough draught of a certain famous line in the "Characters of
Woman"'. The Nick Greene reaction all over again, we observe;
but now, instead of forswearing all human society, she seeks
out a covey of young prostitutes and listens delightedly to their
conversation.

v

Then the Cloud appears—the cloud that marks the beginning of the nineteenth century. The age of damp, and sentiment, and fecundity is upon her.

The great cloud which hung, not only over London, but over
the whole of the British Isles on the first day of the nineteenth

century stayed, or rather, did not stay, for it was buffeted about constantly by blustering gales, long enough to have extraordinary consequences upon those who lived beneath its shadow. A change seemed to have come over the climate of England. Rain fell frequently, but only in fitful gusts, which were no sooner over than they began again. The sun shone, of course, but it was so girt about with clouds and the air was so saturated with water, that its beams were discoloured and purples, oranges and reds of a dull sort took the place of the more positive landscapes of the eighteenth century. Under this bruised and sullen canopy the green of the cabbages was less intense, and the white of the snow was muddied. . . .

Damp makes its way everywhere—into the houses, into the bones, into the intellect. Nothing is clear and defined. 'Love, birth, and death were all swaddled in a variety of fine phrases. The sexes drew further and further apart. No open conversation was tolerated. Evasions and concealments were sedulously practised on both sides.' Even Orlando is affected by the prevailing atmosphere: she becomes more feminine, in the Victorian manner; she begins to think of marriages and wedding-rings. She detests the process, but cannot arrest it. The Zeitgeist has her in its grip. Even her verse, when she tries to write, is morbid and mournful and clinging like ivy. She goes out for a walk—no longer with her old free masculine stride, but timorously. 'At every step she glanced nervously lest some male form should be hiding behind a furze bush or some savage cow be lowering its horns to toss her.' Finally, following the Victorian romantic ideal to its limits, she falls and sprains her ankle; a horseman appears out of the dawn mists, and within a few minutes they are engaged.

Marmaduke Bonthrop Shelmerdine has a ruined castle in the Hebrides, has explored the East, and is now on his way to join his brig at Falmouth. He tells her thrilling stories of sailing round Cape Horn in a storm, of wrecks and rafts and 'peril in the imminent deadly breach'. They are married, for the lawsuit is settled at last and Orlando is given permission to be alive and a woman; and then Shelmerdine sails away. Orlando is left alone, as she has been always alone. The master-theme is still, for Virginia Woolf, Freedom: freedom and bondage, a bondage gladly entered into. But marriage itself has become a fantasy: the problem which has absorbed us in the novels is not met, but parodied. We know next to nothing of Shelmerdine; he is simply a romantic symbol of the perfect husband. Ralph Denham, the intellectual; Richard Dalloway, the politician; Peter Walsh, the failure; Mr Ramsay, the scholar; these, as potential husbands, are recognisable types of everyday life. We can take them seriously. What sort of success will marriage with one of these hold out for the intuitive, freedom-loving woman? But Shelmerdine, prancing out of the dawn on a fiery steed, proposing and being accepted on the spot, sailing off again round the Horn: there is no problem here, and no reality.

However, this is rather like breaking a butterfly on a wheel; although it is well to note that with *Orlando* Mrs Woolf puts behind her the hitherto all-absorbing theme, and passes on, in *The Waves*, to a new vision. The second great period of her work has ended in a dream. With the smoothness of the dream-sequence, the Victorian age passes into the Edwardian, it is not quite so damp now, Orlando bears a son, Shelmerdine returns, and lo! it is the twentieth century, the year 1928. The great house still stands in all its beauty, the symbol of unity and continuity. Finally, too, 'The Oak Tree' is finished, and even published, Nick Greene is now Sir Nicholas, with a Professorship and many critical volumes to his credit. Literature has become respectable, though not so exciting as it used to be. The pageant of history is finished.

CHAPTER VIII

A Room of One's Own

[1929]

IF *Orlando* is an escape from problems, *A Room of One's Own* is a clearing house for ideas. Ostensibly an essay on *Women and Fiction*, it is simply packed with ideas of every sort, though they are most skilfully arranged to illustrate the central theme. It starts off as a tract on the education of women—but how much more witty and urbane than the later *Three Guineas*, where indignation sharpens the gentle voice, and we lose the sense of proportion! How much of life, and literature, and good society, and philosophy, is packed into these hundred and seventy pages!

The essay was presented originally, in a condensed form, as two papers read at Girton and Newnham; and the first chapter is about Cambridge. Though she speaks of Oxbridge, the name only is composite; the place is the university she knew so well. And no one—not even E. M. Forster in *The Longest Journey*—has given us a more understanding portrait of Cambridge and its peculiar flavour. She describes the Cam with its willows 'weeping in perpetual lamentation, their hair about their shoulders'. She is waved off the grass by a beadle; she is refused admittance into Trinity Library. She watches the procession making its way into King's College Chapel, and meditates on the fabric's long history.

> As you know, its high domes and pinnacles can be seen, like a sailing-ship always voyaging, never arriving, lit up at night and visible for miles, far away across the hills. Once, presumably, this quadrangle with its smooth lawns, its massive buildings and the chapel itself was marsh too, where the grasses waved and the swine rooted. Teams of horses and oxen, I thought, must have hauled the stone in wagons from far counties, and then with infinite labour the grey blocks in whose shade I was now standing were poised in order one on top of another, and then the painters brought their glass for the windows, and the masons were busy for centuries up on that roof with putty and cement, spade and trowel.

It is the same consideration aroused in her by the great house in *Orlando*: a mighty image of historical continuity, endowed with the wealth and the blessings of ages: the symbol of masculine education. Against it she is to set the raw red brick edifices of Girton and Newnham, devoid of history, of beauty, of amenities: the makeshift of women's education.

Dinner at Newnham or Girton on plain soup, beef, cabbages and potatoes, followed by prunes and custard, contrasts with the lunch she has had earlier that day in a don's rooms in one of the men's colleges: sole, partridges 'with all their retinue of sauces and salads', followed by 'a confection which rose all sugar from the waves. . . . Meanwhile the wineglasses had flushed yellow and flushed crimson; had been emptied; had been filled. And thus by degrees was lit, halfway down the spine, which is the seat of the soul, not that hard little electric light which we call brilliance, as it pops in and out upon our lips, but the more profound, subtle and subterranean glow which is the rich yellow flame of rational intercourse'.

And so the question arises: for that rational intercourse, for all the leisurely appreciation of life and thought which spells civilisation, is not this material background necessary? Can the soul which is cramped into surroundings which have no amenities, and which is dependent on a body fed on unappetising food, reach its fullest development? More important still: is not the element of security, the possession of, say, five hundred a year, indispensable to the good life which consists in the pursuit of beauty and truth?

She thinks, as always, in pictures first.

> Kings and nobles brought treasure in huge sacks and poured it under the earth. This scene was for ever coming alive in my mind and placing itself by another of lean cows and a muddy market and withered greens and the stringy hearts of old men—these two pictures, disjointed and disconnected and nonsensical as they were, were for ever coming together and combating each other and had me entirely at their mercy.

Then she hears the story of the building of 'Fernham', so different from the story of the founding and endowing of King's: the opposition from the newspapers, the apathy of the public, the struggle to scrape thirty thousand pounds together. And why no endowments for 'Fernham'? Because the women of the race, the only people who could be expected to take an interest in the project, had through the centuries been too busy bringing up families and mending clothes to have any money to bequeath. 'Making a fortune and bearing thirteen children—no human being could stand it.' And all the money made by the husbands had gone to endow Balliol or King's.

Such is the theme—the intellectual subjection of women: but so delicately and wittily does Virginia Woolf touch it, that we are not nauseated by repetition. There is a wealth of imagery and of illustration. And, serious though it is, it is so good-humoured. Seen from a bare 'Fernham' window, the 'famous city' is still lovely and venerable.

> It was very beautiful, very mysterious in the autumn moonlight. The old stone looked very white and venerable. One thought of all the books that were assembled down there; of the pictures of old prelates and worthies hanging in the panelled rooms; of the painted windows that would be throwing strange globes and crescents on the pavement; of the tablets and memorials and inscriptions; of the quiet rooms looking across the quiet quadrangles. And (pardon me the thought) I thought, too, of the admirable smoke and drink and the deep armchairs and the pleasant carpets: of the urbanity, the geniality, the dignity which are the offspring of luxury and privacy and space.

Tinged with regret? yes, that she, a woman, can never know the fellowship of those quiet courts and gardens; but not with envy. The love of spiritual freedom which we have noted in *Jacob's Room* rises again in her heart. 'I thought of the organ booming in the chapel and of the shut doors of the library; and I thought how unpleasant it is to be locked out; and I thought how it is worse perhaps to be locked in. . . .' And so the next step is, as with Jacob Flanders, to London.

ii

In London the context of her meditations widens. In the reading-room of the British Museum she studies the books that men have written about women ('women do not write books about men') and she finds they are full of prejudice and anger. The writers display indignation. They are not at all scientific. As she reads, desultorily, for it is not easy going, her pen draws a face on the paper before her.

It was the face and figure of Professor von X. engaged in writing his monumental work entitled *The Mental, Moral, and Physical Inferiority of the Female Sex*. He was not in my picture a man attractive to women. He was heavily built; he had a great jowl; to balance that he had very small eyes; he was very red in the face. His expression suggested that he was labouring under some emotion that made him jab his pen on the paper as if he were killing some noxious insect as he wrote, but even when he had killed it that did not satisfy him; he must go on killing it; and even so, some cause for anger and irritation remained.

And so it is with all these books by men about women. She finds that 'they had been written in the red light of emotion and not in the white light of truth'. And she asks herself what it was that had made their authors so angry.

It is not long before she discovers the answer. It is sufficiently obvious. The answer is fear. England is a patriarchy. It is rebellion that the male mind fears: a challenge on its own ground of intellect. Men, to be happy, must feel themselves superior; and so they must have a sect to which they can feel themselves superior. This sect is women.

Women have served all these centuries as looking-glasses possessing the magic and delicious power of reflecting the figure of man at twice its natural size. Without that power probably the earth would still be swamp and jungle. The glories of all our wars would be unknown. We should still be scratching the outlines of deer on the remains of mutton bones and bartering flints for sheep skins or whatever simple ornament took our unsophisticated taste . . . That is why Napoleon and Mussolini both insist so emphatically upon the inferiority of women, for if they were not inferior, they would cease to enlarge.

This too explains why men, besides requiring a woman's homage, are so infuriated by her criticism. And there follow some penetrating observations on the love of power and the love of possessions. Women may suffer from the defects of their education, or lack of education. Men suffer from the false ideals education has imbued them with—'the instinct for possession, the rage for acquisition which drives them to desire other people's fields and goods perpetually; to make frontiers and flags; battleships and poison gas; to offer up their own lives and their children's lives'. And the stockbrokers and barristers spend their hours indoors on a May morning to make yet more money when they already have enough to let them enjoy all the beauty and strangeness of life.

In *To the Lighthouse* this theme—woman the mirror of the man —was accepted by Mrs Ramsay and turned into art by Virginia Woolf because there she was dealing with real persons, her own creations that she knew and loved with all their virtues and defects. Here she is treating the theme in the abstract; and though she never loses her poise, she does make an abstract judgment and says, This is wrong, this should not be. There is a better way, a nobler function for the woman *vis-à-vis* the man; and later she will tell us what it is. For the moment she is content to show the futility of the actual situation.

iii

In her third chapter she turns to the testimony of history. The construction of this essay is still peculiarly close to that of *Jacob's Room*: first Cambridge, then London and the British Museum, now retreat into the attic room to study the written records. What have the historians to say about women and their place in the pageant of events? In the Elizabethan age, she reads, they were practically slaves. Wives were beaten regularly; daughters were forced into marriage. And yet, curiously enough, what an important part they play in literature! How dominating are their personalities! Cleopatra, Lady Macbeth, Rosalind; and it is the same with the women characters of all periods, both classical and modern. How explain this paradox?

A very queer, composite being thus emerges. Imaginatively she is of the highest importance; practically she is completely insignificant. She pervades poetry from cover to cover; she is all but absent from history. She dominates the lives of kings and conquerors in fiction; in fact she was the slave of any boy whose parents forced a ring upon her finger. Some of the most inspired words, some of the most profound thoughts in literature fall from her lips; in real life she could hardly read, could scarcely spell, and was the property of her husband.

Can it be, Virginia Woolf wonders, that history has been badly written: has been seen from one angle only, an angle that misses out much of the reality? Certainly history for the historian is a strange thing. 'It often seems a little queer as it is, unreal, lop-sided; but why should they not add a supplement to history? calling it, of course, by some inconspicuous name so that women might figure there without impropriety?'

As it is, almost nothing is recorded of women before the eighteenth century. To make up the gap, Virginia Woolf paints an imaginary portrait—of Shakespeare's sister, whom she calls Judith, who possessed her brother's genius but not his opportunities. She isn't sent to school, and when she tries to read a little at home her parents tell her to mend the stockings or mind the stew. Her genius, which is literary, finds no outlet. In the end (and she is not yet seventeen) when she is threatened with a forced marriage, she runs away to London: she wants to act, she says. The theatre manager laughs at her, and she is driven to become Nick Greene's mistress; she finds herself with child and kills herself. Such, or something like it, would have been the fate of any woman in Shakespeare's day who had had Shakespeare's genius.

The difficulties of writing a work of genius at any time, and for anyone (even a man) are great enough, says Mrs Woolf; and here we have one of those delightful pieces of critical insight which star *A Room of One's Own* and mitigate the monotony of the theme. 'To write a work of genius is almost always a feat of prodigious difficulty. Everything is against the likelihood that it will come from the writer's mind whole and entire. Generally material circumstances are against it. Dogs will bark; people will interrupt; money must be made; health will break down. Further, accentuating all these difficulties and making them harder to bear is the world's notorious indifference.' Towards a woman writer it is worse than indifference: it is positive malevolence. And this malevolence has its repercussions again on the frame of mind of the woman writer. She cannot forget it; it twists her thinking and feeling from the straight. To write well she should have the perfect emotional clarity of Shakespeare.

For though we say that we know nothing about Shakespeare's state of mind, even as we say that, we are saying something about Shakespeare's state of mind. The reason perhaps why we know so little of Shakespeare—compared with Donne or Ben Jonson or Milton—is that his grudges and spites and antipathies are hidden from us. We are not held up by some 'revelation' which reminds us of the writer. All desire to protest, to preach, to proclaim an injury, to pay off a score, to make the world the witness of some

hardship or grievance was fired out of him and consumed. Therefore his poetry flows from him free and unimpeded. If ever a
human being got his work expressed completely, it was Shakespeare. If ever a mind was incandescent, unimpeded, I thought,
turning again to the bookcase, it was Shakespeare's mind.

And, alas! it was Virginia Woolf's mind which in the end, and
in *Three Guineas* especially, found itself overwhelmed with the
sense of grievance which makes pure artistic expression impossible: not a grievance for herself, but for all women who
struggle to be free: the grievance which finds its first full and
ominous, though as yet urbane, unfolding in this very *A Room
of One's Own.*

iv

Now she consults the evidence of writing itself—the writing
of women. There they are, a long and not wholly undistin-
guished company (for are not Jane Austen and Christina
Rossetti among them?): what have they to say for themselves?

They have been twisted, she finds. Twisted by the *res angusta
domi*, by the scoffs of 'the opposing faction', men. They have
been prevented from attaining the impersonality which is
essential to great literature. But, in spite of that, how much they
have accomplished! There is Lady Winchilsea, who wrote some
lines which Pope was not ashamed to appropriate; and the
Duchess of Newcastle, who was driven into eccentricity by
ridicule; and Dorothy Osborne, who thought the Duchess was
crazy to venture to write books, and herself wrote admirable
letters. These are the unsuccessful writers, the inheritors of unfulfilled renown. They are followed by Mrs Aphra Behn, not
wholly estimable, perhaps, but then—how successful! The first
professional woman writer, she marks the turning point.

> The extreme activity of mind which showed itself in the later
> eighteenth century among women—the talking, and the meeting,
> the writing of essays on Shakespeare, the translations of the classics
> —was founded on the solid fact that women could make money
> by writing.

Without Mrs Aphra Behn, there could have been no Jane
Austen, no Brontës, no George Eliot.

Why were they all novelists, these successful writers? 'The

original impulse was to poetry.' It is an interesting critical question; and Mrs Woolf wonders if the explanation may be that these middle-class women of the early nineteenth century were perforce writing in society and of society; they had no room of their own. This is fatal to poetry; less so, possibly, to fiction. Moreover, a woman's training was inevitably in the observation of character and the analysis of emotion: faculties she acquired unconsciously, in the course of her day's activities; and these she could more easily put to use in a novel.

Thus domesticity was not entirely a disadvantage. Yet how much depended on the individual! What does not seem to have irked Jane Austen at all drove Charlotte Brontë to distraction. Jane Austen, it is clear, did not *want* to write about anything but parsonages and tea-parties; but Charlotte Brontë yearned after wider horizons, and the truth and solidity of her creations suffer because she couldn't reach them. 'She knew, no one better, how enormously her genius would have profited if it had not spent itself in solitary visions over distant fields; if experience and intercourse and travel had been granted her.' Thus the range of her work was limited, and its integrity damaged.

V

'I had come at last, in the course of this rambling, to the shelves which hold books by the living; by women and by men; for there are almost as many books written by women now as by men.' She looks carefully through one of these books—a novel by a writer she calls Mary Carmichael: *Life's Adventure*. Is it a good novel? Not very, we gather; its style is jerky, it is ostentatiously modern, it is afraid of being called sentimental. The twist is there: the twist caused by the fear of masculine criticism; but is the writer being herself or someone else? At any rate she is not afraid of a new subject. "Chloe liked Olivia," Mrs Woolf reads. This at least is new—and important. For it denies the masculine premiss that women do not like each other, and find nothing to talk about when they are alone. In masculine novels women are almost exclusively shown in their relation to men. And how wrong this is! Think what would have happened to literature if men had been shown only in their relation to women! 'Suppose, for instance, that men were only represented in literature as the lovers of women, and were never the friends of men, soldiers, thinkers, dreamers.'

From this consideration Virginia Woolf is led to discuss the really vital relations of men with women. Men have again and again sought the companionship of women, not merely for the sensual relation, but for a certain understanding and creative stimulus they cannot get from even the best of their own sex. We have seen that relationship worked out with beautiful completeness and concreteness in *Mrs Dalloway* and *To the Lighthouse*; here she dwells on it for a moment again.

> What they got, it is obvious, was something that their own sex was unable to supply; and it would not be rash, perhaps, to define it further, without quoting the doubtless rhapsodical words of the poets, as some stimulus, some renewal of creative power which is in the gift only of the opposite sex to bestow. He would open the door of drawing-room or nursery, I thought, and find her among her children perhaps, or with a piece of embroidery on her knee —at any rate, the centre of some different order and system of life, and the contrast between this world and his own, which might be the law courts or the House of Commons, would at once refresh and invigorate; and there would follow, even in the simplest talk, such a natural difference of opinion that the dried ideas in him would be fertilised anew; and the sight of her creating in a different medium from his own would so quicken his creative power that insensibly his sterile mind would begin to plot again, and he would find the phrase or the scene which was lacking when he put on his hat to visit her. Every Johnson has his Thrale, and holds fast to her for some such reasons as these, and when the Thrale marries her Italian music master Johnson goes half mad with rage and disgust, not merely that he will miss his pleasant evenings at Streatham, but that the light of his life will be "as if gone out".

This, it seems to me, is one of the key passages of *A Room of One's Own*. This is the relationship, creative and warm and human, which Mrs Woolf would like to see put in the place of the mirror-image function so dear to the indignant writers about women.

vi

Her sixth and last chapter develops the same theme. Again there is a picture to start off the meditation. She looks out of the window, and sees a very ordinary sight. Two people, a man and a woman, come down the street and meet at the corner and get into a cab together. It is an image of co-operation. And more— it is an image of fusion. Like Jung, Mrs Woolf feels assured that the complete, balanced mind is androgynous.

> I went on amateurishly to sketch a plan of the soul so that in each of us two powers preside, one male, one female; and in the man's brain the man predominates over the woman, and in the woman's brain the woman predominates over the man. The normal and comfortable state of being is that when the two live in harmony together, spiritually co-operating. If one is a man, still the woman part of the brain must have effect; and a woman also must have intercourse with the man in her. Coleridge perhaps meant this when he said that a great mind is androgynous. It is when this fusion takes place that the mind is fully fertilised and uses all its faculties.

She sees Shakespeare's mind as the great type of the androgynous. It does not think specially or separately of sex. How different from the writers of our own sex-conscious age! Modern male writers especially (and no doubt she has D. H. Lawrence in the forefront of her mind) seem obsessed with the mechanics of sex and with the 'struggle' between man and woman. Their very indecency—so hard, so brittle, so protesting—is different from Shakespeare's indecency. Virility has become self-conscious. 'Men are now writing only with the male side of their brains.' And this accounts, of course, not only for the imbalance of the notoriously sexual writers like Lawrence, but also for the unsatisfactoriness of the popular novelists like Bennett and Galsworthy. Their minds, unfertilised by the feminine element, deal with the surfaces of things: they lack depth and suggestion.

Prophetically, Mrs Woolf denounces the Fascist age. Mussolini's Italy is a world where masculine values reign supreme; where women are degraded, and violence is all. Over-consciousness of sex and violence do seem to be related. And this over-consciousness is fatal to the writer. Again it seems to us, reading this wise and urbane book, that she is speaking of her own *Three Guineas*, and even of *The Years*.

> It is fatal for a woman to lay the least stress on any grievance; to plead even with justice any cause; in any way to speak consciously as a woman. And fatal is no figure of speech; for anything written with that conscious bias is doomed to death. It ceases to

be fertilised. Brilliant and effective, powerful and masterly, as it may appear for a day or two, it must wither at nightfall; it cannot grow in the minds of others. Some collaboration has to take place in the mind between the woman and the man before the art of creation can be accomplished. Some marriage of opposites has to be consummated. The whole of the mind must lie wide open if we are to get the sense that the writer is communicating his experience with perfect fullness. There must be freedom and there must be peace. Not a wheel must grate, not a light glimmer. The curtains must be close drawn.

Virginia Woolf, alas, is not to have this freedom and this peace. The perfect unfolding of her genius, to which we look forward in the third period of her art, is never to take place: only one masterpiece, *The Waves*, is to come out whole and entire. The world is too much with her; and the monstrous onslaught of diabolism in world affairs is to tear her mind asunder. The golden good-humour of *A Room of One's Own* is submerged by bitterness in *Three Guineas*; the darkness of evil hangs over *The Years*; the mastery of technique falters in *Between the Acts*.

CHAPTER IX

Towards a Pattern

AT the end of our consideration of this second great creative period of Virginia Woolf's work it may be profitable to glance back and sum up our impressions. We have seen the themes which dominate these novels: the life of freedom and the life of bondage in marriage; love, in its ridiculous aspects and its sublime; society and its demands on the individual; the subterfuges of religion; the place of woman; the relations between man and nature; the moment of understanding; time and reality. Let us look at these rather more closely, and see what sort of a philosophy, if we may call it by that name, emerges from the whole.

ii

Most striking, perhaps, is the multifariousness of Virginia Woolf's interests. She doesn't write about action and adventure, nor should we expect her to, for that would be asking her to be a different sort of novelist. But in what concerns *life*, the interior life of the spirit, she leaves few corners unilluminated. She doesn't accept any presuppositions. She tests and compares and revises continually. Her touch is delicate but unflinching. Her glance ranges from consideration to consideration, and her technique makes use of every image and every stylistic device.

The preoccupation of the bulk of novelists with sexual attraction seems to her a limiting factor. Life is so much more than love; and love itself is distorted, if it is detached from the whole of experience. She sees love's ridiculous aspect in *The Voyage Out*: 'the boles of the trees are swollen, are obscene with lovers'. She notes in *Jacob's Room* that sex blurs the vision of reality. In *Orlando* she makes fun of D. H. Lawrence and his gamekeepers. She will not accept sexual passion in itself as admirable: she wants her characters to link it up with life at every point, to integrate it with their other creative activities as rational human beings. Then, as in *Night and Day*, she can show its beauty and sublimity. But it must not distract from reality.

And what is 'reality'? Perhaps we are now in a position to look at this to more advantage.

> What is meant by 'reality'? It would seem to be something very erratic, very undependable—now to be found in a dusty road, now in a scrap of newspaper in the street, now a daffodil in the sun. It lights up a group in a room and stamps some casual saying. It overwhelms one walking home beneath the stars and makes the silent world more real than the world of speech—and then there it is again in an omnibus in the uproar of Piccadilly. Sometimes, too, it seems to dwell in shapes too far away for us to discern what their nature is. But whatever it touches, it fixes and makes permanent. That is what remains over when the skin of the day has been cast into the hedge; that is what is left of past time and of our loves and hates.

So she tells us in *A Room of One's Own*. Reality then is something intangible and indefinable, yet the pearl of great price. We don't usually find it in society or in tumult; and the problem of love and marriage is to find or preserve it in the intercourse of two human beings. *Must* it be solitary? that is the great question, the agonising question. It demands great truthfulness and directness of vision; the rejection of all comfortable beliefs and pretences.

> Think of things in themselves [she urges]; see human beings not always in their relation to each other but in relation to reality; and the sky, too, and the trees or whatever it may be in themselves; if we look past Milton's bogey, for no human being should shut out the view; if we face the fact, for it is a fact, that there is no arm to cling to, but that we go alone and that our relation is to the world of reality and not only to the world of men and women, then the opportunity will come . . .

Such is her testament. There is no Milton's bogey, no ruler and rewarder and punisher of the universe. Each of us, in his relation to reality, is *alone*. And we must base our contacts with the world of men and women (which Virginia Woolf here so carefully distinguishes from the world of reality) on that enduring, austere foundation. Nor can we hope to arrive at any final construction. 'It's life that matters,' she tells us in *Night and Day*, 'nothing but life—the process of discovering—the everlasting and perpetual process, not the discovery itself at all.'

We shall find that, inevitably, we form theories about the nature of reality; but we must not let ourselves be bound down by them. They are not and cannot be ultimate. It is in a later book, her biography of Roger Fry, that she warns us most clearly of the danger.

> From the collision of many converging ideas a theory forms. It may be helpful. For if we allow sensations to accumulate unchecked they lose their sharpness; to test them by reason strengthens and enriches. But fascinating as theories are . . . they too must be controlled or they will form a crust which blocks the way for further experience. Theories must always be brought in touch with facts. The collision may prove fatal to these delicate and intricate constructions. It does not matter. The risk must be run.

Our only escape from the danger is to keep on observing, checking our theories by our sensations. More than any other novelist I know Virginia Woolf has the gift of making us see the thing in itself, and the interpenetration of the thing with a human life. The older novelists, she seems to say, busy with plots, busy with propaganda, have missed something. But let man and nature exist on equal terms, and then let us see what happens.

What happens is a reversal of values. Peter Walsh shows us this in *Mrs Dalloway*.

> A terrible confession it was (he put his hat on again), but now, at the age of fifty-three, one scarcely needed people any more. Life itself, every moment of it, every drop of it, here, this instant, now, in the sun, in Regent's Park, was enough. Too much, indeed. A whole lifetime was too short to bring out, now that one had acquired the power, the full flavour; to extract every ounce of pleasure, every shade of meaning; which both were so much more solid than they used to be, so much less personal.

This view runs right through her writings: the immense depth and solidity of things, and the solitary mind's power of extracting sheer enjoyment from watching them. This explains the great happiness that there is in Mrs Woolf's writing, the controlled ecstasy. She liked looking at things, and writing down just what she saw. We find this simple joy most uncompromisingly set down in *Solid Objects*, that fantasy which is really not so fantastic as it seems. John sees a lump of thick glass buried in the sand; he looks at it with the innocent eye of a child; he sees it, that is, in what Blake would call 'its eternal lineaments'. He feels its satisfying solidity. Happiness seizes him, and he recedes further and further from the world of men, finding his proper life in the collection of such 'solid objects'. The world calls him mad. If he were a painter or a sculptor, he would feel the need to express his intuition of these objects plastically; if he were a writer, he would have to describe them. But John is not an artist. His need is simply for life, and these things, in some odd way, help him to live. We may say that he understands their language; they say something vital to him which nothing else, and nobody else, can say.

Things—natural things, like trees and fishes, and man-made things that have undergone the moulding of nature, like this lump of worn glass—simply are; they neither argue nor invite discussion. Their being is enough in itself to give happiness. Smooth gigantic contours of rock, a leaf sun-flecked twinkling in the wind, the curve of a lizard's body: these things exist in the instant and have no meaning apart from the instant. We cannot abstract them; they do not serve to prove anything. Their reason for being is in themselves. They are not insistent. We can look at them—or we can turn away to a book, to God, to our thoughts. But if we do look, and if we have cleared our minds of cant, and really don't want these things to prove to us that there is a God, or that we have been right in doing what we did yesterday, or that 'everything is for the best in the best of all possible worlds', then they may give us an extraordinary happiness.

But one thing they won't do. They won't make it easier for us to live in the world of men. Human beings come to look so odd, in their clothes and their cars, when one has been gazing for any length of time at 'inanimate objects'. One wants to say to them, 'Stop! don't move about so much! please don't talk, don't move: I cannot see your shape, I don't understand who you are. Why are you not yourselves?' For the oddity of a human being is not the oddity of a tree, for instance, which is inherent in the nature of a miracle: that strange brown pillar sticking up out of the ground, becoming green and leafy at the top. It is rather the oddity of confusion, amorphousness, inconsistency, incompleteness. Things seem to know what they are and what they are about; men and women don't. And things spoil us for conventional civilised living by convincing us that life is really enormously simple—just a matter of a few spatial relations, an inclined plane of rock, say, meeting a horizontal plane of water; a few primary colours, the blue of the sky, a red poppy; certain tactile values, the rough bark of trees, and the cold feet of insects walking over it. Exquisitely simple; but how far removed from the complex life of everyday human affairs! It is difficult for the one world to come to terms with the other.

iv

The technique of Virginia Woolf's novels develops, clearly, with the effort to express more and more exactly the life of the world of things in themselves and in relation to the human world. It develops, too, with the widening of her thought, with the various aspects of the good life that present themselves to her. Both in her thought and in her technique she is ceaselessly experimenting. In her search for values she doesn't cling to one partial solution or another. She gives us the pure observation. When she describes the good life in terms of intellectual striving, when she gives her pictures of lonely students wrestling with Plato and Spinoza, the reader is convinced. Yes, that is the good life, he cries; now I see it clearly. When she describes the good life in terms of fellowship, and pictures friends meeting and discussing until truth is distilled, the reader is convinced. When she shows us a solitary mind engaged not in ratiocination but in the exercise of intuition, sinking down 'into its proper dark', the reader is again convinced. But Mrs Woolf is not convinced: not for long. She cannot cling to any one of these solutions, attractive though each of them is. She is too much aware of the complexity and perplexity of life. She has no ready-made solution to offer; and for this reason the reader is often disappointed and goes to the lesser novelists who are final and consistent.

But this faith in the virtue of things, and seeing things in themselves, is a rock to which she clings; and her writing shows an ever-increasing desire to give the thing in itself perfect portrayal. She is developing a new manner of describing things, and this comes from a growing insight. She sees that one has to enjoy looking at things, just looking, without thought coming in at all; yet looking in the right way takes one deeper into knowing them than any amount of thinking about them. And there is this enjoyment, this extraordinary happiness. What is this right way of looking, which brings such satisfaction? We become aware as we read the novels that it is a mode of being, and of being the thing looked at. It is an identification, in some way not explained, of the seer with the seen. To enter, intuitively, into the life of the thing—that is the secret. To look at the bubbles which rise on the surface of a rain-lashed puddle —and feel oneself into the bubble. This is wisdom—and this, moreover, is freedom. For it is escape from the self. And that is why it brings happiness. The experience of the artist confirms the vision of the sage: to get rid of the self opens every door and floods the spirit with joy. It is of no particular moment whether the thing looked at is a flower or a broken pot. Blake tells us that he could look at a knot in a piece of wood until he was reduced to tears. In practice, of course, it is easier to look at a beautiful thing than at an ugly one; and it is easier to look at a natural object, a stone or a tree-trunk, than at an artificial one, a table-cloth or a pen, because in the latter we have the individualist human element intruding itself, and it is precisely from this that we want to get away.

Human artifacts are so mixed up with emotions, with strivings and with ambitions that they are of little use, for the beginner at any rate—the tyro in the art of seeing. A great artist can look at them and detach them from their impurities of association. But this is an art which has to be learnt. Hence we find Virginia Woolf at first taking us out into the fields and gardens to look at natural forms. She learned a lot about the way to look at them from her painter friends, from her sister Vanessa Bell and from Roger Fry. The Post-Impressionist movement was making itself felt in England at the time when she was beginning to experiment. Cézanne, Gauguin, Van Gogh, Picasso, Matisse, had outraged the British public and the critics at Roger Fry's exhibition at the Grafton Gallery in 1910. For the critic of *The Times*, these painters 'threw away all that the long-developed skill of past artists had acquired and perpetuated'. Wilfrid Blunt saw in the exhibition 'not a trace of sense or skill or taste, good or bad, or art or cleverness. Nothing but that gross puerility which scrawls indecencies on the walls of a privy'. But Roger Fry explains that 'such darts fall wide of the mark, since it is not the object of these artists to exhibit their skill or proclaim their knowledge, but only to attempt to express by pictorial and plastic form certain spiritual experiences . . . These artists do not seek to give what can, after all, be but a pale reflex of actual appearance, but to arouse the conviction of a new and definite reality. They do not seek to imitate form, but to create form, not to imitate life, but to find an equivalent for life . . .'

'To find an equivalent for life'—it is not well-phrased, but Roger Fry has clearly got at the sense of what the Post-Impressionists were trying to do: to express reality rather than appearance. And this is what Virginia Woolf tries to do in, say, *Kew Gardens*. But there is a difference. She is working in terms of words and phrases, not in paint. Therefore she has to *describe* the thing seen—she cannot give a simple impression, as the painter can, for she is not appealing to the eye. Her descriptions must be *both* exact and suggestive. So we find in her descriptions an almost Pre-Raphaelite minuteness which overflows constantly into a world of intuitive reality. The painter can give you his extraordinary joy direct, as it were; you feel the precise vision behind and through the impression. But the writer has a more difficult task: to give you the precise vision first, and then to expand it into joy while you watch. There is a subtle shifting of focus involved, and it is this shifting of focus which makes the excitement of reading Virginia Woolf. Once we have learned to trust her vision, and give ourselves up to her way of seeing things, we are in for adventures; we don't know where the beam of light is going to shift to next, what new shapes and colours it is going to light up. It is in this that she differs from the conventional novelists, whose stock responses to stock situations we know only too well. And it is this, unfortunately, which explains why she will never be popular with the general reading public which likes its emotions to run in the old grooves and demands from the writer the old situations and reactions.

The art of looking at things involves two processes: detachment and identification. Mrs Woolf often stresses detachment as 'the supreme necessity for the artist'. It is first of all detachment from practical concerns and from material cares; the artist cannot carry on his peculiar activity if he is required to worry about drains and tea-parties. It is unfortunate that this should be so, but there it is. Then there is the detachment which is identical with the non-attachment of the saint, the relinquishing of the sense of owning and being owned. The artist cannot be bound to things. 'That rhythm could only grow and expand,' she says in *Roger Fry*, 'if it were detached from the deformation which is possession. To live fully, to live gaily, to live without falling into the great sin of Accidia which is punished by fog, darkness and mud, could only be done by asking nothing for oneself.' And lastly, consequent on this, there is the detachment from the object seen, the refusal to 'bind it to oneself' or mix it up with one's own beliefs and worries and emotions. And here we come to the question of symbolism.

Mrs Woolf's way of seizing on an object and entering into it and expanding it so that it brings joy (I avoid for the moment the question of meaning) has sometimes been called symbolical. It is precisely the opposite. The symbol is a centre around which we organise our beliefs. It is the incarnation of our particular theology. Gerard Manley Hopkins' vision of Nature is symbolical: he sees Christ, the Mass and the Resurrection in everything. He sets out with a body of doctrine in which he believes passionately, and naturally enough that body of doctrine colours everything he sees. He thus makes the universe a comfortable and unified place; but he destroys the sense of adventure. He cannot say to himself, "If I look at that stone long enough it may show me that everything I have believed up to now is a laughable error, and that there is something immeasurably richer and greater behind." He has closed the gates of knowledge. He has made the trees into Gothic columns, the skies into stained-glass windows, and the 'dapple-dawn-drawn Falcon' into an image of Christ. But the universe is not a cathedral, and has very little to do with Christian theology. It is a collection of very varied solid objects bathed in light and suspended in space, which when looked at without preconceptions give an extraordinary joy and, sometimes, the idea of unity.

In *The Waves* (to anticipate a little) the danger of slipping from vision into symbol is explicitly stated. 'So the sincerity of the moment passed; so it became symbolical; and that I could not stand. Let us commit any blasphemy of laughter and criticism rather than exude this lily-sweet glue,' Bernard cries in his summing-up. It is the same reaction as Mrs Ramsay's when, at the close of her mystical experience, she finds herself relapsing into the mood of 'underneath are the everlasting arms'. It is so easy, so comfortable, to slip into symbol, to make the thing seen image the thing believed. But it is fatal to vision. We must be capable of detachment. We must avoid the temptation to 'buckle the shows of things to the desires of the mind'. Only by not twisting the thing seen can we pass into the second stage of the art of seeing, which is identification with the object, a sharing, momentary though it must be, in its peculiar life.

Thus the agnostic's daughter, trained in respect for truth, comes in aid of the visionary, piercing through to reality; and the air she breathes, the indispensable element, is freedom.

V

And now we see more deeply into the nature of Virginia Woolf's aversion from religion. It is a blanket thrown over the curious beauty of the visible world, a pattern of pretence which makes it impossible for the pattern of reality to emerge. *Truth*—intellectual honesty—is not the same as *reality*—the ultimate vision, but it is an indispensable preparation. That is why the masculine intellect of the scholar is admirable and why the sturdy common sense of the business-man or politician is fatal to truth.

> *How should they know*
> *Truth flourishes where the scholar's lamp has shone*
> *And there alone, who have no solitude?*

Whether we suppose reality to flourish in solitude or in society, in the mystic's vision or 'the lover's night', there is no doubt about the climate of truth. It can only be found on the high peaks of solitary thinking. And thus the scholar, the thinker, as well as the artist and the seer, is essential to the good life. He keeps the ports of knowledge clear, he doesn't allow rubbish to accumulate, he prunes and criticises.

There is a kind of detachment which is a species of the first genus I have mentioned (detachment from practical concerns) but it is so important and constitutes such a problem for the artist that it demands a paragraph to itself. This is the detachment from personal relationships. The problem of the individual and the claims of society bulks large in Virginia Woolf's later writings, and we shall have to return to it after a consideration of her final novels. But already, in these first two creative periods, an important issue has been raised. Can the world of things and the world of men exist together—for the artist? Does not the reality of the one destroy the artificiality of the other? When the artist has pursued the other sorts of detachment to a point where the world of things takes on a new significance, the world of persons falls somewhat into the background. The artist who has found his own personality coming in front of his vision, and has found his greatest joy in getting rid of self, will also feel other human personalities, at times, to be an intolerable burden. He has moved far from the position where social conversation seemed important, and he finds himself thinking about the world from an angle which, sometimes, makes other people's thinking appear almost meaningless. Less and less will he be able to fit in. And then there are demands of human emotion, not of society this time, but of a single person (say a husband or wife) or group of persons (a family) to whom he stands in a peculiarly intimate relation. He can only satisfy these claims by going back to a state which he has now left, and in which artistic creation is impossible. How reconcile the claims of art and the claims of society and affection?

It is of these fundamental questions that Virginia Woolf treats in her novels. Those who accuse her of being remote from life do not see that it was precisely the relation between art and life that interested her most; but she refused to deal with life in the surface manner of the popular novelist. She is aware that the artist is an abnormal phenomenon, that he is a human being in an acute state of irritability. He is generally conceded to have a certain value, and he will certainly go on existing whether we want him or not; let us see then, she says, on what terms he may be able to fit in to normal human society. Let us see, in other words, whether the values of art and the values of life have any common basis. She knows very well what the values of art are, and she can see that they don't look at all like the values of life as it is led in society: but may there not be a fallacy here? Perhaps life as it is lived in the first decades of the twentieth century is not the best we can do. Let us, at any rate, look at those hard knots in the cord of living— love, marriage, the family, politics—let us relate them to the activities of the artist and the thinker, and see if we can make a pattern.

It is this experimental tone that gives Virginia Woolf's work its great interest. She isn't dogmatic, she doesn't say, "Things are thus and thus, and I'm going to prove it to you," as Lawrence does. She isn't a preacher. She says rather, "This set of appearances suggests that things are thus, but this other set suggests the contrary. We shall put them together, see them in a clear light, and try to find out how they are related." She wants to accept all the facts. She has her prejudices, of course. She believes in the mind and she doesn't exalt the instincts above reason and imagination. She believes in civilisation. The Greek ideal means a great deal to her. Literature has its value, science too; and there is a beauty in the solitary mind battling for truth to which she always concedes her admiration. The things she doesn't like include war, power politics, successful professional men who are devoid of pity and imagination, religion, and conventional morality, and the purely masculine viewpoint. I have made the lists at random, but these are the things that come to my mind thinking back over the novels and essays. They suggest that Virginia Woolf belongs to the company of the humanists, and there is a real sense in which that is true. If humanism, however, is taken to mean that value resides only in the things of this life it is not true. Virginia Woolf is a mystic, though an incomplete one. I don't think she would have liked being called a mystic, but I can't think of a better word.

vi

Her mysticism is incomplete, for when brought into relation with human suffering and human cruelty it fails in the test. The solitary walking on the beach may think for a moment that his vision of goodness is reflected in the beauty of sky and waves; but it is an illusion; the purple stain on the sea's surface where a submarine has been destroyed mocks his faith. The failure marks a cleavage in Virginia Woolf's mind. As a woman and an artist she is able to accept the thisness of things as satisfying in itself; but there is the other side to her sensitiveness, the quivering nerves of one tortured by the knowledge of pain. She cannot take the final step of the mystic from the Many to the One; she cannot take it consciously, that is to say, for she takes it unconsciously every time she becomes a 'wedge of darkness'. If she took it with full understanding it would bring the faith that is called religious. Such an understanding would dwarf the phenomenal world; a new proportion would be achieved. Had Mrs Woolf become a full mystic it is plain to what order of mysticism she would have belonged. It would not have been the dogmatic kind of Western Christianity. She has the delicacy of observation of the Chinese quietists; she has something of their humour; she has their practical common sense. But, faced with the special horror of modern life, she has not their faith that everything will come all right if you leave it alone, and that the sage has to set the example by loitering under a tree and slapping his thighs. Her pity and her sensitiveness were too much for her.

She could not take the Christian position, that there is a loving Father who cares for each of His children and that the suffering and evil of this world are the result of a Fall. This is the most difficult of all positions to accept intellectually, the easiest to accept emotionally; and it is the position that Mrs Ramsay rejects indignantly when, at the end of her meditation, she finds herself betrayed into the thought, "We are in the hands of the Lord." Nor could she take the Taoist position, though this is, I think, the simplest, that under all phenomena there is a unity, an impersonal force making for good as long as we don't interfere with it. She attained this standpoint in practice, that is quite clear; she attained the ecstasy of absorption into the One; but she could not admit that this ecstasy was its own justification, a guarantee of truth, a proof that happiness and peace somehow lie at the heart of things. She wanted a satisfaction of the intellect; she could not turn her eyes away from suffering; and she felt powerless to help. Even her moments of escape, we suspect, came at the end to seem to her moments of betrayal. In the end it was the inanimate things, and not the One to which they seemed so illusively to point, which were her refuge.

vii

These moments of being, as Virginia Woolf calls them, vary in their context from one period of her work to another. In

her early writing, she reversed the technique of the older novelists, who showed us a stationary world of houses and natural
objects through which human beings passed on their daily
round, and among which they grew up, married, had children,
grew old and died. She, on the contrary, shows us a single
mind, suspended in the instant, through which the flight of
things past and present moves. The flight is at first of images
detached and chaotic, but by and by a significant detail
emerges on which the mind seizes, and then we perceive the
rest to form a pattern round this idea. But the pattern is valid
only for this moment; a gust of wind, an interrupting voice
will blow it all away. In the later novels the technique of
catching the moment is different. Now, we find, both mind
and things stand still. The scheme is an interrelation, not a
stream. Amid a web of things, flowers, trees, rocks, let us say,
the mind sinks into quiet: something flows from the things into
the mind and colours it, changes it; then the mind reflects its
light back upon the things and colours them, changes them.
What emerges is unity. The sensation of unity, which is the
final mystic sensation, brings the highest happiness. Now the
mind is no longer conscious of its own identity amid a flow of
experiences. There is a complete fusion. Again, I must insist,
not through symbolism, but through intuition.

But the moments are fleeting and the reports of intuition
are contradictory. In her next novel, *The Waves*, we feel that
Virginia Woolf is making an experiment of concentration. She
clears out of the way everything that is irrelevant, and gives
us nothing but a series of naked intuitions. There are speakers,
but no plot, no barrier to understanding: the unconscious mind
in each of her six characters wells up and overflows. Do these
six minds all report the same thing? Will a pattern emerge?
That is the question.

III

THE WORLD AND REALITY

CHAPTER X

The Waves

[1931]

IN *The Waves* Virginia Woolf carries her mastery, both in
thought and in technique, to its ultimate point. Beyond this
there is no development, though there is still experimentation.
In this novel the old shackles which she has so often resented
—plot, dialogue, exterior descriptions—all disappear. She has
achieved a new mode of communication. And what is com-
municated is not action, or sayings, or thoughts even, but pure
being: the hidden life. The nerves of her six characters are laid
bare, not by the scalpel, but by the X-ray of intuition. These
persons—Bernard, Louis, Neville, Rhoda, Jinny, Susan—are
revealed in their inner life from the nursery to middle age.
We come to know them very well: and indeed the value of the
book is largely psychological. We learn from it. We learn to
know ourselves and our friends. The guiding lines of personality are traced, the superfluities are brushed away. Each of
the six characters is slowly, meticulously, elaborately built up
from glimpses through the minds of the other characters. So a
constant process of adjustment and readjustment of focus is
going on.

The psychological process is from simplicity—the childhood
simplicity of pure sensation and emotion—to complexity in
adolescence, and back to a new kind of simplicity in the vision
of maturity. This is achieved only once, at the end of the book,
by Bernard. Bernard is the writer, the phrase-maker, and in
his all-embracing mind the other five characters, in a sense,
exist. The experiment which Virginia Woolf is carrying out
here is a contrapuntal one: a synthesis of the textures of life—
the interrelations not only of six human beings, but of those
human beings with *things*, sun and stars and trees and sea and
sky.

This is what is meant by living, she seems to say: this con-
tinual awareness, this ruthless clinging to the truth of thoughts
and sensations and emotions. The rest is superficial. And in her
presentation she shows a consummate mastery of technique.

The number of threads in her hand is enormous, but she has them firmly grasped and not one is allowed to fall. The web she weaves is full of colours and sounds and scents. It is no barren, abstract analysis. It lives and moves. And behind all the colour we sense 'the white radiance of eternity', the presence of Reality itself. For it is in this novel (if we can call it a novel) that Mrs Woolf gets most closely to grips with the problem of reality. Will any of these six minds attain, we wonder, the vision of the white radiance itself?

Yes, one of them does: Bernard. But again the old dilemma presents itself: reality and society do not go together. The delight of friendship brings warmth and beauty, but these things also vanish, as the comfort of marriage vanished in the earlier novels. The solitary mind alone can glimpse ultimate truth. Mrs Woolf shows us these six persons, vividly alive, dwelling in full community with one another, yet at bottom feeling themselves separate, 'each in himself alone'; and the sense of reality comes only hand in hand with the sense of dereliction.

Structurally, as we can see, Mrs Woolf has devised a new method. She gives us an exploration of six minds from childhood to adulthood. There is no narrative. In *The Waves*, in fact, she is carrying into practice the suggestion she made in *A Room of One's Own*: the suggestion that the woman novelist needs to work out a new form of her own, since the masculine novel is not wholly adaptable to her kind of sensibility. For the male writer the important thing is action, or else preaching: usually a combination of the two. For the woman novelist—at least for Mrs Woolf—the important thing is observation leading to vision. Hitherto she has followed the masculine model, though with important modifications: describing her settings from the outside, while letting her characters be seen from many personal angles, as Mrs Ramsay is seen through Lily Briscoe's musings.

In *The Waves* she works from the inside outwards, showing us first the sensations of the children, then something of the environment, then something of their physical appearances. This is the reverse of the traditional method, where the novelist first builds up a scene, then puts a person into it, complete with Norfolk jacket and drooping moustache, then twitches the string and makes him speak and act, and sometimes, *ab extra,* tells us his thoughts. *The Waves* is all thoughts; there is no direct speaking or acting, no direct descriptions (except in the exordium to each section). It is an attempt at painting the pure perception.

But there has to be something definite, some foundation under the shifting currents of thought. This foundation, which for the older novelist was a religion, a cosmogony, a social conviction, is for Mrs Woolf in *The Waves* the simple progress of a day. The novel has nine parts, each division being marked by a sort of prologue or exordium; in these exordiums we see the sun rising higher and higher, then sinking again. The rhythm of the day is reflected in the lives of the six characters, and these lives are quintessentialised in their thoughts. In each exordium we are looking out over the sea. In the first we see the sea as 'undistinguishable from the sky, except that the sea was slightly creased as if a cloth had wrinkles in it'. Then we are shown the waves beating gently on the shore. 'The wave paused, and then drew out again, sighing like a sleeper whose breath comes and goes unconsciously.' The ascent of the sun from below the horizon is as though a woman were raising her hand which holds a lamp. Then we turn our gaze from the sea and look round at the house and garden, becoming distinct under the morning sun.

> The light struck upon the trees in the garden, making one leaf transparent and then another. One bird chirped high up; there was a pause; another chirped lower down. The sun sharpened the walls of the house, and rested like the tip of a fan upon a white blind and made a blue finger-print of shadow under the leaf by the bed-room window. The blind stirred slightly, but all within was dim and unsubstantial. The birds sang their blank melody outside.

'Their blank melody', we note. The wealth of impressions we are given here has not yet been co-ordinated into any sort of pattern. That will come when the blind is drawn, and the human consciousness is awake to things. We note, too, the impressionistic technique of *Jacob's Room*, the painter's eye. We are given the object direct.

Inside, the children are sleeping, like the waves. They awake, and their thoughts, or rather sensations, are presented: sensations evoked by the entrance of the sunbeam, the singing of the birds, and the noise of the waves, now become audible.

"I see a ring," said Bernard, "hanging above me. It quivers and hangs in a loop of light."

"I see a slab of pale yellow," said Susan, "spreading away until it meets a purple stripe."

"I hear a sound," said Rhoda, "cheep, chirp; cheep, chirp; going up and down."

"I see a globe," said Neville, "hanging down in a drop against the enormous flank of some hill."

"I see a crimson tassel," said Jinny, "twisted with gold threads."

"I hear something stamping," said Louis. "A great beast's foot is chained. It stamps, and stamps, and stamps."

These are the first impressions, the fruit of the immediate contact of senses with phenomena. The word 'said' does not of course refer to spoken words; these are inarticulate sense-perceptions. As the book goes on, we find that the things 'said' are often unconscious; they represent the life which goes on beneath the surface of direct communication. This, indeed, is the novel about 'Silence, the things people don't say', that Terence Hewlet wanted to write.

The next six impressions, given without any traditional passage of description, without any typographical break even, are those of children who are up and looking out of the window. Bernard sees the spider's web with its beads of water; Susan, the leaves like pointed ears round the window; Louis, a shadow bent across the path; Rhoda, islands of light swimming on the grass; Neville, the bright eyes of birds in the tunnels between the leaves; Jinny, the short harsh hairs on the flower-stalks. Then a further chain of perceptions makes it clear that the children have run out of doors. And so the series continues, registering at first these direct sense-impressions, with the personalities of the children hardly differentiated; then, little by little, the human passions are brought in: we see Louis as the solitary one, conscious of his inner loneliness, yet feeling himself deeply rooted in the earth; Jinny, impulsive, kissing Louis because she finds him alone and pities him; Susan, jealous; Bernard, consoling, making comforting phrases, making stories; Rhoda, living in the world of the imagination; Neville, loving precision and order. We are made aware of their reactions to their governess, to the sight of birds digging their beaks into fat worms; Neville has 'heard about the dead man through the swing-door last night when cook was shoving in and out the dampers. He was found with his throat cut. The apple-tree leaves became fixed in the sky; the moon glared; I was unable to lift my foot up the stair. He was found in the gutter. His blood gurgled down the gutter. His jowl was white as a dead cod-fish. I shall call this stricture, this rigidity, "death among the apple-trees" for ever. . . . We are doomed, all of us, by the apple-trees, by the immitigable tree which we cannot pass.' And Susan sees the kitchen boy kissing the kitchen maid behind the currant bushes. "He was blind as a bull, and she swooned in anguish, only little veins streaking her white cheeks red."

These experiences enter the minds of the children and remain there to recur, as Neville predicts, at critical moments throughout life: and also to aid in fashioning life's very pattern. The life of things and the life of the mind are interwoven. The attitudes now assumed will persist. Joy and sorrow, success and failure, are being created now, in the garden. We become aware of the scope of each of the children, and of their several limitations; we can say, now, there you will succeed, or, beyond that point you will not pass. But life, blowing through them, convinces them all that in spite of weaknesses and fears they will achieve happiness, will become famous or deeply loved.

What is Mrs Woolf trying to do in this first section of *The Waves*? She is still pursuing her search for value. She is going back to the beginning. She is using her intuition into the child mind, and her observation of children, to give us their world, without adult comment. She shows us this world as far as she can, drawing upon memory, intuition, observation; she shows us the vividness of early sense-impressions, the keenness of early emotions. She shows us that it is all under the stress of an inexorable destiny. The waves are breaking higher and higher upon the shore; the birds that sang so purely at dawn are digging their beaks into the festering bodies of slugs; the picture of the man with his throat cut lying under the apple-tree will stick in the mind.

And we cannot stay for ever in the world of the child. Louis, Neville and Bernard go to a boys' school, Jinny, Susan and Rhoda to a girls'. We are given the moments of leaving home and arriving at school, the first impressions of headmaster and headmistress. School chapel brings out the boys' varying reactions to Christianity. Bernard is still making his telling phrases: in this lies his power to provide escape for them all.

Percival—a new character, and never quite one of the circle
—is introduced: he is beautiful and pagan, and Neville loves
him: Neville, who is to go through life attaching himself to one
person. Percival, we are made aware, is an *ordinary* person; and
by this sheer ordinariness he is fascinating to these six who are
not ordinary. He provides for them a point of contact with
simple living.

An important turning-point in the book arrives now in
Louis's soliloquy. Louis, the solitary one, becomes aware of
moments in the flux and sees them as points of integration and
disintegration. Once they have passed, nothing will be the same
again.

> Here on this ring of grass we have sat together, bound by the
> tremendous power of some inner compulsion. The trees wave, the
> clouds pass. The time approaches when these soliloquies shall be
> shared. We shall not always give out a sound like a beaten gong
> as one sensation strikes and then another. Children, our lives have
> been gongs striking; clamour and boasting; cries of despair; blows
> on the nape of the neck in gardens.
> Now grass and trees, the travelling air blowing empty spaces
> in the blue which they then recover, shaking the leaves which
> then replace themselves, and our ring here, sitting, with our arms
> binding our knees, hint at some other order, and better, which
> makes a reason everlastingly. This I see for a second, and shall try
> tonight to fix in words. . . .

The child himself, then, realises that he must leave the world
in which colours are vivid, emotions sharp. The forms of nature
'hint at some other order, and better, which makes a reason
everlastingly'. It is the old search for value—not to be found,
then, in the world of the child?

The waves beat on the shore; the tide of life surges in, over
rocks and sand. The chained beast is stamping still, when the
time comes for school life to end and Cambridge to begin. And
now there is to be a separation; for all cannot go to Cambridge.
Neville and Bernard and Percival are there together; Louis is
in an office; Susan is finishing her education in Switzerland;
Jinny is enjoying life at balls; Rhoda is also at the ball, but not
enjoying it. At this point Mrs Woolf subtly reminds us of those
very first impressions the children woke to in the nursery.
Neville, we remember, saw a globe; and now he wants to feel
himself a unity. Bernard, who had seen a ring, quivering,
envisages experience as 'a drop that forms on the roof of the

soul in the evening, round, many-coloured'. Louis, who had heard the great beast stamping, sits in a City restaurant and listens to the multitude passing, and feels menaced by them. Susan, whose image was 'a slab of pale yellow', identifies herself with things, and thinks of 'crusts of bread and butter and white plates in a sunny room'. Her thoughts are already turning to love and motherhood. Jinny (she saw 'a crimson tassel twisted with gold threads') enjoys her dance, moving about amid gilt chairs and glasses of red wine. Rhoda heard birds chirping through the nursery window; and now, in the ball-room, she thinks: 'I am fixed here to listen.'

Moreover, the hint conveyed in Louis's soliloquy: 'the time approaches when these soliloquies shall be shared', is reinforced by the note in the exordium to this third section: 'In the garden the birds that had sung erratically and spasmodically in the dawn on that tree, on that bush, now sang together in chorus, shrill and sharp.' The purely solipsist stage has passed; now, for good or ill, the six are responsible members of society. So now Virginia Woolf can present her dilemma under its sharpest aspect: the world and reality. And the note of horror too is emphasised in a new description of the birds.

Now glancing this side, that side, they looked deeper, beneath the flowers, down the dark avenues into the unlit world where the leaf rots and the flower has fallen. Then one of them, beautifully darting, accurately alighting, spiked the soft, monstrous body of the defenceless worm, pecked again and yet again, and left it to fester. Down there among the roots where the flowers decayed, gusts of dead smells were wafted; drops formed on the bloated sides of swollen things.

'The complexity of things becomes more close,' says Bernard. These young men at Cambridge are trying to puzzle out this complexity, trying to understand who they themselves are, fitting on the masks of Byron and Tolstoy and Meredith. Bernard is like that, but Neville feels himself always as one person, attached to one person: Percival.

And in the fourth section (the scene is now transferred to London, with Cambridge already in the past) it is Percival who holds them all together when they meet again at a dinner party to bid him goodbye; for he is going off to India. Bernard is engaged; and the sense of fulfilment is upon him. He is one with the purposes of life. 'Life for me is now mystically prolonged.' Susan too is looking forward to 'the bestial and beautiful passion of maternity'. Rhoda remains unattached, unhappy. Jinny, as always, is an arrow pointed at a certain goal. But all of them are united by the presence of Percival. The moment of meeting is felt as an eternal moment. The mind of each goes back to the essential childhood experience. 'From these close-furled balls of string we draw now every filament, remembering, when we meet,' says Louis. 'We have come together (from the North, from the South, from Susan's farm, from Louis's house of business) to make one thing, not enduring—for what endures?—but seen by many eyes simultaneously.' This phrase of Louis might be the motto of *The Waves* itself.

But Percival goes; and, in the fifth section, he is dead. The force which had held the circle together, 'making this moment out of one man', is destroyed. As in *The Voyage Out*, and *Jacob's Room*, and *To the Lighthouse*, we are made aware of the pathos of promise unfulfilled. 'The waves fell; withdrew and fell again, like the thud of a great beast stamping.' Everything is stupid and meaningless. Neville watches 'women shuffle past the window as if there were no gulf cut in the street; no tree with stiff leaves which we cannot pass'. There is worse than meaninglessness: there is malignity. 'There is something sneering behind our backs.'

The sixth chapter of the novel shows us maturity—'the finished man among his enemies'. Louis is a successful business-man, but he realises that his success is merely a compensation for childhood hurts; and success tends to cut out Plato. Its rewards are 'a chair and a rug; a place in Surrey with glass houses, and some rare conifer, melon or flowering tree which other merchants will envy'. Yet the life of the mind and the life of the senses have not been wholly extinguished.

> I still keep my attic room. There I open the usual little book; there I watch the rain glisten on the tiles till they shine like a policeman's waterproof; there I see the broken windows in poor people's houses; the lean cats; some slattern squinting in a cracked looking-glass as she arranges her face for the street corner; there Rhoda sometimes comes. For we are lovers.

Susan's fulfilment is in marriage and maternity. The house is her kingdom; and 'steam has obscured the window'. She is shut off from any other awareness than that of her baby. Jinny, on the other hand, is still exploring the world of love, still adventurous and free. 'Beauty must be broken daily to remain beautiful,' she thinks. And Neville's need is still to be alone with the one friend. He always finds a successor to Percival, but the old agony remains. 'Our lives have meaning only under the eyes of love,' he says. So his life is a series of emotional disturbances. The pattern of the six lives, so closely knit in childhood, is cracked and starred now, and the pieces fly in all directions. Even Louis's love affair with Rhoda is to turn to tragedy.

After maturity, decline. In the seventh section they are 'no longer young'; the tide is going out, the petals are falling. We see 'time tapering to a point'. Disillusion is upon them all. Bernard, in Rome, feels utterly detached from all the life around him. 'Things have dropped from me. I have outlived certain desires; I have lost friends, some by death—Percival—others through sheer inability to cross the street. I am not so gifted as at one time seemed likely. Certain things lie beyond my scope. I shall never understand the harder problems of philosophy.' Yet this moment of detachment, he knows, is transitory. People will always be necessary to him: people in all their variety, for he can never, like Neville, attach himself to the single love.

This moment of escape is a perception of the discreteness of things: there is no pattern, unless it be imposed by the mind. Things remain only in themselves, not in their connections. 'This bare visual impression is unattached to any line of reason.' And with this, for the moment, he is content. 'Why impose my arbitrary design?' The bare impression is filed away in the mind, to take its place among other impressions, waiting however for the final statement which will reconcile them all.

To Susan, too, disillusionment has come.

I ask now, standing with my scissors among my flowers, Where can the shadow enter? What shock can loosen my laboriously gathered, relentlessly pressed down life? Yet sometimes I am sick of natural happiness, and fruit growing, and children scattering the house with oars, guns, skulls, books won for prizes and other trophies. I am sick of the body, I am sick of my own craft, industry and cunning, of the unscrupulous ways of the mother who protects, who collects under her jealous eyes at one long table her own children, always her own.

This then is the answer Virginia Woolf gives to that idyll in *To the Lighthouse*, that delightful scene of the mother among her children, giving and receiving so much. In the former novel it was something precious and natural to set against the monomaniac demands of Mr Ramsay; but here, in *The Waves*, it is rejected. It is not enough. Into this relationship also, ownership and injustice enter: there is no purity.

What then of Jinny's solution—the butterfly life?

> Look—there is my body in that looking-glass. How solitary, how shrunk, how aged! I am no longer young. I am no longer part of the procession. . . . Little animal that I am, sucking my flanks in and out with fear, I stand here, palpitating, trembling. But I will not be afraid. I will bring the whip down on my flanks. I am not a whimpering little animal making for the shadow. It was only for a moment, catching sight of myself before I had time to prepare myself for the sight of myself, that I quailed. It is true; I am not young—I shall soon raise my arm in vain and my scarf will fall to my side without having signalled. I shall not hear the sudden sigh in the night and feel through the dark someone coming.

Still courageous, then; but she knows that the life of the body has failed.

For Neville, life has proved the loss of glory. 'When we were young we sat anywhere, on bare benches in draughty halls with the doors always banging.' He knows now that finality and completeness are unobtainable: all that remains is to accept. We are not responsible (and by 'we' he means people of his type, and Bernard's and Neville's) for the horror of the world, he cries. 'We are not judges. We are not called upon to torture our fellows with thumbscrews and irons; we are not called upon to mount pulpits and lecture them on pale Sunday afternoons. It is better to look at a rose, or to read Shakespeare as I read him here in Shaftesbury Avenue.' It has not been possible, after all, to reshape the world.

Louis has parted from Rhoda, and his mistress is a little actress with a cockney accent who drops her dirty underlinen about the floor. He is immensely successful in business. But the attic room is still there, at enmity with success.

> I open a little book. I read one poem. One poem is enough.
>
> *O western wind . . .*
>
> O western wind, you are at enmity with my mahogany table and spats, and also, alas! with the vulgarity of my mistress, the little actress . . .

It is for Rhoda that he longs.

Rhoda, with whom I shared silence, when the others spoke, she who hung back and turned aside when the herd assembled and galloped with orderly, sleek backs over the rich pastures, has gone now like the desert heat. When the sun blisters the roofs of the city I think of her; when the dry leaves patter to the ground; when the old men come with pointed sticks and pierce little bits of paper as we pierced her—

> O western wind, when wilt thou blow,
> That the small rain down can rain?
> Christ, that my love were in my arms,
> And I in my bed again!

I return now to my book, I return now to my attempt.

Rhoda has fled to Spain from her anguish, but it pursues her. In her words, more perhaps than in those of the others, it is Virginia Woolf we hear speaking: a sorrowful condemnation of humanity.

None had the courage to be one thing rather than another. What dissolution of the soul you demanded in order to get through one day, what lies, bowings, scrapings, fluency and servility! How you chained me to one spot, one hour, one chair, and sat yourselves down opposite! How you snatched from me the white spaces that lie between hour and hour and rolled them into dirty pellets and tossed them into the wastepaper basket with your greasy paws. Yet those were my life.

Accompanied by her anguish then, she climbs a Spanish hill that looks out over Africa; and her thoughts are of death.

In the next chapter there is a reunion—at Hampton Court. A reunion—but no real unity: for Percival, whose strong humanity had linked them all together in the first reunion, is dead. The sun is sinking now. There is an air of immobility about everything. And again, as in the first reunion, Virginia Woolf stresses, though subtly, her references to those first sense-perceptions in the nursery.

Bernard ('a ring, quivering') is conscious of their precarious union. 'How many telephone calls, how many post cards, are now needed to cut this hole through which we come together, united, at Hampton Court?' He is conscious, too, of how little he has done with his life. The others have made something: Louis, a great business: Susan, a home: Neville, a literary reputation. He has made only phrases.

Neville ('a globe hanging down in a drop against the enormous flanks of some hill') also seeks unity amid chaos. What have they all done with their lives? he asks. 'Sometimes one trembling star comes out in the clear sky and makes me think the world beautiful and we maggots deforming even the trees with our lust.'

Susan ('I see a slab of pale yellow') opposes Neville's vision of life as intimacy with the single beloved person.

> Lying deep in a chair with one person, one person only, but one person who changes, you see one inch of flesh only; its nerves, fibres, the sullen or quick flow of blood on it; but nothing entire. You do not see a house in a garden; a horse in a field; a town laid out, as you bend like an old woman straining her eyes over her darning. But I have seen life in blocks, substantial, huge; its battlements and towers, factories and gasometers; a dwelling-place made from time immemorial after an hereditary pattern. These things remain square, prominent, undissolved in my mind. I am not sinuous or suave; I sit among you abrading your softness with my hardness, quenching the silver-grey flickering moth-wing quiver of words with the green spurt of my clear eyes.

She sees life in the round, in its completeness; this vision has been brought her by maternity.

Rhoda ('a sound, cheep, chirp; cheep, chirp; going up and down') is most cut off from the others. 'Inwardly I am not taught; I fear, I hate, I love, I envy and despise you, but I never join you happily. . . . I have no face.' When the others go down towards the lake in the evening light, she remains with Louis, detached, and the old bird image returns. 'What song do we hear—the owl's, the nightingale's, the wren's?' There is a moment of communion with Louis; a moment which the others break with their return.

Louis ('I hear something stamping. A great beast's foot is chained. It stamps, and stamps, and stamps') has heard nightingales singing among the trampling feet, and now, contrariwise,

> this moment of reconciliation, when we meet together united, this evening moment, with its wind and shaking leaves, and youth coming up from the river in white flannels, carrying cushions, is to me black with the shadows of dungeons and the tortures and infamies practised by man upon man. So imperfect are my senses that they never blot out with one purple the serious charge that my reason adds and adds against us, even as we sit here. What is

the solution, I ask myself, and the bridge? How can I reduce these dazzling, these dancing apparitions to one line capable of linking all in one?

Jinny, finally ('a crimson tassel, twisted with gold threads'), who is never alone, says: 'I see what is before me, this scarf, these wine-coloured spots. This glass. This mustard pot. This flower. I like what one touches, what one tastes.' She gulps down her life entire. 'My imagination is the body's.' The torments and divisions which the others have suffered have been solved for her by bodily contacts.

Now I turn grey; now I turn gaunt; but I look at my face at midday sitting in front of the looking-glass in broad daylight, and note precisely my nose, my chin, my lips that open too wide and show too much gum. But I am not afraid.

What is the meaning of it all? Bernard is the only speaker in the final section: he sums up, he tries to explain his own life, and by implication the lives of the others: 'the illusion is upon me that something adheres for a moment, has roundness, weight, depth, is completed'. But the illusion does not last. He sees that all his life he has been consoling himself with phrases and stories. Truth lies, perhaps, in tumult, in disintegration? He thinks of a stormy day, and its exhilaration. His mind goes back to the nursery, and a life made up of 'arrows of sensation'; with pity and love, and the determination to fight the brute forces of the world. 'We suffered terribly as we became separate bodies.' But Bernard is the artist standing apart; he is not hurt so easily. Over schooltime his memory wanders, over Cambridge and philosophy. It is all a flux, no pattern anywhere. Yet outside objects, like a willow-tree, seem to stand out of the flux and can thus be clung to.

I saw the figures beneath the beech-trees at Elvedon. The gardeners swept; the lady at the table sat writing. But I now made the contribution of maturity to childhood's intuitions—satiety and doom; the sense of what is unescapable in our lot; death; the knowledge of limitations; how life is more obdurate than one had thought it. Then, when I was a child, the presence of an enemy had asserted itself; the need for opposition had stung me. I had jumped up and cried, 'let's explore'. The horror of the situation was ended.

But now he knows there is nothing to end, nothing to explore. There is only noise and confusion. And only once has he known peace, 'a space cleared in the mind'. It was when, leaning over a gate, he found that his self had disappeared, lost—not, as the sages say, in a larger whole—but in nothingness, desertion.

> The woods had vanished; the earth was a waste of shadow. No sound broke the silence of the wintry landscape. No cock crowed; no smoke rose, no train moved. A man without a self, I said. A heavy body leaning on a gate. A dead man. With dispassionate despair, with entire disillusionment, I surveyed the dust dance; my life, my friends' lives, and those fabulous presences, men with brooms, women writing, the willow-tree by the river—clouds and phantoms made of dust too, of dust that changed, as clouds lose and gain and take gold and red and lose their summits and billow this way and that, mutable, vain. I, carrying a notebook, making phrases, had recorded merely changes; a shadow, I had been sedulous to take note of shadows. How can I proceed now, I said, without a self, weightless and visionless, through a world weightless, without illusion?

This was the end, he had thought: this dereliction. But in reality he was undergoing an experience (may we call it purgation?) preparatory to the end: the shedding of the self. There is a vision beyond this vision. Suddenly, there comes the experience of moving about in 'the world seen without a self'. It is only when the self has been destroyed, indeed, that a new world can be seen. What he has been pursuing all these years, trying to piece glimpses of self-coloured illumination into a whole, is the wrong track. But now the lost landscape returns.

> So the landscape returned to me; so I saw fields rolling in waves of colour beneath me, but now with this difference; I saw but was not seen. I walked unshadowed; I came unheralded. From me had dropped the old cloak, the old response; the hollowed hand that beats back sounds. Thin as a ghost, leaving no trace where I trod, perceiving merely, I walked alone in a new world, never trodden; brushing new flowers, unable to speak save in a child's words of one syllable; without shelter from phrases—I who have made so many; unattended, I who have always gone with my kind; solitary, I who have always had someone to share the empty grate, or the cupboard with its hanging loop of gold. But how describe the world seen without a self? There are no words. Blue, red—even they distract, even they hide with thickness instead of letting the light through. How describe or say anything

in articulate words again?—save that it fades, save that it under-
goes a gradual transformation, becomes, even in the course of one
short walk, habitual—this scene also. Blindness returns as one
moves and one leaf repeats another. Loveliness returns as one
looks, with all its train of phantom phrases. One breathes in and
out substantial breath; down in the valley the train draws across
the fields lop-eared with smoke.

But for a moment I had sat on the turf somewhere high above
the flow of the sea and the sound of the woods, had seen the house,
the garden, and the waves breaking. The old nurse who turns the
pages of the picture-book had stopped and had said, 'Look. This
is the truth.'

Yes, the vision is fleeting, passing 'even in the course of one
short walk': but it is not, as the others were, partial. It is all-
embracing and, while it lasts, all-satisfying. This is because the
partial illuminations have been given up. They had been seen
through the distorting medium of the self; the personality had
got mixed up in them. But here the self is lost. Moreover, the
nature of the true revelation is to be seen in its fruits, lasting
beyond the revelation itself; and now Bernard tells us what
these fruits are.

The first is indifference to what happens. 'It does not matter
whom I meet. All this little affair of "being" is over.' The
second is unconsciousness of where one is. 'Nor do I know
exactly where we are. What city does that stretch of sky look
down upon? Is it Paris, is it London where we sit, or some
southern city of pink-washed houses lying under cypresses,
under high mountains, where eagles soar? I do not at this
moment feel certain.' The third is doubt about the reality of
the material world. 'I begin now to forget; I begin to doubt
the fixity of tables, the reality of here and now, to tap my
knuckles smartly upon the edges of apparently solid objects and
say, "Are you hard?" ' The fourth is the sense of identity with
others. 'And now I ask, "Who am I?" I have been talking of
Bernard, Neville, Jinny, Susan, Rhoda and Louis. Am I all of
them? Am I one and distinct? I do not know. We sat here
together . . . This difference we make so much of, this identity
we so feverishly cherish, was overcome.' The fifth fruit is the
acceptance of every component of one's nature, even the most
animal. 'There is the old brute, too, the savage, the hairy man
who dabbles his fingers in ropes of entrails; and gobbles and
belches; whose speech is guttural, visceral—well, he is here . . .

That man, the hairy, the ape-like, has contributed his part to my life.' The sixth fruit is an intense unselfish interest in things. 'When I look down from this transcendency, how beautiful are even the crumbled relics of bread! What shapely spirals the peelings of pears make— how thin, and mottled like some sea-bird's egg. Even the forks laid straight side by side appear lucid, logical, exact; and the horns of the rolls which we have left are glazed, yellow-plated, hard. I could worship my hand even, with its fan of bones laced by blue mysterious veins and ability to curl softly or suddenly crush—its infinite sensibility.' The seventh fruit is the loss of desires. 'Immeasurably receptive, holding everything, trembling with fullness, yet clear, contained—so my being seems, now that desire urges it no more out and away; now that curiosity no longer dyes it a thousand colours. It lies deep, tideless, immune, now that he is dead, the man I called Bernard . . .' The eighth fruit is the feeling of omniscience. 'Let a woman come, let a young man in evening dress with a moustache sit down; is there anything that they can tell me? No! I know all that, too. . . . The shock of the falling wave which has sounded all my life, which woke me so that I saw the gold loop on the cupboard, no longer makes quiver what I hold.'

The moment of vision is transitory; these resultant moments of peace, with whatever they may owe to the fine old brandy and the quails, can be broken by a face coming in at the door. But they come together again, in silence, in solitude. Once the self has been lost, the secret is found. It is with a song of glory that the book ends.

Let me now raise my song of glory. Heaven be praised for solitude. Let me be alone. Let me cast and throw away this veil of being, this cloud that changes with the least breath, night and day, and all night and all day. While I sat here I have been changing. I have watched the sky change. I have seen clouds cover the stars, then free the stars, then cover the stars again. Now I look at their changing no more. Now no one sees me and I change no more. Heaven be praised for solitude that has removed the pressure of the eye, the solicitation of the body, and all need of lies and phrases.

Only one desire remains to break this calm: the desire to conquer Death. And thus the book ends.

Death is the enemy. It is death against whom I ride with my spear couched, and my hair flying back like a young man's, like Percival's, when he galloped in India. I strike spurs into my horse. Against you I will fling myself, unvanquished and unyielding, O Death!

CHAPTER XI

Criticism and Biography

VIRGINIA WOOLF enjoyed reading, and her characters, we find, enjoy reading too. We seldom picture them without a book in their hand. They are intellectual creatures, most of them: the kind of people Mrs Woolf knew and moved amongst: men and women interested in thought. Mr Ramsay, with all his rationalism and his logic, sheds tears over the superb realism and pathos of Scott; Bernard presses flowers between the pages of Shakespeare's sonnets; Jacob retires to his attic room to ponder Plato and Spinoza. The world of literature and the world of life are fused. Life informs literature; literature elucidates and broadens the vision of life. And behind it all, solid and bright, lies the great terraced landscape of Greece; close at hand are the Elizabethan oceans and deserts, and the trim formal gardens of Pope, Montaigne and Mme de Sévigné. There is no lack of variety.

Indeed, what strikes us at once is the range of Mrs Woolf's interests. In the two volumes of *The Common Reader*, and the essays collected posthumously in *The Death of the Moth*, there is hardly a period of English literature without its comment. And she goes further afield. The survey begins with the Greeks. It is to the Greeks that we always return, she tells us, when we are sick of the heart-searchings and the personalities, 'the vagueness, the confusion, the Christianity and its consolations, of our own age'. For Greek is pre-eminently the hard impersonal literature. Its tragedy is bare and universal; its philosophy is engaged in the unremitting search for truth. How well she describes the Socratic method!

It is an exhausting process; to concentrate painfully upon the exact meaning of words; to judge what each admission involves; to follow intently, yet critically, the dwindling and changing of opinion as it hardens and intensifies into truth. Are pleasure and good the same? Can virtue be taught? Is virtue knowledge? The tired or feeble mind may easily lapse as the remorseless questioning proceeds; but no one, however weak, can fail, even if he does not learn more from Plato, to love knowledge better. For as the argument mounts from step to step, Protagoras yielding, Socrates

proper to man; she who in sheltered bays reared to womanhood beautiful girls unfathomable and austere'.

Finally, there is the individual in society. We know how much this problem meant to Virginia Woolf in her novels: they are built almost entirely around it. And so in her criticism we find her examining with intent interest the writers who have worked out this counterpoint: Jane Austen, Henry James, the Brontës, George Eliot, Meredith, E. M. Forster. These are the social psychologists: they show us how far the human spirit can attain maturity and be itself in the milieu of the family, the social group, the school and university, the state. Jane Austen 'knew exactly what her powers were, and what material they were fitted to deal with as material should be dealt with by a writer whose standard of finality was high'. She was not cramped by her environment, by her family sitting-room; though there are suggestions in the last novel, Mrs Woolf thinks, that she might have been 'the forerunner of Proust and of Henry James' by developing detachment and a severer satire —had she lived. George Eliot and the Brontës, on the other hand, obviously were restricted by their surroundings, and the individual stands out in their pages as opposed to the group. They are caught irresistibly in the whirlpool; while Henry James, by contrast, stands outside and gives us the quintessence of recollection. 'With all the creative power at his command he summons back the past and makes us a present of that.' E. M. Forster, again, is somewhere in between the two positions: he is deeply concerned for personal relationships and for candour and reality, he is embedded in the time process, but his mind never loses its detachment and sometimes he stands too far away from his characters.

Mrs Woolf's feminism (she detested the word, but there really isn't any other) comes out plainly in her critical work. We have only to count the number of essays dealing with women writers, and then to look at the remainder and note the part women play in them, to see how large this interest bulked. As in *A Room of One's Own*, she discusses and rediscusses the conditions which have made women novelists what they are, and the conditions which will give them a chance to be different. Sometimes the discussion becomes wearisome; but when she manages to detach it from the purely personal and carping, when she is led to make penetrating comment on, say, the technical differences between the masculine and feminine way of writing, she keeps our interest. The male intellect is rational, and it is devoted to action; the female is intuitive, and concerned with being. These differences must be reflected in both the subjects and the forms of the novel. It is useless, she tells us in *A Room of One's Own,*

it is useless to go to the great men writers for help, however much one may go to them for pleasure. Lamb, Browne, Thackeray, Newman, Sterne, Dickens, De Quincey—whoever it may be— never helped a woman yet, though she may have learned a few tricks of them and adapted them to her use. The weight, the pace, the stride of a man's mind are too unlike her own for her to lift anything substantial from him successfully. The ape is too distant to be sedulous. Perhaps the first thing she would find, setting pen to paper, was that there was no common sentence ready for her use. All the great novelists like Thackeray and Dickens and Balzac have written a natural prose, swift but not slovenly, expressive but not precious, taking their own tint without ceasing to be common property. They have based it on the sentence that was common at the time . . . [It] is a man's sentence . . . unsuited for a woman's use. . . . Moreover, a book is not made of sentences laid end to end, but of sentences built, if an image helps, into arcades or domes. And this shape too has been made by men out of their own needs for their own uses. There is no reason to think that the form of the epic or of the poetic play suit a woman any more than the sentence suits her. But all the older forms of literature were hardened and set by the time she became a writer. The novel alone was young enough to be soft in her hands—another reason, perhaps, why she wrote novels. Yet who shall say that even now "the novel"˙. . . is rightly shaped for her use? No doubt we shall find her knocking that into shape for herself when she has the free use of her limbs; and providing some new vehicle, not necessarily in verse, for the poetry in her. For it is the poetry that is still denied outlet.

That is a long extract; but what it says is important, not only for Virginia Woolf's attitude towards the women writers she talks about but also, of course, for her own work. It makes explicit what she has been trying to do in the novel; it explains that ceaseless experimentation and rejection of one form after another. And when she says of Jane Austen that 'she would have devised a method, clear and composed as ever, but deeper and more suggestive, for conveying not only what people say, but what they leave unsaid; not only what they are, but what life is', we feel that in *The Waves* Virginia Woolf succeeds in doing what Jane Austen did not live to do.

Mrs Woolf's criticism of masculine authors like Bennett, Wells and Galsworthy is not that they cannot do the things women writers can do, but that they do not do well the things they ought to be doing: building characters, giving vigorous action, and penetrating by force of intellect into the nature of reality. They are all materialists, occupied with the surface of life. 'They write of unimportant things; they spend immense skill and immense industry making the trivial and the transitory appear the true and the enduring.' They construct magnificent 'apparatus for catching life' but life just refuses to live there. And the reason? First, of course, this preoccupation with the transitory. But, also, the elaboration and complexity of their 'apparatus'. Their novels are made to a recipe: plot, comedy, tragedy, love interest, a happy ending. It is admirably done; but is it life?

> Look within and life, it seems, is very far from being "like this". Examine for a moment an ordinary mind on an ordinary day. The mind receives a myriad impressions—trivial, fantastic, evanescent, or engraved with the sharpness of steel. From all sides they come, an incessant shower of innumerable atoms; and as they fall, as they shape themselves into the life of Monday or Tuesday, the accent falls differently from of old; the moment of importance comes not here but there; so that, if a writer were a free man and not a slave, if he could write what he chose, not what he must, if he could base his work upon his own feeling and not upon convention, there would be no plot, no comedy, no tragedy, no love interest or catastrophe in the accepted style, and perhaps not a single button sewn on as the Bond Street tailors would have it. Life is not a series of gig lamps symmetrically arranged; life is a luminous halo, a semi-transparent envelope surrounding us from the beginning of consciousness to the end. Is it not the task of the novelist to convey this varying, this unknown and uncircumscribed spirit, whatever aberration or complexity it may display, with as little mixture of the alien and external as possible? We are not pleading merely for courage and sincerity; we are suggesting that the proper stuff of fiction is a little other than custom would have us believe it.

The proper stuff of fiction! This is what it is for her, then: the luminous halo of life that surrounds consciousness. But where is she to find this proper stuff described and analysed, outside her own work? Well, she has found it in Montaigne, and Sterne, and Emily Brontë, and De Quincey. Among the moderns she finds it in Proust, Forster, and James Joyce—and the Russians. Especially the Russians. They are the master-delineators of the soul. With them, 'the accent falls a little differently; the emphasis is upon something hitherto ignored; at once a different outline of form becomes necessary, difficult for us to grasp, incomprehensible to our predecessors'. So masterly are the Russians, she says, that if they are mentioned 'one runs the risk of feeling that to write of any fiction save theirs is waste of time. If we want understanding of the soul and heart where else shall we find it of comparable profundity? If we are sick of our own materialism the least considerable of their novelists has by right of birth a natural reverence for the human spirit'. Their minds are inconclusive: questioned, they honestly reply that there is no answer. Still, there is something in English fiction that the Russians haven't got. Doesn't the eternal insistence on the soul become a little wearisome? Don't we turn back with relief to the energy and warmth of the great English novelists? It would be stupid to compare the two types, but don't let us despise 'our natural delight in humour and comedy, in the beauty of earth, in the activities of the intellect, and in the splendour of the body'.

And this brings me to the second criterion that Mrs Woolf applies to literature. It must be alive. She delights in truth, yes; but she revels too in colour, and movement, and extravagance. We see it in her praise of Conrad, of Homer, of Defoe, writers who give us real human beings in all their variety. Of Defoe's prostitutes and highwaymen she says:

> Their courage and resource and tenacity delighted him. He found their society full of good talk, and pleasant stories, and faith in each other, and morality of a home-made kind. Their fortunes had that infinite variety which he praised and relished and beheld with wonder in his own life. These men and women, above all, were free to talk openly of the passions and desires which have moved men and women since the beginning of time . . .

We see this love, too, in her own writing. She delights in pictures of indomitable old women, who sell flowers or sing in the gutter, or, sweeping a room, re-create a whole past in their bewildered brains. In Chaucer, as in Defoe, she praises the all-embracing mind which rejects nothing as common or unclean. She draws back from Christina Rossetti, great poet as she was, because that 'something dark and hard, like a kernel', which was religion, had closed her eyes to more than half of human experience.

It is for their colour, their extravagance, their variety, that she comes back again and again to the Elizabethans. They lack all the things the Greeks have; Tolstoy beats them hollow for 'depth, range, and intricacy'; they hold tracts of unmitigated dullness. But, when all is said and done, they have poetry—and strangeness—and, as Keats said, 'the indescribable gusto of the Elizabethan voice'; and these are enough. What they meant to Virginia Woolf as a writer is evident from her first novel to her last. Yet she learned nothing from them of her own peculiar art, the analysis of moments of being. Their view of reality was quite alien to hers. Hers is a technique of realisation, of savouring the very essence of the moment as it is caught by the alert consciousness. Theirs is an art of fantasy, of escape, which she imitates only once: in *Orlando*.

> Exquisite is the delight, sublime the relief of being set free to wander in the land of the unicorn and the jeweller among dukes and grandees, Gonzaloes and Bellimperias, who spend their lives in murder and intrigue, dress up as men if they are women, as women if they are men, see ghosts, run mad, and die in the greatest profusion on the slightest provocation, uttering as they fall imprecations of superb vigour or elegies of the wildest despair.

It is because it is such a relief, and also because behind the embroidered speech she can hear the shouting and cat-calls of the audience, that she returns to the Elizabethans. The poetry, 'the word-coining genius', is terrific; and so is 'that broad humour based upon the nakedness of the body'. Even reading an Elizabethan play, in the study, we are conscious of the vivid life which ran through the age; we are not alone, we feel ourselves part of an excited crowd. But it can only be for a moment. Modern ears, studious bespectacled ears, could not bear that hullabaloo. A new desire seizes us.

> What is it that we are coming to want so persistently, that unless we get it instantly we must seek elsewhere? It is solitude. There is no privacy here. Always the door opens and someone comes in. All is shared, made visible, audible, dramatic. Meanwhile, as if tired with company, the mind steals off to muse in solitude; to think, not to act; to comment, not to share; to explore its own darkness, not the bright-lit surfaces of others. It turns to Donne, to Montaigne, to Sir Thomas Browne, to the keepers of the keys of solitude.

Yet even here, among the solitaries, there are certain qualities she demands: the qualities of strangeness, of eccentricity. She loves to describe the whimsical and the unbalanced. Jack Mytton, on whom she writes an amusing essay, does not belong to the company of the anchorites—he stands with the Elizabethans as a fantastic of the active life. But there are plenty of genuine hermits to choose from in her pages. Some of these names are unknown to fame: Lætitia Pilkington, for example, and Lady Dorothy Neville. Others have their undisputed niche: Dr Bentley, Richard Lovell Edgeworth, Thomas Day: solitaries less in practice than in inclination. Then come the parsons, James Woodforde and John Skinner. Immured in their country rectories, they built a world of fantasy which a breath was enough to blow into ruin. And, of course, the great fantastic clergymen: Donne, Swift and Sterne. How she loves them because they are not like clergymen at all! 'It was a daring thing for a clergyman to perceive a relationship between religion and pleasure,' she writes of Sterne. And as we read through the critical essays we become slowly conscious of the great gap in her sympathies. She has no place for the devotional writers. Hooker's clarity, William Law's marvellous prose, Andrewes' sinuous winding into the subject cannot get them a hearing. She passes over Herbert, Vaughan, Traherne, Crashaw, and the Donne of the Holy Sonnets, in silence. We have found her blind spot. Leslie Stephen's daughter pauses on the steps of St Paul's, and turns away. It is a pity, for in many ways the great mystics were trying, within their limitations, to do very much what Virginia Woolf was attempting within hers. But unfortunately she never seemed able to distinguish between good devotional writing and bad, or between the spirit of Christianity and its practitioners. Oddly, the figure of the Reverend Mr Bax of *The Voyage Out*, came between her and William Law or William Blake: and she saw the great mind through a mist of the little mind.

But with those writers to whom she did allow herself access —and they are many—how immediate the contact! This is the best thing her criticism gives us: the sense of immediacy. She responded directly and with all her being to the writers she loved. She was continually alert. And she has the art of passing her findings over to us, of making us feel the immediate impact of mind on mind. Thus we too learn the art of 'reading, not to acquire knowledge, not to earn a living, but to extend our intercourse beyond our own time and province'. Among critics, Virginia Woolf stands in the class of the interpreters. She doesn't lay down rules about how poems or novels should be written. Nor does she try to improve writers by pointing out their individual faults. She never stands on the defensive, as a fellow-writer, and says, 'Your novel is a bad one but mine is a good one.' No, she is admirably detached and alert; and it is this very detachment from personal ends which enables the writer's impact to be as immediate as we have seen it to be. She does not forget her own work altogether; and feminism will creep in; but she avoids the personal fallacy. We feel, as we read her, the working of a great critical integrity.

It was a year after the publication of the second volume of *The Common Reader* (October 1932), that her first full-length biography appeared: the story of Elizabeth Barrett Browning's dog, Flush. It was a disappointment after *The Waves*. This was not what her readers had been hoping for. And looking back from her death in 1941, they were still more inclined to grumble. "You had so little time left—couldn't you have given us another novel?" It was natural to feel like that; yet *Flush* is a perfect success. It does admirably what it sets out to do. It is an exercise in virtuosity and an act of piety at the same time. Elizabeth Barrett Browning is an interesting figure among the women writers of England. Virginia Woolf had already given her high praise in *The Common Reader*. Her story held the elements of drama, of romance and suspense. It has proved excellent material for the stage and the screen. But Mrs Woolf does not take the obvious course, does not give us the straight-forward story. The problem she set herself was to tell the story as it passed through the mind of a dog. She tries to see the world as a dog's world, and this means an upsetting of human values. Smells and tastes are more important than sights and sounds, instincts dominate thoughts. *Flush* is not really outside the main current of her writing; she is simply, here, trying her hand at giving the flavour of another world, another set of values, a glimpse of canine reality. We have seen her painting the lover's world, the scholar's world, the world of the child. But where those constructions were works of imagination this (to use Coleridge's blessed distinction) is a work of fancy. We believe her when she says, 'The child's mind works something like this,' because she has her own childhood to draw upon as well as her observation and her intuition. But *Flush* is Aesopian. We accept it as a fable, a fairy tale, but we miss the feeling that we get from the novels that we are penetrating into deeper and deeper layers of reality. We remain on the surface, and are entertained and amused as at a play.

That is not to say that *Flush* is without its darker side. If the profound reality of the world of the spirit is absent, the realisation of evil (which was growing more and more on the author, and was to dominate her next novel) is made fully apparent. The massive respectability of Wimpole Street is real; the sordid horror of its immediate neighbourhood is also real. Mrs Woolf's social conscience is very active. London is a monument of civilisation; it is also a den of vice. Two people live in each seven feet of space. A child drinks from a bright-green stream. Thieves, beggars and prostitutes are everywhere. When Miss Barrett forgets to lead Flush on a chain, he is stolen. It is only a glimpse we are given of this London underworld, but it makes us wonder if *Flush* itself, with all its sentiment and prettiness, is not Mrs Woolf's momentary escape from consciousness of 'the misery of the world'. It is a necessary let-down of tension between the concentrated intuition of *The Waves* and the dully insistent recognition of futility and evil in *The Years*. The shadow cast before by *The Years* is this episode of Flush in Mr Taylor's cellar. Flush bolting indoors 'with one spring' from the sinister figure, leering, which 'issues from the public house at the corner', is the anticipation of little Rose Pargiter running home from the sexual maniac who stands under the street-lamp. And something of the atmosphere of Wimpole Street is reproduced in the first part of *The Years*. The situation is in a way inverted, though not the meaning. In the Barrett household it is the daughter who is confined to her bed, her life drawn from her by the egotism of an all-too-living parent. In Abercorn Terrace it is the dying parent who feeds on the servitude of her children, 'an impediment to all life'.

Her next attempt at biography, *Roger Fry*, did not appear until 1940; but it will be convenient to glance at it now. It is a solid, an attractive, but not a brilliant book. Virginia Woolf undertook it at the request of the family, and one feels throughout it the absence of a really strong driving force. It is competently put together in an easy conversational style, but it gives no opportunity for Mrs Woolf's special gifts. There is no vision, as in the novels; no penetrating and enthusiastic criticism, as in the critical essays; no fantasy, as in *Orlando* and *Flush*. Only the record, painstaking and complete, of a life distinguished enough but without the striking qualities, the eccentricities and the greatnesses, which make a biography absorbingly interesting. It is the life of a critic, and Virginia Woolf is at her best when she is writing about an original genius: then she catches the spark and produces something original herself. Roger Fry does not come to life in these pages. There is absolutely no dramatic force in the book. There is no point at which we wonder eagerly what is going to happen next. We accept the account she gives as veracious, we are mildly interested in the battle of the Post-Impressionists and the portrait of Pierpont Morgan. But when we have finished the book and laid it aside, I doubt if any permanent impression of its central figure remains.

The low temperature at which Virginia Woolf was writing is apparent in much of the phrasing. Take this description of Fry's house 'Durbins'. 'There were paintings and carvings, Italian cabinets and Chippendale chairs, blue Persian plates, delicately glazed, and rough yellow peasant pottery bought for farthings at fairs. Every sort of style and object seemed to be mixed, but harmoniously. It was a stored, but not a congested house, a place to live in, not a museum.' Virginia Woolf here is saying all the right things, one feels; that last phrase is exactly the one called for; and for that very reason it is not what one expects from her. It is too slick.

There are things that are interesting—for example, the account of Roger Fry's childhood in a Quaker household; and the interest comes from the implicit contrast with Virginia Woolf's own upbringing. We compare in our minds the boy's life, overshadowed by religion, cramped intellectually (even at Cambridge his thinking is parent-dominated) with that of the girl, Leslie Stephen's daughter, reading voraciously and without let in a library of eighteenth-century classics. But even here the story lacks the point of energy which would have gripped us: we look for rebellion, for the hot reaction of youth; but there is none of it. When his father forbids him to paint from the female nude, he acquiesces; 'men', Professor Middleton had agreed, 'have much better figures as a rule in England and are more useful to practise drawing on'. And this is towards the end of residence in Cambridge! At thirty he wants to marry; but the girl has no money, she is an artist, and Sir Edward Fry holds the purse-strings. "Don't think," he writes, "I don't feel sufficiently the humiliation of having to appeal to father's generosity —I know that I am at his mercy and that if he chooses to cut off my allowance the whole thing must be broken off. We are neither of us very young nor very rash . . ." After this we expect little from Roger Fry's painting, and not very much more from Virginia Woolf's autobiography.

Reading through this very sober account of an art-critic's career, however, there is one thing we come to realise; and that is that Virginia Woolf's friendship with Roger Fry must plainly have meant a great deal to her as a writer. In fact, the fire and the imagination which we miss in the biography have been aroused long before, and have gone into the novels. Fry's life at Cambridge has gone into *Jacob's Room*; the struggles with family conditions have gone into *Night and Day*. And the interest in painting and its technique, and above all in Post-Impressionism, has made its mark on the writing of the novels. Roger Fry was not a big enough figure, it seems, to move Virginia Woolf to produce a masterpiece of biography; but as a catalyst his influence was of the first importance.

CHAPTER XII

The Years

[1937]

IT is Virginia Woolf's last novel but one; it follows *The Waves* at an interval of six years; and like that novel it is dominated by the conception of time. As in *The Waves*, each of the sections has a little prologue, in which our mind is allowed to stray from its fierce concentration on a single family and look at what the world outside is doing. But there is a difference. In that novel it was the voice of the sea we heard, a rhythmical voice pulsing through the action of the book and suggesting that somehow, somewhere there is a pattern; the waves beat slowly in towards the shore, and then as slowly retreat; the sun makes his portentous transit of the heavens. Here, however, there is no pattern. Instead of the waves, we have the seasons, but in no natural order: Spring 1880, Autumn 1891, Summer 1907, Spring 1910, Summer 1911, Spring 1914, Winter 1917 and then Summer at the present day (1937). The rhythm has been deliberately destroyed. Order and coherence have vanished.

Vanished too, pretty completely, are beauty and significance. The six persons of *The Waves* were given a fair chance of ordering their lives. They lived amid beauty; some of them experienced Cambridge, others travelled; none was cramped unduly by poverty. It was some inner compulsion which robbed them of happiness. Now Mrs Woolf is going to wrestle with the graver problem which she has touched on again and again in her essays and discussion books: the wrong done to the individual by society, by the system to which he (or more often she) is compelled to submit. She is going to make a novel out of *A Room of One's Own* and the darker pages of *Flush*.

ii

She is plunging right into what she has avoided up to now: unintellectual male society. The book opens in a Piccadilly club. We are introduced to Colonel Abel Pargiter, who has a dying wife (who won't die) at Abercorn Terrace, and a mistress, Mira, who is forty but much younger than he, at No. 30 in a little street under the shadow of the Abbey. We visit Mira with Colonel Pargiter. And now something very strange happens: something for which we, her readers, are not prepared. Virginia Woolf attempts a new world, a new picture of life. Desire, furtive, animal, senile and deformed, has found a place in her canvas. Lust in a dirty house.

In this small room, so close to the other houses, dusk came quickly; and the curtains were half drawn. He drew her to him; he kissed her on the nape of the neck; and then the hand that had lost two fingers began to fumble rather lower down where the neck joins the shoulders.

We ask ourselves, Can she bring it off? And the first thing we see is that Colonel Pargiter is a 'flat' character. In drawing him Virginia Woolf has crossed the frontier of her own experience. Her aim is, partly, and in this particular incident, to show masculine lust; partly, in the novel as a whole, to show masculine stupidity crushing feminine initiative: she has, then, to draw us a stupid male. Unfortunately, she doesn't know any well, and her mind lacks the vital materials out of which to create one. This doesn't mean at all that Colonel Pargiter is unconvincing: it means that he is convincing only as a type, a 'humour'. He has all Mrs Woolf's experience as a novelist, all her art behind him; but he hasn't all her insight and experience as a woman. He lives in the novel, then, in a different way from that in which his daughters, Milly, Delia, Eleanor and Rose live. He is a typical retired soldier, and his mannerisms sometimes pass over into caricature. His wife is dying slowly; he is waiting for her to die, and his family is waiting with him. There is no nobility and no pathos. The children are tied to their mother's bedside. Her relapses are greeted with intense hope, her rallies with scarcely concealed disappointment. Nor are the children very loving among themselves, sucked dry as they are by the incubus upstairs. The first conversation we listen to among them is conducted in these terms: ". . . Delia said irritably . . . said Milly severely . . . said Rose, the little girl, grumpily . . . she said gloomily . . . said Delia severely . . . Blast that kettle, said Martin turning away sharply . . . Milly reproved him." All they are talking about is a kettle that won't boil: yet there is intense negative emotion.

But perhaps, outside the house of the invalid, "somewhere there's beauty, Delia thought, somewhere there's freedom". Is there? We are quickly shown. If the world of Abercorn Terrace is full of suffering, and hatred, and hypocrisy, and blind revolt (" "No, no, no," said Delia, stretching her arms out, "it's hopeless . . ." "), the world outside is saturated in evil. The little girl Rose steals out to run down the street.

> "I am Pargiter of Pargiter's Horse," she said, flourishing her hand, "riding to the rescue!" She was riding by night on a desperate mission to a besieged garrison, she told herself. She had a secret message—she clenched her fist on her purse—to deliver to the General in person. All their lives depended upon it. The British flag was still flying on the central tower . . .

We are in the secret world of childhood, which Virginia Woolf paints so well. We hope we shall be allowed to stay there for a time, for the atmosphere of the adult world has become too oppressive. But no: we are recalled with a grim flash of evil. The figure of a man emerges suddenly in Rose's path from under a gas-lamp.

> "The enemy!" Rose cried to herself. "The enemy! Bang!" she cried, pulling the trigger of her pistol and looking him full in the face as she passed him. It was a horrid face: white peeled, pockmarked; he leered at her. He put out his arm as if to stop her. He almost caught her. She dashed past him. The game was over.
> She was herself again, a little girl who had disobeyed her sister, in her house shoes, flying for safety to Lamley's shop.

And as she comes back from Lamley's shop, with fear in her heart, the lamps seem very far apart, the pools of darkness in between very black. She begins to run. The man is waiting for her.

> He was leaning with his back against the lamp-post, and the light from the gas-lamp flickered over his face. As she passed he sucked his lips in and out. He made a mewing noise. But he did not stretch his hands out at her; they were unbuttoning his clothes.

As she runs home she thinks she hears the man come padding after her. That night as she sleeps the face comes back. She wakes; and there is a masterly touch of pure horror.

She made herself think of a flock of sheep penned up in a hurdle in a field. She made one of the sheep jump the hurdle; then another. She counted them as they jumped. One, two, three, four —they jumped over the hurdle. But the fifth sheep would not jump. It turned round and looked at her. Its long narrow face was grey; its lips moved; it was the face of the man at the pillar-box, and she was alone with it.

In this novel, then, for the first time in Virginia Woolf's writing, the note of sexual evil in its extreme form is struck. Of sex she had written often enough before: but it was of sex as energy, not as frustration and corruption. She has seen sex as bawdry and she has seen it as something ridiculous and she has also seen it as beauty. Now she sees it as evil. This extreme note is not sounded again; but it is enough to trouble the harmony of the whole book. Rose cannot tell her sister, when she comes to the nursery, what has frightened her. The horrible vision stays deep down in her mind, poisoning the springs of consciousness.

Ugliness without corresponds with ugliness within. Mrs Pargiter has to be tended. 'Her face was pouched and heavy; the skin was stained with brown patches; the hair which had been red was now white, save that there were queer yellow patches in it, as if some locks had been dipped in the yolk of an egg.' It is curious how in this book Mrs Woolf forces herself to delve into the unpleasant. Mrs Pargiter's face, the pervert's face, the Colonel's mutilated hand, Uncle Horace's glass eye, the dark stain on the chair-back where the Colonel has rested his head: they are all crowded in upon us. Finally, in this same year 1880 in which the story opens, Mrs Pargiter dies. It is a painful scene. Delia can feel no emotion but relief, yet admires the perfection of her father's play-acting.

"Rose!" he cried. "Rose! Rose!" He held his arms with the fists clenched out in front of him.

You did that very well, Delia told him as he passed her. It was like a scene in a play. She observed quite dispassionately that the raindrops were still falling. One sliding met another and together in one drop they rolled to the bottom of the window-pane.

In Oxford too it is raining. Edward is there, an elder brother. He is reading Greek: the *Antigone*. He entertains his friends. But what has happened? we wonder. The old atmosphere has vanished, the warmth and the reverence and the delight in learning. It is Oxford now, not Cambridge; therefore without emotion. The Greek is being swotted, not lived—it is for a prize. Friendship is tainted with jealousy. 'He had had two rows with Ashley about Gibbs already this term.' The life of the spirit, then, like the life of the family, is a sham. So Oxford appears to Kitty Malone, the daughter of a college head, who reads history with Miss Craddock in the suburbs, and admires Jo Robson, who is handsome but not Eton or Winchester, and is admired in her turn by her cousin Edward Pargiter. 'All seemed to her obsolete, frivolous, inane. The usual undergraduate in cap and gown with books under his arm looked silly. And the portentous old men, with their exaggerated features, looked like gargoyles, carved, mediaeval, unreal. They were all like people dressed up and acting parts, she thought.'

Thus in *The Years* she seems to be travelling back through her novels and turning them over, showing us the obverse of all the situations she has created hitherto. The family of *To the Lighthouse* and *The Waves* is turned inside out; the University ideal of *Jacob's Room* is exposed as a sham; childhood itself is tainted by evil.

iii

The second section is full of symbolism. Rain, dismal, depressing, had swept through 1880; it is smoke that obscures the outlines of reality in 1891. Everywhere they are burning weeds in gardens. 'One must burn one's own smoke,' Colonel Pargiter thinks regretfully, feeling alone and deserted. His mistress is old and fat now; though she has had an affair with another man, she is clamouring for an allowance. The past is eddying its smoke over the present.

And now the battalions of good and evil are more sharply defined than ever before. Mrs Woolf puts them plainly before us. On the one hand, the forces of society in all its forms. Colonel Pargiter reading the *Financial Times*; his son, Morris, a barrister tied day after day to 'the vast funereal mass of the Law Courts'; the bright Kitty, now Lady Lasswade, having married neither Edward nor Jo; Edward, academically distinguished at Oxford; Sir Digby Pargiter, the Colonel's brother, deep in politics. On the other hand, the individual, struggling against servitude. Eleanor, almost an old maid, tied to her ageing father as she was tied to her dying mother. Delia, the rebel, who has left home. Martin, the younger brother, now enjoying adventure in India. Eugenie, Sir Digby's wife, on holiday in Venice. The death of Parnell.

Underneath the shows of society corruption is everywhere. Slums and sickness, the inhumanity which forbids the incurable to end it all. Poor children crowd round a pony but daren't stroke its nose. 'Here a church raised its filigree spire. Underneath were pipes, wires, drains . . .' Eugenie's child is physically deformed, as Rose was spiritually by her experience of evil. 'She had been dropped when she was a baby; one shoulder was slightly higher than the other.' Everywhere there are stains on ceilings, stains in human lives. And Eleanor is acutely conscious of the chasm between her own life and the life of freedom. 'She stopped at the entrance to Charing Cross station. The sky was wide at that point. She saw a file of birds flying high, flying together; crossing the sky. She watched them. Again she walked on. People on foot, people in cabs were being sucked in like straws round the piers of a bridge.' And when she hears the news of Parnell's death: 'He's dead, she said to herself, still conscious of the two worlds; one flowing in wide sweeps overhead, the other tip-tapping circumscribed upon the pavement.'

The symbolism is almost too evident, the contrast too clearly drawn. The writing itself is full of pain. Virginia Woolf is feeling the futility and the injustice too acutely, and her novel in consequence lacks the detachment of great art. It lacks too those overtones, those suggestions of a meaning beyond the transitory, which gave her previous work its special value. The world of men has been allowed to crowd the world of things out of the picture. No longer does she move from plane to plane, altering the focus of her writing to show now the snail moving under the sunny leaf, now the sea heaving at dawn, now the child running after a hoop, now the meditation of the solitary mind. The masculine world has devoured it all. Society with all its weight has come down on the delicate spirit. The bird is caught in the cage and cannot sing.

THE WORLD AND REALITY

iv

Midsummer, 1907. The dull weight is lifted for a moment, for now Virginia Woolf is going to give us one of her favourite situations—the situation which, in *A Room of One's Own*, she described as marking a revolution in fiction: a conversation between two young women. They are Maggie and Sally, Eugenie Pargiter's daughters. Maggie has been to a dance; Sally, who was dropped as a baby, has had to lie still in bed. She has been reading a little brown book of philosophy, and she has looked into the *Antigone* of Sophocles. An image of horror arises from the printed page.

> The unburied body of a murdered man lay like a fallen tree-trunk, like a statue, with one foot stark in the air. Vultures gathered. Down they flopped on the silver sand. With a lurch, with a reel, the top-heavy birds came waddling; with a flap of the grey throat swinging, they hopped—she beat her hand on the counterpane as she read—to that lump there. Quick, quick, quick, with repea⁺ed jerks they struck at the mouldy flesh. Yes. She glanced at the tree outside in the garden. The unburied body of the murdered man lay on the sand. Then in a yellow cloud came whirling—who? She turned the page quickly. Antigone? She came whirling out of the dust-cloud to where the vultures were reeling and flung white sand over the blackened foot. She stood there letting fall white dust over the blackened foot. Then behold! there were more clouds; dark clouds; the horsemen leapt down; she was seized; her wrists were bound with withies. . . . She was buried alive. The tomb was a brick mound. There was just room for her to lie straight out. Straight out in a brick tomb, she said.

When Maggie comes back from the ball, she says nothing to her about the image of horror, but asks her about her partner, and whether anyone offered her his broken heart, and picks up the little book of philosophy.

' "This man," she said, tapping the ugly little brown volume, "says the world's nothing but thought, Maggie." ' And they discuss the question until their mother comes in. There is no trace of bitterness or jealousy. It is not Maggie who has done Sara this wrong, but the world itself, which is nothing but thought. And what if that thought be changed, what if men and women agree to think in a different way? That is the question that runs through the book. She will take it up more

fully and explicitly in *Three Guineas*. How can we induce people
to think otherwise than they do, and so make it impossible for
young women to be walled up in brick tombs?

v

First, the rain, then the smoke, and now the wind. It is a
sordid wind. The image from the *Antigone*, horrible though it
was, had a certain grandeur; but now we are back again in the
yellow-stained atmosphere of modern life. It is a year later:
March, and the wind is blowing.

Had it any breeding-place it was in the Isle of Dogs among tin
cans lying beside a workhouse drab on the banks of a polluted
city. It tossed up rotten leaves, gave them another span of
degraded existence; scorned, derided them, yet had nothing to
put in the place of the scorned, the derided. Down they fell.
Uncreative, unproductive, yelling its joy in destruction, its power
to peel off the bark, the bloom, and show the bare bone, it paled
every window; drove old gentlemen further and further into the
leather smelling recesses of clubs; and old ladies to sit eyeless,
leather cheeked, joyless among the tassels and antimacassars of
their bedrooms and kitchens. Triumphing in its wantonness it
emptied the streets; swept flesh before it; and coming smack
against a dust cart standing outside the Army and Navy Stores,
scattered along the pavement a litter of old envelopes; twists of
hair; papers already blood smeared, yellow smeared, smudged
with print and sent them scudding to plaster legs, lamp-posts,
pillar-boxes, and fold themselves frantically against area railings.

The wind cleanses nothing; but it has blown many things
away. Sir Digby and Eugenie are dead; the Colonel has had a
stroke, and his vitality is very low, though he still manages to
draw a good deal from Eleanor. She too is feeling worn and
tired. Martin is back from India, and out of the army. Rose, a
handsome girl but over forty now, has been addressing meetings
in the North. In the next section we find them all at a
Suffragette meeting: Rose, Eleanor, Sally, Kitty, Martin. And
the King dies, in 1910. A year later Colonel Pargiter is dead too,
and Eleanor gets away for a holiday to Greece and Spain: but
when she returns the problem confronts her, what to do with
her life? She is fifty-five. Life has gone on for all of them, as it
had proceeded for the six characters of *The Waves*: but in *The*

Years everything is on the surface, is meaningless. Things happen, but have no connection with each other. Where we get a glimpse of depths, they are always dark and smelly. There is no repose. Nor, on the other hand, is there variety. There are none of those portraits of intelligent young men that Mrs Woolf delighted us with in her earlier novels. The Colonel, Morris, Edward—all are mere 'humours'. The masculine world is a pasteboard construction surrounding the feminine world in which the author is really interested. And what shall we say of this monotonously feminine world? Its inhabitants do not live with the intense and profound life Mrs Woolf has hitherto given to her creations. We do not feel we know Eleanor, Rose or Sally as we knew Jinny and Susan, Mrs Dalloway, or even Katharine Hilbery and Lily Briscoe. The subtle flame of life does not burn through them. We neither see each in herself, nor through the eyes of the others.

Moreover there is little connection in the plot, if we may call it a plot. Detached situations follow one another, but there are no climaxes. No particular scene grips us, to open a window on life. There is no heightening of the understanding. Where shall we find a central *motif* around which to group these detached situations? Nowhere: or if at all, only in that initial shock of horror, that trauma, which scarred the child mind of Rose Pargiter. Yes, it is from this that the succeeding incidents stem, and with this that the mainsprings of the other characters are to be compared. Rose, Eleanor, Sally: all are blighted: Rose by a mental shock, Sally by a physical, Eleanor by the slow process of exhaustion. For these three the normal development of womanhood is barred. They are enclosed, living, in the brick tomb ordained by Creon, by male society.

vi

The stress on unpleasantness does not diminish as the narrative proceeds. Martin takes Sally out to lunch. The waiter tries to cheat him, and he goes away in anger without leaving a tip. He feels conscience-stricken afterwards, and tries to make up for it by putting sixpence into a violet-seller's tray. But here too is corruption.

He dropped a sixpence in her tray to make amends to the waiter. He shook his head. No violets, he meant; and indeed they were faded. But he caught sight of her face. She had no nose; her face was seamed with white patches; there were red rims for nostrils.

And if there is a breathing space, if we are taken away with Kitty to her great house in Yorkshire, to smell the clean air again and find the peace of the wolds—it is only to make the final shock more terrific. For now it is 1914. Air-raids drive them into the cellar: Eleanor and Maggie and Sally, and Nicholas, the young Pole, and René, Maggie's French husband. Stupidity and malice, the attributes of society, have come to a head. "I have spent the evening in a coal cellar while other people try to kill each other above my head," René says suddenly. Nicholas is hopeful about the new world that will come after the war.

"The soul—the whole being," he explained. He hollowed his hands as if to enclose a circle. "It wishes to expand; to adventure; to form—new combinations?"

"Yes, yes," she said, as if to assure him that his words were right.

"Whereas now,"—he drew himself together; put his feet together; he looked like an old lady who is afraid of mice—"this is how we live, screwed up into one hard little, tight little—knot?"

"Knot, knot—yes, that's right," she nodded.

"Each is in his own little cubicle; each with his own cross or holy book; each with his fire, his wife . . ."

vii

Such was the hope: to expand, to form new combinations. In the last section, The Present Day, we learn what is the reality. The yellow stain is still there. Sara, unmarried, lives alone. 'There was no sign of dinner . . . only a dish of fruit on the cheap lodging-house tablecloth, already yellowed with some gravy stain.' It is true there are aeroplanes, cars and radios: but is this really the new world Nicholas had promised? Eleanor wonders, looking up at the sky. Mussolini bellows and gesticulates in the newspaper, and she tears the paper across. 'It was as if she still believed with passion—she, old Eleanor—in the things that man had destroyed.'

"You see," Eleanor interrupted, as if she wanted to explain her words, "it means the end of everything we cared for."

"Freedom?" said Peggy perfunctorily.

"Yes," said Eleanor. "Freedom and justice."

If there is no sequence, there is certainly repetition. Scenes are repeated, the same yet with subtle distortions, from generation to generation. Rose and Delia have disappeared from the stage early, but all are together again in the party which ends the book. Eleanor, for a brief moment, seems to catch a glimpse of a pattern.

Does everything then come over again a little differently? she thought. If so, is there a pattern; a theme, recurring, like music; half remembered, half foreseen? . . . a gigantic pattern, moment- arily perceptible? The thought gave her extreme pleasure: that there was a pattern. But who makes it? Who thinks it? Her mind slipped. She could not finish her thought.

She falls asleep at the party, and an extraordinary feeling of happiness comes to her: the feeling that one can be 'happy in this world, happy with living people'. But Peggy, her niece, cannot see it. How is it possible, in a world full of egotism and possessiveness?

How can one be "happy"? she asked herself, in a world bursting with misery. On every placard at every street corner was Death; or worse—tyranny; brutality; torture; the fall of civilisation; the end of freedom. We here, she thought, are only sheltering under a leaf, which will be destroyed. . . . Thinking was torment; why not give up thinking, and drift and dream? But the misery of the world, she thought, forces me to think.

That voice, Virginia Woolf's own voice, now moves over to the lips of North, Peggy's brother. How is the world to be saved?

Not halls and reverberating megaphones; not marching in step after leaders, in herds, groups, societies, caparisoned. No; to begin inwardly, and let the devil take the outer form, he thought. . . . Not black shirts, green shirts, red shirts—always posing in the public eye; that's all poppycock. Why not down barriers and simplify . . . make a new ripple in human consciousness, be the bubble and the stream, the stream and the bubble—myself and the world together—he raised his glass. Anonymously, he said, looking at the clear yellow liquid. But what do I mean, he wondered—I, to whom ceremonies are suspect, and religion's dead; who don't fit, as the man said, don't fit in anywhere.

How much *The Years* lacks of what the earlier novels had is obvious enough. The life of things, the life of love and friendship, the life of solitary fulfilment: all these are absent. There is little colour and no music. We feel that we have stepped across a threshold: a certain view of reality, or the possibility of reality, has been abandoned. London, and London in its darkest and direst guise, is the setting: the theme is the power of society to thwart and to crush. And we ask ourselves, Is this the end? Does this mark the jettisoning of the old dream of discovering that somehow, somewhere, beauty is truth, truth beauty? The answer to that question, a very partial answer, will come in *Between the Acts*. Meanwhile there is still 'purgatory blind' to go through. *Three Guineas* will mark the nadir of Virginia Woolf's circle of understanding.

CHAPTER XIII

An Indictment of Society

THE grim picture of society which Virginia Woolf gives in *The Years* has not come upon us unheralded and unexpected. From the beginning she has been working up to this picture, trying to turn her eyes away from this picture, protesting that she will have nothing to do with it for it is meaningless and obscene—yet filled all the time with a horrible fascination. Against the irrational and brutal organism called society she has set up all her private worlds: love, scholarship, art, things, the family. And she has seen society invading and crushing them all.

Essentially, Virginia Woolf's writing is a search for value. In what does value consist? she seems to ask. In beauty? in intellect? in understanding? Does it reside in the service of one's country, or of a cause? Is it a personal thing, bound up with the cultivation of personal life? Can we find it in love, or in art, or in work? Is it easiest to discover in a community like Cambridge; or shall we find it alone in an attic room in a London street?

For most thinkers the enquiry is a religious one; but Virginia Woolf was far, both by upbringing and by temperament, from the orthodox religious position. The Christian solution appeared too crude and too fantastic; she cannot observe in the behaviour of Christian people that their sense of values is particularly acute, or that they have attained any pearl of great price. On the contrary, they seem obtuse, stupid and malevolent. Her best characters, such as Mrs Ramsay and Mrs Dalloway and Eleanor Pargiter, reject the Christian outlook with violence. They feel it as a sort of defilement, a sticky paste of humbug and spite that leaves its slime on the mind even if it touches only for a moment. There are no nice Christians among her *dramatis personae*, though she can see some good in every other class of human beings. The solitary exception will be Mrs Swithin in *Between the Acts*.

Virginia Woolf's aversion from Christianity springs first, then, from her hatred of hypocrisy. It springs also from her sensitiveness to unpleasantness and pain. These things are, artistically, outside her scope. She knows they are there; and, as we have seen, she is even too acutely conscious of them. They contradict her vision of beauty and significance. They worry her; she feels she must put them in her picture. So, conscientiously, in they go, the nasty aspects of life: the rim of grease round the bath and the hairs left by Abrahamson, the commercial traveller, in *The Years*, the birds pecking at snails in *The Waves*. But the glimpse is fleeting, or else too general. There is no penetration into evil: for that we must go to T. F. Powys in one *genre* or to Joyce in another. Virginia Woolf cannot detach herself personally from evil as these writers do. She cannot stand aside, even for a moment as the artist has to do if he is to make evil an integral part of his picture. When she does try, when she forces herself to linger, she becomes involved with her material: pain and cruelty and obscenity swell into a great black cloud which overshadows her mind and blots out everything else.

Her dislike of Christianity, I repeat, has its roots here. For Christianity puts pain in the forefront: the symbol of the crucified Lord, the doctrine that suffering is salutary, the description of this world as a vale of tears, the barren asceticism: all the nay-saying that for her was blasphemy. She strikes back passionately against it. The voice of the Reverend Mr Bax drones away; meanwhile, St John Hirst reads the verses of Sappho and writes a poem against God. He represents intelligence in revolt against stupid orthodoxy. Mrs Ambrose is afraid that her children at home may be taught the Lord's Prayer while she is away; and later, in the fourth novel, we find an embittered and bigoted spinster trying to win Mrs Dalloway's daughter away from her 'to God'. The anti-clericalism is cruder in these early novels than it is later, when the element of pain rather than stupidity becomes stressed. Neville, in *The Waves*, detests the gilt crucifix which heaves on Dr Crane's waistcoat.

> I gibe and mock at this sad religion, at these tremulous, grief-stricken figures advancing, cadaverous and wounded, down a white road shadowed by fig-trees where boys sprawl in the dust —naked boys; and goat skins distended with wine hang at the tavern door. I was in Rome travelling with my father at Easter; and the trembling figure of Christ's mother was borne niddle-noddling along the streets; there went by also the stricken figure of Christ in a glass case.

Unpleasantness is perceived swiftly, briefly, and turned away from: but the defilement of the glimpse persists and spreads. Nobody is immune. Nothing can wash out the stain. Those who have seen participate in the guilt. Evil which comes from humanity is shared by all human beings. In *The Years* Sara looks out of the window and sees a drunken man being thrown out of a pub.

> There he came, staggering. He fell against a lamp-post to which he clung. The scene was lit up by the glare of the lamp over the public house door. Sara stood for a moment at the window watching them. Then she turned; her face in the mixed light looked cadaverous and worn, as if she were no longer a girl, but an old woman worn out by a life of childbirth, debauchery and crime. She stood there hunched up, with her hands clenched together.
>
> "In time to come," she said, looking at her sister, "people, looking into this room—this cave, this little antre, scooped out of mud and dung, will hold their fingers to their noses"—she held her fingers to her nose—"and say 'Pah! They stink!' "

Yet in this same *The Years* we find that Virginia Woolf is by no means insensitive to the charm there is in Christianity, to the beauty of old buildings, old words and old music. A boy's voice floating round the dome of St Paul's like a wandering dove had delighted her before; and now the words of the burial service: 'I am the Resurrection and the Life . . . And fade away suddenly like the grass, in the morning it is green, and groweth up; but in the evening it is cut down, dried up and withered.' The words are beautiful, but they do not continue to speak truth.

> "We give thee hearty thanks," said the voice, "for that it has pleased thee to deliver this our sister out of the miseries of this sinful world——"
>
> What a lie! she cried to herself. What a damnable lie! He had robbed her of the one feeling that was genuine; he had spoilt her one moment of understanding.

This is the trouble, this mixture of truth and falsehood, of simplicity and hypocrisy: how disentangle them in the woof of religion?

> She had always wanted to know about Christianity—how it began; what it meant, originally. God is love, The kingdom of

heaven is within us, sayings like that she thought, turning over the pages, what did they mean? The actual words were very beautiful. But who said them—when? . . . It was what a man said under a fig-tree, on a hill, she thought. And then another man wrote it down.

She cannot get over the contrast between the simplicity of Christ's teaching and the wealth and pomp of the Church. For the clergy, the ministers of religion, the priests, she has nothing but scorn. She feels that they are either stupid, repeating words whose meaning they do not grasp; or hypocritical, repeating words they do not believe; or fanatical and cruel. The sincere, intelligent mind cannot accept their findings.

In these dilemmas [thinks Bernard] the devout consult those violet-sashed and sensual-looking gentry who are trooping past me. But for ourselves, we resent teachers. Let a man get up and say, 'Behold, this is the truth', and instantly I perceive a sandy cat filching a piece of fish in the background. Look, you have forgotten the cat, I say.

Religion misses out the cat. It shuts its eyes to life, and lives in a world of make-believe. Virginia Woolf quotes with approval, in her essay *Two Antiquaries*, the bold words of Horace Walpole:

Church and presbytery are human nonsense invented by knaves to govern fools. *Exalted notions of church matters* are contradictions in terms to the lowliness and humility of the gospel. There is nothing sublime but the Divinity. Nothing is sacred but as His work. A tree or a brute stone is more respectable as such, than a mortal called an archbishop, or an edifice called a church, which are the puny and miserable productions of men. . . . A Gothic church or convent fills one with romantic dreams—but for the mysterious, the Church in the abstract, it is a jargon that means nothing or a great deal too much, and I reject it and its apostles from Athanasius to Bishop Keene.

It is not, then, in religion that value is to be found. And as for the talk about a loving Father watching over the universe—

a drunk man staggers about with a club in his hand—that is all.

ii

Mrs Woolf has been called a psychological novelist, because of the subtlety and intricacy of her character-drawing: she has been ranked with Proust and Henry James. But I am inclined to see her much more as a philosophical novelist, in the sense that she is engaged throughout her work in an enquiry which is strictly metaphysical. In E. M. Forster's novels we have another enquiry in the background: what is the good life, and how do we achieve it? And the answer comes: in personal relationships, in tolerance and sympathy. Further into the ultimate Forster does not seek to go. But Virginia Woolf was tortured by the disparity of life: the existence of beauty and the existence of evil side by side, running in and out of each other; by the uncertainty of human aims; by the pity for human failure. What is truth, what is reality? she asks. And in a series of incomparably vivid situations she shows us the several facets, not of truth itself, for the question remains unanswered, but of the question.

The question remains unanswered. These novels form the analysis of incompleteness. In *The Voyage Out* she tries to see the answer as love; but love is not allowed to complete itself; the curtain falls on the first act and does not rise again. There is a terrible sense of waste. Who is responsible? God? Nature? Society—for the doctor is incompetent? In *Night and Day* the issue is not so clear-cut; love is set side by side with work: Ralph's writing and Katharine's mathematics; the book ends on a question mark—will the marriage be a success? For note: it is society which is forcing them into marriage, into an indissoluble union. Katharine envisages simply living together, without the ceremony; but society, in the shape of Mrs Hilbery, says no. And thus the problem is raised: can two minds of such equal force and sincerity live together, or does marriage imply that leaven of pretence, of compromise, that neither is prepared to give? In *Jacob's Room*, again, society takes a hand in shattering the pattern: Jacob dies in battle, his promise unfulfilled.

This incompleteness is of the essence of Virginia Woolf's vision of life and that is why her novels are, to some people, so unsatisfying. She cannot pretend, she cannot draw a complete design where she does not see it. Life is like this, she seems to say, endlessly fascinating and beautiful, tantalisingly suggesting a whole, significant in patches, self-contradictory. Human beings do not fit perfectly together. Terror suddenly darkens out of a sea and sky which, a moment before, had proclaimed peace, ecstasy, goodness. The philosophies over which young men rack their brains in lonely rooms are partial and distorting mirrors. So her novels too are partial, tentative. But they are full of a great integrity. Her vision, we feel, can be trusted: she will not try to twist it for any reason whatever.

iii

In what single fact, or in what conjunction of circumstances, will value be found? Will it flash out upon us in the light of nature, or are we to look for it in the depths of the human soul? It is this enquiry which is at the bottom of her delicate character-drawing, in which she seems to trace the very cells and nerves of her *dramatis personae*. Shall we arrive at the truth (which will suddenly illuminate the universe, and reveal the unity which binds together all appearances) in the intellection of the masculine mind or in the intuition of the feminine—or in the combination of both? The solidity and tranquillity of *things*, perhaps, will provide the best ground for the mind to rest on; but one cannot put one's conviction about this into words—and has one the right to withdraw while the world goes on striving and suffering? And then there are people: friends in whose eyes one reads joy and understanding; perhaps they have the secret. Let us make contact with their minds, then. And the world of children, so happy and creative: is it the return to the child mind that we want? Alas, here too, as she demonstrates in *The Years*, society plants its corruption.

Thus the counterpoint of situations and people, of things and ideas, of the masculine understanding and the feminine, is woven into the intricate stuff of Virginia Woolf's writing. And because her knowledge was broadening and deepening all the time, the chief interest in reading her work lies in seeing how this texture varied: how at first one strand is prominent, then another. She is never wholly detached; it is life she is dealing with, and suffering. She cannot take the gently ironic attitude which is plain in Forster's novels. The dilemma which presented itself in its crudest form at the beginning of her career—

art or the suffragettes—is always present. Always she sees the brute force of society pressing down on these values as they emerge one by one, like flowers opening, from consciousness.

iv

What does it mean, this intense sensibility—what is its effect on Virginia Woolf's writing as a whole? Well, it means in the first place that with all her respect for the classics, and with all her real graces of lucidity and reasonableness, she is not a 'classical' writer. She is a romantic. Her emotions and intuitions dominate; she is not detached or impersonal. However much she may understand and admire the masculine virtues of hard thinking and scientific precision, she could never be mistaken for anything but a woman writer. This is not a criticism. Mrs Woolf's intuition goes deeper, it seems to me, than the reasoning detachment of most masculine writers. But we must beware of supposing that, because she has presented the picture of young men engaged on the arduous pursuit of truth with such vividness and sympathy, she herself espouses the intellectualist point of view. Her novels give us many facets; she considers each in turn, and rejects them all. There is no conclusion. But her own approach was clearly through sensibility and intuition.

Her awareness of, her defencelessness against stupidity and cruelty (the vices of society rather than of individuals) brings another consequence with it: a certain lack of balance. She could not absorb and transmute everything. She did not see life steadily or see it whole, because some things in life—what I have called unpleasantness—burst out of the frame. There are certain writers who can afford to be indignant: they are the satirists, whose art is controlled by a cold and deadly intensity. The heart feels, but the head rules. Pope, Swift, Dryden—they are all classical writers. Their framework is tight enough, impersonal enough, to prevent the indignation from breaking through and becoming something that is not art—an infant crying in the night, or a woman's scream. The romantic writer who turns to satire in his indignation rarely succeeds. We have only to put Shelley's denunciations of the Lord Chancellor side by side with Dryden's *MacFlecknoe* to see what happens. There is a lack of balance, a failure to control.

V

Since, therefore, she felt acutely this power of society to throw her off her balance and destroy the symmetry of her work, Mrs Woolf tries to stand back from society and to some extent from her characters. 'Removed, and to a distance that was fit.' There they are, men and women, working and playing and falling in love, listening to music and painting pictures; but not too emphatically, not with an insistence that dwarfs the non-human actors. Mrs Woolf isolates them, puts a buffer of nature between them and society. For the older novelists, like Dickens and Meredith and Jane Austen, nature served as a background, and the human beings kept the centre of the stage. What we remember when we have read the book is the men and women. The rest slips out of our mind. It is true that this is not the case with Hardy: Egdon Heath broods and dominates, even in retrospect, the puppets which dance and weep upon it. But Egdon Heath is itself a symbol, a concrete expression of the something dark and enormous and terrible that broods over human destiny. It does not exist in the novel by virtue of itself. In Virginia Woolf's writing, however, trees and rivers and curves of shore do exist of themselves, and transmit a peculiar joy. Here is a man, she says, here is a rock. Let us consider their relations.

Now this new vision of the world is precisely the thing the artist is there to give us; and unless he presents us with that, unless he makes it possible for us to see the common things in a new way, we get tired of him and forget him. This is his great virtue, this new slant on life. What we are all doing is trying to get our own individual views of the world, and we are helped and encouraged when we see others succeeding. For a certain number of people in every age the old views have lost their significance; and they have to construct new ones. They look about eagerly to see how their companions are getting on with the job. The job really consists in putting ordinary things in a strange light and showing that they are related one to another in ways which before have hardly been suspected. This and this together do not mean *that*, says the new writer or the new painter, they mean *this*. Of course a lot of people will be perfectly content with the old way of looking at things, and they will be annoyed with the new way which seems to threaten the old: hence the opposition to new artists.

Virginia Woolf's eye seems to me a painter's eye as much as a writer's. Her values are those of a plastic artist. She is interested in colours, shapes, masses. She is not interested in plots, that is, in the experiences men and women undergo as active members of society; she is interested in character, in psychology, which she interprets as the relation of man to his non-human as much as to his human environment. Her new slant on life shows the intersection of the human and the non-human; and both planes are of equal significance. Her outlook is Impressionist, not Symbolist; she doesn't in the least want to put meaning into things. She will wait, yes, to see whether meaning will emerge at odd moments; but the search after meaning blurs and distorts the pure lines of life. All her men characters who go a-whoring after meanings and philosophies are shown as unbalanced creatures, often delightful and lovable, noble and brave, but not poised, not firmly rooted in reality as the women are. Mrs Ramsay, Mrs Dalloway carry about with them an atmosphere of spiritual health: they are for ever righting the balance which is for ever being upset by their menfolk. It is the feminine world of her novels which is in almost perfect relationship with the non-human world; and the plane of the masculine, artificial world cuts into this, sometimes with brutal violence. The child James sees it all in *To the Lighthouse*.

> If he put implicit faith in her, nothing should hurt him; however deep he buried himself or climbed high, not for a second should he find himself without her. So boasting of her capacity to surround and protect, there was scarcely a shell of herself left for her to know herself by; all was so lavished and spent; and James, as he stood stiff between her knees, felt her rise in a rosy-flowered fruit tree laid with leaves and dancing boughs into which the beak of brass, the arid scimitar of his father, the egotistical man, plunged and smote, demanding sympathy.

This is not a sentimentalising or idealising of women; we find this virtue of reality somehow in women who are presented as far from admirable; and Virginia Woolf finds much to admire and even to envy (for there are remarkable virtues entirely masculine) in the young thoughtful men she knew so well. She granted them their courage, their sincerity, even their foolish enthusiasms for meanings (no one has spoken better about

Plato), their physical beauty. Yet the two worlds are strange, distinct from each other: the world of women, trees, rivers, music; the world of men, committees, wars, government.

The function of women, perhaps, is to bridge the gap between men and the natural world, to keep men sane and prevent them from losing themselves in abstractions and possessions. Women do this in some obvious ways: through sex, by running a home, by bearing children. But there are less obvious ways. Woman has to help man to get rid of his manias. She does this by being herself, by providing a *punctum indifferens* in relation to which man's exaggeration comes to seem even to himself exaggerated. Among these manias the lust for power stands out. The lust for power has the western world in its grip. To dominate, to crush, to convert—in exchange for these delights men are willing to sacrifice the best of human relationships, the most serene of contemplative joys. But from woman he can still learn that human relationships and right contact with natural things are the stuff of living. The sad thing is that in her unending fight with male manias woman exhausts herself; and, in addition, she is constantly being called upon for sympathy, advice, comfort and praise. What wonder that, like Mrs Ramsay, she sinks under the strain? Life proceeds, it is true; and something of Mrs Ramsay, Lily Briscoe thinks, persists in tree and air and house:

> This, that, and the other; herself and Charles Tansley and the breaking wave; Mrs Ramsay bringing them together; Mrs Ramsay saying "Life stand still here"; Mrs Ramsay making of the moment something permanent (as in another sphere Lily herself tried to make of the moment something permanent)—this was of the nature of a revelation. In the midst of chaos there was shape; this eternal passing and flowing (she looked at the clouds going and the leaves shaking) was struck into stability. Life stand still here, Mrs Ramsay said.

vi

This catching of the moment that Lily Briscoe describes is what Mrs Woolf tried to do in all her novels. To catch the moment, to understand its significance, its ecstasy, and slowly to distil its essence—that for her was the artist's task. The rest is superfluous. It is success in this attempt, like Mrs Ramsay's success, that gives Virginia Woolf's novels their supreme value. No one else has done anything like it in prose. It requires a sensitiveness abnormal, almost morbid; an intuition of the finest; a style the most lucid and precise that can be found. For now she has come to feel that it is in the moment alone that value subsists. We must not attempt to make a generalisation, or construct a system. We must be content with fragments of meaning. They are all we shall get. And we shall not get even these if we stay in the world of men, in the cities where the manias of power, and possessiveness, and cruelty pullulate. So in these novels of her middle years she takes us out to the islands, or into the countryside, or beside the sea, and sets us to watch 'Nature's gentle doings'. She observes, she connects. There is an order. Willows droop over streams, birds in flight make a pattern against the sky. And there is a rhythm. There is first the great sequence of the seasons, imposing itself, willy-nilly, upon the lives of men. And there is the rhythm of man's life itself—childhood, maturity, old age and death. These great facts are easily related to one another and to the non-human world. So why bother to concentrate your attention on the unessentials, the surface of life, money-making, social success, moral codes (she is thinking of the Galsworthys and the Bennetts) when you have these deeper tracts to deal with?

One is reminded of the parallel instance of William and Dorothy Wordsworth. It is when he is sickened by the failure of the French Revolution and has 'given up moral questions in despair' that Wordsworth turns to the quiet observation of nature, under the guidance of his sister. 'She gave me eyes, she gave me ears.' In the majestic forms of mountains, in the quiet of the lakes, he found that dignity and order which eluded him in the world of men. Then, gradually, he began to build up his own world of men to fit in with the mountains; and he took the people who were on the spot: the lakeland shepherds. He never came very directly into contact with them, and so he was able to idealise them and to 'naturalise' them—to make them rather more like rocks and trees than they really were. Dorothy never does this: her observation is much purer than William's; she doesn't contaminate it by moralising. She gives you the thing seen—and how vividly seen!—for its own sake. William was too soon to take up again the moral questions he had abandoned in despair; he was not content to observe and to enjoy. Coleridge expects him to write a long philosophical poem; he must penetrate more deeply into the life of things, and find hidden there the doctrines of Hartley and Godwin.

Mrs Woolf is saved from this danger by the non-moral character of the age she lives in. The writer is no longer expected to find a spiritual purpose in nature. Darwin has replaced the idea of a moral order by that of an evolutionary process. Moreover (and perhaps this is still more important) she is a novelist, not a poet. Her business is with character and incident. She need not have a message. Fielding and Jane Austen had none; and if Dickens and Meredith had, some people think it spoiled their power as novelists. She can use nature as background, if she wants, as they did in the eighteenth century, and nobody is going to scold her. She needn't be solemn and Wordsworthian about mountains and fields. She can use them in a decorative way, she can even be witty about them. She can show them up. An enormous range of possibilities is open to her.

What she does, in fact, is choose the Wordsworthian approach with a bias to its Dorothy side. She observes, reports, connects, but she doesn't moralise. Wordsworth falsified his fine intuitions of 'the life of things' by reading into them his own ethical prejudices and those of his age. Thus, when reading him, we are constantly coming bump against a hard knot of moralising in the midst of his finest passages of insight; or else we unexpectedly find ourselves caught up into the seventh heaven after page upon page of tedious preaching. Dorothy doesn't give us the splendid flights, but she doesn't bore us either. Moreover, she has a more real interest in human beings as individuals, not in 'the still sad music of humanity', but in the immediate misery of the beggars and gipsies who passed her cottage door. Mrs Woolf has noted this with approval in her essay on Dorothy Wordsworth in the second *Common Reader*. Dorothy had an eye for the unusual in human beings, she had an ear for the striking phrase. And for these we turn to her journal when her brother's sublimities are tiring us a little.

In her use of the external world as an ingredient of the novel, Virginia Woolf introduces neither sublimities nor moralisings. The essence of the sublime is that the mind of the observer should be dominated, overborne, enslaved to the thing seen.

There is nothing of this in the novels. There is observation, enquiry (has this any meaning? she asks), and an attempt to connect. Let us look at these three ingredients in turn.

First, the observation. This is perhaps what strikes the reader most when he comes fresh to Virginia Woolf. How clearly she sees! with what minuteness of detail, and with what enjoyment of the simple act of looking! Yet is it so simple after all? Why can't we look and see like that? After a time we come to ask this question, and the answer is interesting. We see that for Mrs Woolf nothing is allowed to come between her and the object. All complications have been swept away for the moment of seeing. The mind behind the eye has become the child mind. It is interested in the thing in itself, in its attractions of colour and shape. But it differs from the child mind in that it doesn't want to own the things it sees. It escapes 'the deformation which is possession'. It is contented to look and enjoy. The child stretches out its hands to the moon. The poet folds his hands. And this, we may say, is the one reward of experience. Life heaps up in our minds a lot of rubbish, we become entangled with emotions and passions and ambitions, and most of us get mixed up with possessions. But a few of us, the wise ones, learn the art of freedom, and drop the habit of wanting and owning.

At the moment of seeing, then, the mind asks nothing better than to observe and enjoy. This is sufficient in itself to bring 'an extraordinary happiness'. That things exist, that their appearances are so various and so interesting, and that one is privileged to stand and stare at them—isn't this enough? Certainly Mrs Woolf makes us think so: and in many a passage of the novels the intensity of her emotion is such that she is able, by means of a very adequate technique, to convey to us something of the same emotion. More than that: she makes us put the book down, get up from our chairs, and go to the window. Yes, that is what the world is like—'so various, so beautiful, so new'. How is it that we had not seen it like that before? We feel that we have been made free of a new order of experience. And this, I repeat, is Mrs Woolf's greatest virtue, in the long run: to make us see common things more clearly and intensely. In the long run, it doesn't matter so much whether we agree with her taste in characters, or find her hesitant philosophy satisfactory—we all have to build our own, anyway. But the world she looks at is our world too.

Various, beautiful and new—but also, and in equal proportion, Mrs Woolf shows us, cruel, unpleasant and strange. She reports 'a snail shell, rising in the grass like a grey cathedral, a swelling building burnt with dark rings and shadowed green by the grass'; she also reports 'yellow excretions exuded by slugs', and 'drops forming on the bloated sides of swollen things'. The two exist side by side. She reports with the impartiality of a Thoreau; but does she delight, as he seemed to delight, in these starker manifestations of life? One remembers the gusto with which he tells of a beaver full of maggots, and a turtle with its inside eaten out. Plainly she does not revel in this ugliness and savagery. But we are assured that she is not a sentimentalist, she will not falsify her vision or leave anything out. That is important, for half the trouble about letting oneself be carried away by the spell that Wordsworth or Keats weaves is that one is always interrupting with a "Yes, but . . ." Mrs Woolf does not let us down in that way.

vii

No, it is she herself who is let down, who comes, in the end, to see that the terrible dilemma, the conflict, is inherent in the nature of things. Every value collapses. Over against the human values of love, friendship, thought, kindness, she has seen the huge bulk of Society, an inhuman monster devouring the wise and the good. She has thought to fly for healing to the 'calm oblivious tendencies' of nature, to the life of things: and there too she has found cruelty enthroned. She is too wise to try to make a philosophy out of the fleeting 'moments of being' that have come to her in the fields and by the sea-shore. They are too discrete, too contradictory. And they may come just as persuasively in a London 'bus. In fact, she grows to see that while *things* may give human beings the insight into order, they cannot give them the pattern itself. That has to be created by human effort. If there is a meaning, it has to be worked out by human skill and good will. Reality is not immanent, but emergent. The great human activities, the solitary student distilling truth, the courage of the explorer, the radiance of the family circle: these still remain as the crown of life. And if men show these qualities, if through the long human centuries these activities have existed, why, she cries, why do I look around me and still see wars, famine and torture?

What is the canker at the heart of society?

Her considered answer to this question comes in *Three Guineas* (1938). The book is an overflow from *The Years*; it treats the themes of that novel in their sternest form, without admixture of humour, or imagination, or tolerance. It is the hardest of all Virginia Woolf's books to read, because it is so uncompromising. The creator's wand has become the surgeon's scalpel. For the time is late, the disease far advanced. 'The black night that now covers Europe', the night which has already blotted out so much pity, and beauty, and civilisation: this is her theme. And she pursues it from its overt form in international politics into its concealed forms in English society and in the human heart.

She shows us two pictures. The first comes at the beginning of the book. It is a photograph from Spain, a collection of photographs. They come every week, by the post.

> They are not pleasant photographs to look upon. They are photographs of dead bodies for the most part. This morning's collection contains the photograph of what might be a man's body, or a woman's; it is so mutilated that it might, on the other hand, be the body of a pig. But those certainly are dead children, and that undoubtedly is the section of a house. A bomb has torn open the side; there is still a bird-cage hanging in what was presumably the sitting-room, but the rest of the house looks like nothing so much as a bunch of spillikins suspended in mid air.

The second photograph she shows us at the end of the book. But in the subject of the second photograph we recognise the cause of the first.

> It is the figure of a man; some say, others deny, that he is Man himself, the quintessence of virility, the perfect type of which all the others are imperfect adumbrations. He is a man certainly. His eyes are glazed; his eyes glare. His body, which is braced in an unnatural position, is tightly cased in a uniform. Upon the breast of that uniform are sewn several medals and other mystic symbols. His hand is upon a sword. He is called in German and Italian Führer or Duce; in our language Tyrant or Dictator. And behind him lie ruined houses and dead bodies—men, women and children.

And now, she asks (and this is the great question of the book), how has this figure, unnatural and glaring, arisen? how has it managed to impose itself on millions of people, after three thousand years of civilisation?

She replies that it has always been there—in the patriarchal system, in the very framework of society. The force that subdued Antigone and shut her up living in the tomb is the same force that held Elizabeth Barrett prisoner in a sick-room and forbade Sophia Jex-Blake to earn her own living. She has shown this same force at work in *The Years*: the tyrant in the home. 'There we have in embryo the creature, Dictator as we call him when he is Italian or German, who believes that he has the right, whether given by God, Nature, sex or race is immaterial, to dictate to other human beings how they shall live; what they shall do.' And the women who fought against that tyranny were the advance guard of the fight against Fascism. They were the allies of the men of good will who in the present day are fighting tyranny in the international sphere.

> The daughters of educated men who were called, to their resentment, 'feminists' were in fact the advance guard of your own movement. They were fighting the same enemy that you are fighting and for the same reasons. They were fighting the tyranny of the patriarchal state as you are fighting the tyranny of the Fascist state. Thus we are merely carrying on the same fight that our mothers and grandmothers fought; their words prove it; your words prove it. But now with your letter before us we have your assurance that you are fighting with us, not against us. . . . Abroad the monster has come more openly to the surface. There is no mistaking him there. He has widened his scope. He is interfering now with your liberty; he is dictating how you shall live; he is making distinctions not merely between the sexes, but between the races. You are feeling in your own persons what your mothers felt when they were shut out, when they were shut up, because they were women. Now you are being shut out, you are being shut up, because you are Jews, because you are democrats, because of race, because of religion.

If dictatorship is to be fought, then, it must be fought first of all at home. Injustice cannot be fought with injustice, force with force. That is her thesis. It must be fought first in the private house. 'The fear which forbids freedom in the private house . . . is connected with the other fear, the public fear . . .' A woman who is looking after a house and family, who is bearing children, has a right to a private income: she must not be dependent on her husband's generosity. Her profession is a valuable one to the State. It must be fought too in the professions. Equal services are entitled to equal wages, whatever the sex of the person who renders them. It must be fought in the Universities. Women are still excluded from membership of the University of Cambridge [1]; their numbers at Girton and Newnham are rigidly restricted by university statute; they are given only the 'titles' of degrees. The battle has not yet been won, not by a long way.

And what, she asks, is the root of this injustice? The answer is, Fear. The fear of being dispossessed from an age-long position of superiority. It has become necessary to man's self-esteem to possess a mirror in which his glory may be reflected, an inferior province of humanity over which he can rule. Hence the opposition to every effort women have made to educate themselves, to make themselves independent. Women have been starved of education so that their brothers might go to Oxford and Cambridge, to Eton and Winchester. They have been starved of freedom and money. Heavy fathers have frowned on their efforts to achieve independence; even, sometimes, on their desire to marry. For domination and possessiveness are integral qualities of the masculine mind. 'What we have we hold.'

Virginia Woolf, we learn, has received a letter. She has left it unanswered for over three years. 'But there it is with its question—How in your opinion are we to prevent war?' She is not acquainted with the writer: it is a circular letter, it seems; and that makes it all the harder to answer. One thing is certain: the writer is a man; she is a woman. Can her answer, then, be of much value? For it is from a woman's standpoint that she must answer, if at all. And she must point to the qualities in the masculine character which, while they remain uncorrected, seem to her to make war inevitable. There follows a searching diagnosis.

In the first place, the male love of fighting. This is incomprehensible to a woman. 'Here . . . are three reasons which lead your sex to fight; war is a profession; a source of happiness and excitement; and it is also an outlet for manly qualities, without which men would deteriorate.' She quotes Mussolini, she

[1] This anomaly is now (1947) on the eve of being rectified.

quotes Hitler. But there are dissentient voices too, even from men. Wilfred Owen, who was killed in the First World War, thinks fighting unnatural, inhuman, insupportable, horrible, beastly and foolish.

Then there is patriotism, which exalts England above every other country, which identifies the pride and prestige of the individual with the pride and prestige of the fatherland. How can a woman feel that emotion? Is she a daughter of England? She has only recently acquired the vote, at the expense of what blood and tears; she has no property; she has no education and her earning powers are unnaturally restricted. Patriotism is for her an unreal loyalty.

She has no place in the world of professional life. And what a strange world that is!

Your world, then, the world of professional, of public life, seen from this angle undoubtedly looks queer. At first sight it is enormously impressive. Within quite a small space are crowded together St Paul's, the Bank of England, the Mansion House, the massive if funereal battlements of the Law Courts; and on the other side, Westminster Abbey and the Houses of Parliament. There, we say to ourselves, pausing, in this moment of transition on the bridge, our fathers and brothers have spent their lives. All these hundreds of years they have been mounting those steps, passing in and out of those doors, ascending those pulpits, preaching, money-making, administering justice. It is from this world that the private house (somewhere, roughly speaking, in the West End) has derived its creeds, its laws, its clothes and carpets, its beef and mutton. And then, as is now permissible, cautiously pushing aside the swing doors of one of these temples, we enter on tiptoe and survey the scene in greater detail. The first sensation of colossal size, of majestic masonry is broken up into a myriad points of amazement mixed with interrogation. Your clothes in the first place make us gape with astonishment. How many, how splendid, how extremely ornate they are—the clothes worn by the educated man in his public capacity! Now you dress in violet; a jewelled crucifix swings on your breast; now your shoulders are covered with lace; now furred with ermine; now slung with many linked chains set with precious stones. Now you wear wigs on your heads; rows of graduated curls descend to your necks. Now your hats are boat-shaped, or cocked; now they mount in cones of black fur; now they are made of brass and scuttle-shaped; now plumes of red, now of blue hair surmount them . . .

With her pungent satire she is pricking the bubble of male display. But not for amusement: there is a serious purpose behind it. Virginia Woolf ponders the reason for this display. In woman variety and colourfulness and beauty of dress are easily explained: they 'create beauty for the eye, and attract the admiration of your sex. Since marriage until the year 1919—less than twenty years ago—was the only profession open to us, the enormous importance of dress to a woman can hardly be exaggerated'. But in men gorgeousness of dress is an advertisement. 'It serves to advertise the social, professional, or intellectual standing of the wearer.' Or again, it glorifies the great profession of war. 'Your finest clothes are those you wear as soldiers. Since the red and the gold, the brass and the feathers are discarded upon active service, it is plain that their expensive and not, one might suppose, hygienic splendour is invented partly in order to impress the beholder with the majesty of the military office, partly in order through their vanity to induce young men to become soldiers.' Thus in the soldier dress is used to advertise war; in the professional man to advertise rank and distinction. The one use is immediately, the other more remotely connected with hatred and violence. For by advertising his superiority, the professional man emphasises the inferiority of others. He fosters the emotions of pride, arrogance, competition, jealousy, hatred and fear. He makes division among men.

Another letter lies on Mrs Woolf's table. It comes from the honorary treasurer of a women's college, asking for a subscription towards rebuilding. What can the answer be? If it is to the qualities of hatred and violence that education leads, then that education must be altered. There must be no subscription unless a promise is given that education will be reformed. 'Since history and biography . . . seem to prove that the old education of the old colleges breeds neither a particular respect for liberty nor a particular hatred of war it is clear that you must rebuild your college differently.'

It must be an experimental college, an adventurous college. Let it be built on lines of its own. It must be built not of carved stone and stained glass, but of some cheap, easily combustible material which does not hoard dust and perpetuate traditions. Do not have chapels. Do not have museums and libraries with chained books and first editions under glass cases. Let the pictures and the books be new and always changing. Let it be decorated afresh by each generation with their own hands cheaply. The work of the living is cheap; often they will give it for the sake of being allowed to do it. Next, what should be taught in the new college, the poor college? Not the arts of dominating other people; not the arts of ruling, of killing, of acquiring land and capital. They require too many overhead expenses; salaries and uniforms and ceremonies. The poor college must teach only the arts that can be taught cheaply and practised by poor people; such as medicine, mathematics, music, painting and literature. It should teach the arts of human intercourse; the art of understanding other people's lives and minds, and the little arts of talk, of dress, of cookery that are allied with them. The aim of the new college, the cheap college, should be not to segregate and specialise, but to combine. It should explore the ways in which mind and body can be made to co-operate; discover what new combinations make good wholes in human life.

The importance of this statement on education can hardly be exaggerated: it sums up all the scattered dicta we have found in Virginia Woolf's novels, and it indicates a new hope for the future. Education is to be restricted to the essentials, and focused upon the arts of living. This statement, in its context, calls for reading and re-reading. It is unnecessary to comment on it, for its implications are crystal-clear. It is the first constructive suggestion in the book: a suggestion towards a cure of the disease which is afflicting society in the twentieth century; which is still, and even more urgently after the Second World War, afflicting society. But who will have the courage to build the new college, the poor college?

Who, indeed? Virginia Woolf does not shut her eyes to the hard facts. What influence women have today is dependent on their power to earn their own living; and that power is dependent on their learning the kind of subjects that are commercially profitable in the modern world, and on their flaunting the qualifications which universities have to give. Therefore the new college cannot come into being at once. There must be a compromise. The daughters of educated men cannot ask any sacrifice of their sisters who are in process of being educated.

It appears that we can ask them to do nothing; they must follow the old road to the old end; our own influence as outsiders can only be of the most indirect sort. If we are asked to teach, we can examine very carefully into the aim of such teaching, and refuse to teach any art or science that encourages war. Further, we can pour mild scorn upon chapels, upon degrees, and upon the value of examinations. . . . And, of course, if we are offered offices and honours for ourselves we can refuse them—how, indeed, in view of the facts, could we possibly do otherwise?

This is the first suggestion towards the prevention of war. Is there anything more that women can do? Cannot they work through the professions? 'Our only weapon,' she ponders, is 'the weapon of independent opinion based upon independent income'; and that weapon surely they possess, for the professions have been open to women for the past twenty years?

But on examination the facts take on a different aspect. There is a serious discrepancy between the salaries women can expect to earn and those earned by men. There is a serious prejudice against the employment of women at all in the higher branches, say, of the Civil Service. The Church closes her doors. And, more important still, there is an ugly doubt. What will the highly paid professions do to women if ever they get into them? For they too, like the universities, are breeding-grounds of negative emotions. Are we wise 'to encourage people to enter the professions if we wish to prevent war'?

For what are the facts? The first fact is that professional life induces a combative, a competitive spirit. It is a struggle against rivals. For centuries professional men have kept their preserves to themselves, and in particular they have striven to exclude women. 'There was the battle of Westminster. There was the battle of the universities. There was the battle of Whitehall. There was the battle of Harley Street. There was the battle of the Royal Academy. Some of these battles, as you can testify, are still in progress.' Do we want women to acquire these combative qualities which lead to war?

Then, again, there is the question of the handsome incomes which attach to successful professional life. It seems unlikely, but it is possible, that one day women may be earning salaries of a thousand, two thousand, even three thousand a year.

In short, we may change our position from being the victims of the patriarchal system, paid on the truck system, with £30 or £40 a year in cash and board and lodging thrown in, to being the champions of the capitalist system, with a yearly income in our own possession of many thousands which, by judicious investment, may leave us when we die possessed of a capital sum of more millions than we can count.

Is this a desirable prospect? 'A great authority upon human life, you will remember, held over two thousand years ago that great possessions were undesirable.' Moreover, to make all that money women will have to accept the same conditions of labour as men: they will have to shut their eyes to the sun and moon, stop looking at the apple-blossom in spring, leave the house at nine and come back to it at six—and do a great deal of overtime into the bargain. Life, in fact, will cease to be living and become money-making: nothing else. There will be certain ceremonies to be observed, certain loyalties to be professed. These facts, then,

> cause us to doubt and criticise and question the value of professional life—not its cash value; that is great; but its spiritual, its moral, its intellectual value. They make us of the opinion that if people are highly successful in their professions they lose their senses. Sight goes. They have no time to look at pictures. Sound goes. They have no time to listen to music. Speech goes. They have no time for conversation. They lose their sense of proportion—the relations between one thing and another. Humanity goes. Money making becomes so important that they must work by night as well as by day. Health goes. And so competitive do they become that they will not share their work with others though they have more than they can do themselves. What then remains of a human being who has lost sight, and sound, and sense of proportion? Only a cripple in a cave.

It is a terrible, a biting indictment. For to these professional men, to these moral and intellectual cripples, nations entrust their fortunes, their very lives and happiness. To have made money is considered as in itself excellent, and as fitting the maker for the highest offices in the State. To these men without a sense of humanity or proportion are entrusted the delicate tasks of diplomacy. Thus through the professions, as through the universities, human values are upset and the negative emotions flourish. That is the dilemma.

> Behind us lies the patriarchal system; the private house, with its nullity, its immorality, its hypocrisy, its servility. Before us lies the public world, the professional system, with its possessiveness, its jealousy, its pugnacity, its greed. The one shuts us up like slaves in a harem; the other forces us to circle, like caterpillars head to tail, round and round the mulberry tree, the sacred tree, of property. It is the choice of evils. Each is bad. Had we not better plunge off the bridge into the river; give up the game; declare that the whole of human life is a mistake and so end it?

What is the solution to the dilemma? Enter the professions women certainly must, for on their economic independence rest their freedom and their influence to effect events, such as it is. But they must enter on their own terms, as 'civilised human beings', not as haters, money-grubbers and loyalty-mongers. They must refuse to exclude others from their own privileges; they must keep 'free from unreal loyalties'; they must not earn a penny more than is sufficient to be independent, healthy, leisured and civilised; they must refuse to sell their brains for money, that is, do work they are not interested in for financial profit; they must pour scorn on advertisement, badges, orders and degrees.

> If you agree to these terms then you can join the professions and yet remain uncontaminated by them; you can rid them of their possessiveness, their jealousy, their pugnacity, their greed. You can use them to have a mind of your own and a will of your own. And you can use that mind and will to abolish the in-humanity, the beastliness, the horror, the folly of war.

Here, then, is the second constructive proposal that Virginia Woolf has made. Again it is perfectly straightforward; and it is easier to carry into effect than the first. For it depends on the individual conscience. We can see that it is a moral, even a religious proposal. It implies the doctrine of Jesus. Great possessions are evil, and engender evil. Life is more than riches. Brotherhood means the sharing of opportunities. Men and women find their true nature in this sharing, this sense of proportion which leads them to live in the present moment with all the intensity the present moment can bring, in the simplicity and variety of life.

The first letter, asking for subscriptions, had also invited Mrs Woolf to join a certain society whose aims were peace and liberty. Shall she do so? At first sight the answer seems obvious. She, like them, is in support of these aims. But what of the means? She hasn't a man's belief in societies, and discussions, and committees. Is it likely that any society will succeed now in doing what Oxford and Cambridge have failed to do after seven hundred years? The influence of a woman within any male society would be negligible. Women are not counted fit to teach in public schools.

> For us to attempt to reform the education of our brothers at public schools and universities would be to invite a shower of dead cats, rotten eggs and broken gates from which only street

scavengers and locksmiths would benefit, while the gentlemen in authority, history assures us, would survey the tumult from their study windows without taking the cigars from their lips or ceasing to sip, slowly as its bouquet deserves, their admirable claret.

The sarcasm is bitter; but, surely, merited. The universities, which might be expected, if any society may be expected, to uphold liberty and culture, are notably hotbeds of advertisement, intrigue, monopoly and hatred. Is it likely that any other male society will be free of these things? No, the contribution of women to the fight for culture and intellectual liberty must be something apart. 'We can only help you to defend culture and intellectual liberty by defending our own culture and our own intellectual liberty.' Women must refuse to write for the sake of money. They must not commit 'adultery of the brain'.

Money is not the only baser ingredient. Advertisement and publicity are also adulterers. Thus, culture mixed with personal charm, or culture mixed with advertisement and publicity, are also adulterated forms of culture. We must ask you to abjure them; not to appear on public platforms; not to lecture; not to allow your private face to be published, or details of your private life; not to avail yourself, in short, of any of the forms of brain prostitution which are so insidiously suggested by the pimps and panders of the brain-selling trade; or to accept any of those baubles and labels by which brain merit is advertised and certified —medals, honours, degrees—we must ask you to refuse them absolutely, since they are all tokens that culture has been prostituted and intellectual liberty sold into captivity.

And thus she comes to make her third constructive proposal, which she calls the Outsiders' Society. A society of women, 'without office, meetings, leaders or any hierarchy, without so much as a form to be filled up, or a secretary to be paid'. A society of private individuals, working for liberty and against war in divers ways. Partly by abstaining: by refusing to attend lectures that prostitute culture; by not subscribing to papers that encourage intellectual slavery; by showing indifference to appeals to patriotic emotion. 'For psychology would seem to show that it is far harder for human beings to take action when other people are indifferent and allow them complete freedom of action, than when their actions are made the centre of excited emotion. The small boy struts and trumpets outside the window; implore him to stop: he goes on; say nothing: he stops. That the daughters of educated men then should give their brothers neither the white feather of cowardice nor the red feather of courage, but no feather at all; that they should shut the bright eyes that rain influence, or let those eyes look elsewhere when war is discussed—that is the duty to which outsiders will train themselves in peace before the threat of death inevitably makes reason powerless.'

Partly, of course, by action. There is the private printing press: why not use it to distribute propaganda? Or get a room and speak the truth about pictures, books and music—for this is defending intellectual liberty too. Deflate patriotism by comparing English music with German music, English painting with Italian painting. Press for a living wage in the professions now open to women: including the professions of marriage and motherhood. The Outsiders should also 'bind themselves to obtain full knowledge of professional practices, and to reveal any instance of tyranny or abuse in their professions'.

They would be creative in their activities, not merely critical. By criticising education they would help to create a civilised society which protects culture and intellectual liberty. By criticising religion they would attempt to free the religious spirit from its present servitude, and would help, if need be, to create a new religion based, it might well be, upon the New Testament, but, it might well be, very different from the religion now erected upon that basis.

And in all this they would be helped by their obscurity, by not belonging to any overt society. Secrecy is essential. There will be no pageantry, no personal distinctions. The human mind needs darkness if it is to create and to move into new paths. Obscurity and integrity live together, and it is in the darkness that the seed germinates. In the darkness, too, are to be found the roots of 'a unity that rubs out divisions as if they were chalk marks only', and the springs of 'the capacity of the human spirit to overflow boundaries and make unity out of multiplicity'.

It is a sombre book, this *Three Guineas*. But it is, in its own way, a great book. It is full of a massive integrity. 'Not here, O Apollo, are haunts fit for thee'; not in these pages does Virginia Woolf give us her glimpses of the life of things, or of music, or of friendship. She has come, here, face to face with horror: the photographs from Spain will not be expunged from her mind. She sets her frail but steadfast vision of reality against the lie of society; and in the end, for that vision, she was content to die. By death she set the seal on the sincerity of her vision.

CHAPTER XIV

Between the Acts

[1941]

WHATEVER the *mise en scène* of Virginia Woolf's novels, the sea is never far distant. The sea is the great renewer, the source of life, the cleanser flowing over white bare sands. It is, considered under its aspect of vastness and homogeneity, the image of eternity and of unity. Considered as a concourse of waves ever arising and ever disappearing, it is the image of change and diversity. Thus it is Mrs Woolf's most permanent image: for her thought, as we have seen, is constantly occupied with the problem of the One and the Many. We have traced in these pages the progress of her search for a unifying talisman. We have seen her weighing the claims of love, of family life, of thought, of art, of solitude. And we have seen each of these things fail her, shattered by two overwhelming forces: the irreducible alogicality of the universe, and the incorrigible unreasonableness of society.

In the end she sets aside the glimpses of unity which have been brought to her in 'moments of being'. On these glimpses, contradicted as they are by every brute fact, she cannot build a philosophy. Her vision has pointed her to Monism: her observation binds her down to Pluralism. The universe is a manifold of separate events, suggesting discrete and disparate values. There is no connecting link. 'Only connect' can no longer be the watchword: 'only accept' must be put in its place. And thus the virtue of tolerance, which has always stood high in her scheme of morality, now takes the highest place. There are many worlds. We must learn to accept and value them all. And individuals contain highly contradictory worlds within themselves. We must try not to oversimplify. In the end we may establish a new sort of connection, based not on unity but on the acceptance of diversity.

In *Between the Acts*, the sea divides and isolates. They are talking about it early in the book. Isa is speaking.

"Are we really," she said, turning round, "a hundred miles from the sea?"

"Thirty-five only," her father-in-law said, as if he had whipped a tape-measure from his pocket and measured it exactly.

"It seems more," said Isa. "It seems from the terrace as if the land went on for ever and ever."

"Once there was no sea," said Mrs Swithin. "No sea at all between us and the continent. I was reading that in a book this morning. There were rhododendrons in the Strand; and mammoths in Piccadilly."

Mrs Swithin is an older, a more tired Mrs Ramsay; with all Mrs Ramsay's courage and genius for understanding and tolerance. But she has something which Mrs Ramsay hasn't got: religion. Here Virginia Woolf is making her own effort at understanding. To her, Mrs Swithin's creator, religion means nothing, or something unpleasant, as we have seen. But she has come to see that there are people, good and understanding people, to whom religion does mean something. And now she accepts this. Now, without satire or bitterness, she puts Mrs Swithin, with her gold crucifix and her prayers, in the centre of the picture.

Mrs Swithin has courage. When her brother, Mr Oliver of the Indian Civil Service, retired, attacks her faith, she does not lose heart. The situation is curiously repeated from *To the Lighthouse*.

"It's very unsettled. It'll rain, I'm afraid. We can only pray," she added, and fingered her crucifix.

"And provide umbrellas," said her brother.

Lucy flushed. He had struck her faith. When she said "pray", he added "umbrellas". She half covered the cross with her fingers. She shrank; she cowered; but next moment she exclaimed:

"Oh there they are—the darlings!"

The perambulator was passing across the lawn.

Isa looked too. What an angel she was—the old woman! Thus to salute the children; to beat up against those immensities and the old man's irreverences her skinny hands, her laughing eyes! How courageous to defy Bart and the weather!

Bart, Mr Oliver, is the destructive type in contrast to his sister Lucy. Like Ramsay in *To the Lighthouse*, he is incapable of entering the world of the child. There is a lovely picture at the beginning of the book showing that world: George, Isa's little boy, bending over a hollow of wild flowers, and apprehending form and colour and texture as a perfect unity.

George grubbed. The flower blazed between the angles of the roots. Membrane after membrane was torn. It blazed a soft yellow, a lambent light under a film of velvet; it filled the caverns behind the eyes with light. All that inner darkness became a hall, leaf smelling, earth smelling of yellow light. And the tree was beyond the flower; the grass, the flower and the tree were entire. Down on his knees grubbing he held the flower complete. Then there was a roar and a hot breath and a stream of coarse grey hair rushed between him and the flower. Up he leapt, toppling in his fright, and saw coming towards him a terrible peaked eyeless monster moving on legs, brandishing arms.

"Good morning, sir," a hollow voice boomed at him from a beak of paper.

The old man had sprung upon him from his hiding-place behind a tree.

The child's world, as significant to him as the world of *The Times* and memories of India is to the old man, has been wantonly destroyed. Staggered by the shock, he bursts into tears. The old man walks on disgruntled, muttering "Cry-baby!" There is no effort at understanding. The two worlds have met and collided: George's real world of beauty, and Bart's imaginary world of how small boys should be amused and delighted by their grandfathers dressed up as demons.

Yet this old man, so obtuse in one direction, can be most delicately perceptive in another. Miss La Trobe has organised and produced her pageant: no one has understood what she has been trying to say. Certainly not Mrs Swithin. But in the kindness of her heart she wishes to thank her.

"Oughtn't we to thank her?" Lucy asked him. She gave him a light pat on the arm.

How imperceptive her religion made her! The fumes of that incense obscured the human heart. Skimming the surface, she ignored the battle in the mud. After La Trobe had been excruciated by the Rector's interpretation, by the maulings and the manglings of the actors . . . "She don't want our thanks, Lucy," he said gruffly. What she wanted, like that carp (something moved in the water) was darkness in the mud; a whisky and soda at the pub; and coarse words descending like maggots through the waters.

That is real understanding; as real, in its way, as the understanding Mrs Swithin gives earlier in the day to the unfortunate homosexual William Dodge. Like Mrs Ramsay, she is a healer.

He saw her eyes only. And he wished to kneel before her, to kiss her hand, and to say: "At school they held me under a bucket of dirty water, Mrs Swithin; when I looked up, the world was dirty, Mrs Swithin; so I married; but my child's not my child, Mrs Swithin. I'm a half-man, Mrs Swithin; a flickering, mind-divided little snake in the grass, Mrs Swithin; as Giles saw; but you've healed me . . ."

These are a few of the worlds contained within the microcosm of *Between the Acts*; but there are others, and within the limits of a single June day in 1939 we are shown these several worlds meeting but never uniting, while behind it all is the horror of the dark night that covers Europe. There are the worlds of the separate individuals, and the separate worlds inside those individuals. There are the several worlds within Pointz Hall itself: the drawing-room, the kitchen, the barn, the garden, the lily-pond. The cowman, Bond, 'thought very little of anybody, simples or gentry. Leaning, silent, sardonic, against the door he was like a withered willow, bent over a stream, all its leaves shed, and in his eyes the whimsical flow of the waters'. Lucy may be Mrs Swithin in the drawing-room, but she is Old Flimsy to the servants in the kitchen, a figure of fun. Miss La Trobe, the would-be creator of a unified vision (in whom we see something of an autobiographical caricature), is called Bossy in the bar parlour of the village pub. She goes there for her drink, but sits apart. The two worlds do not mingle. The Rev. G. W. Streatfield is 'ignored by the cows, condemned by the clouds which continued their majestic rearrangement of the celestial landscape; an irrelevant forked stake in the flow and majesty of the summer silent world'.

The diversity of ideas, the multiplicity of worlds within a single mind is stressed again and again. Candish, the servant, 'loved flowers, and arranging them, and placing the green sword or heart shaped leaf that came, fitly, between them. Queerly, he loved them, considering his gambling and drinking'. We must not expect people to be consistent. Ideas melt imperceptibly into one another. 'Why's stale bread, she mused, easier to cut than fresh? And so skipped, sidelong, from yeast to alcohol; so to fermentation; so to inebriation; so to Bacchus; and lay under purple lamps in a vineyard in Italy, as she had done, often . . .' Incongruous ideas are juxtaposed. 'It was a summer's night and they were talking, in the big room with the windows open to the garden, about the cesspool'—such are the book's opening words. The pattern of the book, then, is to be allowed to form itself as far as possible; there is to be no set symbol around which the various ideas shall group themselves. And, in fact, *Between the Acts* does give us more an impression of impromptu than any other of the novels. It seems to have grown with perfect naturalness from a single mood of the author's, a mood which though single held within itself the greatest diversity and fluidity of ideas. The struggle for unity is abandoned.

The seekers for unity within the story itself are mildly satirised. Mrs Swithin is one, of course. Her brother, Bart, watches her as she sits listening to waltz music. 'She was thinking, he supposed, God is peace. God is love. For she belonged to the unifiers; he to the separatists.' And later, during the pageant, when they are waiting between the acts:

> Mrs Swithin caressed her cross. She gazed vaguely at the view. She was off, they guessed, on a circular tour of the imagination— one-making. Sheep, cows, grass, trees, ourselves—all are one. If discordant, producing harmony—if not to us, to a gigantic ear attached to a gigantic head. And thus—she was smiling benignly —the agony of the particular sheep, cow, or human being is necessary; and so—she was beaming seraphically at the gilt vane in the distance—we reach the conclusion that *all* is harmony, could we hear it. And we shall.

It is the attitude that Virginia Woolf has always hated: the ability to close the eyes to unpleasant truths, to believe what we want to believe; but now she does not hate the person. Mrs Swithin remains admirable and lovable.

This 'one-making', the disease of the congenital monists, affects Isa, old Mr Oliver's daughter-in-law, as well. She too is a curious mixture. She feels a violent sensual passion for a gentleman farmer, Rupert Haines, though they have scarcely had a word together. 'She had met him at a Bazaar; and at a tennis party. He had handed her a cup and a racquet—that was all. But in his ravaged face she always felt mystery; and in his silence, passion.' This crude Ethel M. Dell emotion persists in her consciousness along with the most perfectly civilised feelings—feelings which Virginia Woolf herself admires supremely. When old Bart tells her how little George cried when he sprang out upon him, she frowned. He was not a coward, her boy wasn't. And she loathed the domestic, the possessive; the maternal. And he knew it, and did it on purpose to tease her, the old brute, her father-in-law.

That is all. Yet she too, tormented by her love for Haines, longs for the unchanging land, the abode of unity.

"Where do I wander?" she mused. "Down what draughty tunnels? Where the eyeless wind blows? And there grows nothing for the eye. No rose. To issue where? In some harvestless dim field where no evening lets fall her mantle; nor sun rises. All's equal there. Unblowing, ungrowing are the roses there. Change is not; nor the mutable and lovable; nor greetings nor partings; nor furtive findings and feelings, where hand seeks hand and eye seeks shelter from the eye."

Finally, Miss La Trobe. It is she who organises the pageant, and attempts to give a unity to history, and in the end shows the present time its scattered individualities. She is the queerest mixture of them all. No one knows where she came from; some people suspect she has Russian blood in her veins. There are rumours that she kept a tea-shop in Winchester, that she had been an actress, that she had bought a four-roomed cottage and shared it with an actress, and then quarrelled with her. She strides about the fields with a whip in her hands and uses very strong language. Perhaps she isn't quite a lady. 'At any rate, she has a passion for getting things up.' She produces a pageant of English history: a dramatic version of *Orlando*. While the acting is in progress, all the diverse elements of her audience are held together. This is her triumph. She is creating unity. These are the significant moments of time. But there are the intervals: between the acts. Here the audience falls apart and the individuals lead their own lives. Unity is destroyed, and has to be painfully built up again in the next act.

Now Miss La Trobe stepped from her hiding. Flowing, and streaming, on the grass, on the gravel, still for one moment she held them together—the dispersing company. Hadn't she, for twenty-five minutes, made them see? A vision imparted was relief from agony . . . for one moment . . . one moment. Then the music petered out on the last word *we*. She heard the breeze rustle in the branches. She saw Giles Oliver with his back to the audience. Also Cobbet of Cobbs Corner. She hadn't made them see.

It was a failure, another damned failure! As usual. Her vision escaped her.

It is, of course, the eternal cry of the artist; and we shall not be going far astray in this instance in reading the passage as autobiographical. The life's work of Virginia Woolf was precisely the effort to make people see: to make them see a world of values different from the common values: a world simplified in its human activities, infinitely enriched in its relations with natural things and its adventures of understanding and connecting. And in this effort she felt, in the first years of the war, she had failed. The old unreal complexities, the cherished negative emotions, persisted. There was no hope anywhere at all.

What is the purpose of *Between the Acts*—the idea behind it? Is it an allegory, a tract for the times, a mirror for the age's futility? It seems to be all these. The prevailing sentiment in the book is of impotence and remoteness. Pointz Hall is a backwater, a beautiful old house buried in the heart of England. Beautiful, but what opportunities have been lost in its building! It is in a hollow; it faces north; there is a magnificent terrace, but no one has thought to build on it. Or perhaps someone had, but the idea never came to anything. 'A wall had been built continuing the house, it might be with the intention of adding another wing, on the raised ground in the sun. But funds were lacking; the plan was abandoned, and the wall remained, nothing but a wall.' Then what of the inside of the house? The library, say. 'Books are the mirror of the soul.'

In this case a tarnished, a spotted soul. For as the train took over three hours to reach this remote village in the very heart of England, no one ventured on so long a journey, without staving off possible mind-hunger, without buying a book on a bookstall. Thus the mirror that reflected the soul sublime, reflected also the soul bored. Nobody could pretend, as they looked at the shuffle of shilling shockers that week-enders had dropped, that the looking-glass always reflected the anguish of a Queen or the heroism of King Harry.

The inhabitants of the house too are impotent and remote. Here in the library old Bart comes to nod in the early morning after he has destroyed the little boy's world: he dreams of past greatness, **Imperial greatness,** drowsily seeing as in a glass, its lustre spotted, himself, a young man helmeted; and a cascade falling. But no water; and the hills, like grey stuff pleated; and in the sand a hoop of ribs; a bullock maggot-eaten in the sun; and in the shadow of the rock, savages; and in his hand a gun. The dream hand clenched; the real hand lay on the chair arm, the veins swollen but only with a brownish fluid now.

'Mirror on mirror mirrored is all the scene'—Yeats' line aptly describes the unreal dream-world of this English country house. While old Bart relives his youth in India, his sister loses herself in an Outline of History and watches mastodons demolishing trees 'in the green steaming undergrowth of the primeval forest'. Isa is lost in an unreal dream of love. Her husband, Giles Oliver, was meant for a farmer but finds himself in a stockbroker's office. 'Given his choice, he would have chosen to farm. But he was not given his choice. So one thing led to another; and the conglomeration of things pressed you flat; held you fast, like a fish in water.' And into this world of unreality come the two figures—Mrs Manresa and William Dodges—from the outside world; but that world is also a world of pretence. Mrs Manresa ('lust', as Giles Oliver sums her up) affects to be the 'simple child of nature'; William Dodges ('perversion') has been twisted in his boyhood, and bundled into an office when he should have been an artist. Thus a variety of negative emotions are aroused by the contact: and Miss La Trobe's effort to unite her audience in a single vision is defeated by the powerful subterranean feelings of lust (Isa's for Rupert Haines, Giles's for Mrs Manresa, William's for Giles) and hatred (Giles's for William, Mrs Haines's for Isa) which emerge and triumph in the intervals between the acts.

And all live under the shadow of the future. 'The future shadowed their present, like the sun coming through the many-veined transparent vine leaf; a criss-cross of lines making no pattern.' The future is there in the present. In *The Times* that morning they read of the rape of a girl by the troopers at Whitehall. Europe is being raped by the dictators. As for the English countryside, 'at any moment guns would rake that land into furrows; planes splinter Bolney Minster into smithereens and blast the Folly'.

In spite of these divergences, these impotences and mutters of violence, the book has its form and its unity. It is held together by a 'triple melody': the beauty of the setting—rural England; the quiet coming on of evening as the pageant proceeds; and music itself. Music is the great unifier, but only while the music lasts.

> Music wakes us. Music makes us see the hidden, join the broken. Look and listen. See the flowers, how they ray their redness, whiteness, silverness and blue. And the trees with their many-tongued much syllabling, their green and yellow leaves hustle us and shuffle us, and bid us, like the starlings, and the rooks, come together, crowd together, to chatter and make merry while the red cow moves forward and the black cow stands still.

Or if the music stops, if the villagers' song is inaudible as they pass in and out of the trees in the background, then nature herself steps in and takes a hand in supporting the illusion of unity. There are gaps between the different episodes of each act, and Miss La Trobe is in agony to think that her audience's attention is slipping. 'Then suddenly, as the illusion petered out, the cows took up the burden. One had lost her calf. In the very nick of time she lifted her great moon-eyed head and bellowed. All the great moon-eyed heads laid themselves back. From cow after cow came the same yearning bellow. The whole world was filled with dumb yearning. It was the primeval voice sounding loud in the ear of the present moment. . . . The cows annihilated the gap; bridged the distance; filled the emptiness and continued the emotion.' At yet another point Miss La Trobe is preparing to confront the audience with themselves. She is going to send little imps among them holding up mirrors. She wants to shut out the environment. Here the cows and the trees and the swallows are a nuisance.

> Panic seized her. Blood seemed to pour from her shoes. This is death, death, death, she noted in the margin of her mind; when illusion fails. Unable to lift her hand, she stood facing the audience.
> And then the shower fell, sudden, profuse.
> No one had seen the cloud coming. There it was, black, swollen, on top of them. Down it poured like all the people in the world weeping. Tears. Tears. Tears.

Then it stops. Nature has once more taken Miss La Trobe's part. The illusion is sustained.

Yet it is only an illusion. Mrs Swithin, Bart, Isa, William,

Giles, Mrs Manresa, these are spectators only; an audience looking on at old, forgotten, far-off things. 'This is the burden that the past laid on me, last little donkey in the long caravanserai crossing the desert,' says Isa. Does the way to unity and reality come, then, through throwing away the past, renouncing possessions, as the sages have said? The question presents itself to Isa, as she stands alone, between the acts.

> "It's a good day, some say, the day we are stripped naked. Others, it's the end of the day. They see the Inn and the Inn's keeper. But none speaks with a single voice. None with a voice free from the old vibrations. Always I hear corrupt murmurs; the chink of gold and metal. Mad music . . ."

And in the end she counsels herself ("On, little donkey, patiently stumble") not to hearken to the voices of the leaders who point to a spurious unity, not to shut her eyes to the irreducible diversity and hardness of things.

Between the Acts is the most lyrical of Virginia Woolf's novels. Its prose slips easily into poetry: in parts it *is* poetry, not poetry pretending to be prose. There are Isa Oliver's thoughts; she is a poet, and writes her thoughts down in a little book bound like an accounts book so that her husband won't suspect. There are the verse parts of the pageant script. All this is excitingly experimental. The book has the looser texture which characterises verse. It flows from point to point, it is not built up, it has a natural rather than an artificial rhythm. Of course it lacks the solidity of the great novels: *Mrs Dalloway, To the Lighthouse, The Waves*. In comparison with these, it is slight. The interest is wholly in ideas and atmosphere. There is no depth of characterisation. In spite of their complexity, Mrs Swithin, Mr Oliver, Isa and Miss La Trobe are 'flat' figures. They do not live for us as individuals. It seems as if in *Between the Acts* Mrs Woolf were feeling her way to yet a further development of the novel. In *The Waves* she cut out plot, description, conversation, link-passages; here she is making shift to do without characterisation too. The process is of course in its early stages: we do not see how far it might have been carried, or with what success. But when a master of characterisation like Mrs Woolf gives us figures as flimsy as these we may be assured there is purpose behind it. She is working her way towards the lyrical novel.

We shall never know what the outcome would have been. As on Rachel Vinrace and Jacob Flanders, so too on their creator the curtain falls between the acts: the page is torn across and the story left untold. Behind the lyrical grace of this last novel the dark shadow lies plain enough to be seen.

CHAPTER XV

The Achievement

OF the real achievement of Virginia Woolf's writing it is
hard to speak. Exposition, however subtle, could not do it
justice. It is something felt, something in which the reader steeps
himself as though it were life, something which enters into the
texture of his own life. Perhaps the best thing we can say is
that she achieved in her art what in her metaphysical search
she could not attain: reality. There is an extraordinary richness
and integrity of vision. It all seems to grow, spontaneously, out
of a single moment, around which the quintessence of other
moments is organised with consummate art. Let us put it in
this way: there is no decoration, only organic form. She has
the power which only the greatest artists have, of flowering at
every vital moment into scenes and pictures and images which
not only suggest an amazing richness of experience beneath
them, but also illuminate one another as they stand related in
the novel.

More than that. Her work is a whole, in that each scene and
image is related to other scenes and images throughout all the
novels, and we understand *Jacob's Room* the better for having
read *Between the Acts*, and we see the germ of the later works in
their predecessors. There is an intense feeling of *growth*, like
the atmosphere of a spring day: we can sense the creative
activity working right out beyond the bounds of the novel we
are reading to embody itself in the next. Never do we get the
sense of striving or of poverty. Never does the vision which
worked through her falter in its choice of a direction or a
channel. It is for ever overflowing its banks, but cleanly, not
blurring outlines, for there is already a new mould prepared
for it.

This implies a mastery of form; and that is one of the virtues
which strikes one most forcibly in Virginia Woolf's work. In
spite of the fact that she was experimenting all the time, seeking
to develop her own medium, her own kind of novel-form, she
never hesitates or fumbles. There is development, but each
stage of that development is perfect in its kind, as the egg, the

caterpillar and the butterfly are each perfect in their kind. She likes to draw a steady bounding-line round her *mise en scène*: she groups her characters on an island, in a country house, in a South American town, or in London. Then she sets to work to relate character to character, character to environment, character to the world of things. We see each person through the eyes of the other persons, or from the viewpoint of a snail or a bird; we see their reactions to solitude, and to society; we penetrate into their thoughts and emotions, and build up a world from within outwards. All the time Mrs Woolf is interested in the mind as in itself a creative power, not a mere instrument for sensation and classification. What kind of worlds does it bring into being as it operates on that great unknown which lies 'outside'? What relations have these worlds to 'reality'? How can they be combined to add to the sum of human happiness? And this interest is so unusual in the novel that we might expect, if we were told of it before we had read any of Mrs Woolf's work, that her writing would be vague, inconclusive and formless. But on the contrary we find that the metaphysical interest is embodied in purely human and personal terms, that the bounding-line of art remains unbroken, that the concrete images which are the very stuff of art are never sacrificed to abstraction, but are indeed more in evidence than in the work of such writers as Bennett and Wells. She has chosen for her theme the inner life of the mind—and lo! the outer life of tree and stream, of bird and fish, of meadow and sea-shore crowds in upon her and lends her image after image, a great sparkling many-coloured world of sight and scent and sound and touch. This is the miracle of her work.

'Princes appear to me to be Fools. Houses of Commons and Houses of Lords appear to me to be fools,' wrote William Blake, 'they seem to me to be something Else besides Human Life.' Virginia Woolf was of this opinion also. The romance of big business, the adventure of science, the drama of politics and social reform, as exploited by the Wellses, the Galsworthys, the Bennetts, seemed to her something else besides human life: and human life was her theme. She didn't want to scratch about on the surface, to glue incidents together into plots, and plaster the plots with information and propaganda and prophecy. She wanted to reveal the springs of action, to show men and women living, alone and in society, and dealing with ordinary human things; she wanted to bring in the world of children and the great non-human world too, on equal terms with men and women. She had an original vision of life, or rather a series of original visions, to impart; and for that she had to stand aside from contemporary fiction and create her own form. In that attempt she was magnificently successful.

'Detachment is the supreme necessity for the artist,' she writes. She doesn't mean detachment from life, from men and women. She means detachment from personal prejudices, from personal end-seeking, and from the spirit of the age if that spirit is antagonistic to the kind of creation that the artist is set upon. Personal prejudices: the commitment to a single world-picture, a snug hide-out from the storms of thought; attachment to unreal loyalties; irrational hatreds and affections. Personal end-seeking: the exploitation of one's artistic gifts to make money or gain influence. The spirit of the age: commercialism, the implication that art is a side-line, the growing inhumanity of centralised power, the belief that the group is more important than the individual. And so on. All these considerations weigh heavily upon the writer. He must seek detachment.

That detachment Virginia Woolf attained: and it is no small part of her achievement. From the first we feel that she is writing to fulfil an ideal which exists in her own mind: she is not writing to give vent to some personal grudge, or mania, or to please a party, or to form one of a school, or to make money, or to get fame. Her work is pure expression of an individual vision. And for this reason we feel we can always trust her: we know she will give us nothing but the naked vision, the pure intuition. She will never twist her focus to serve any purpose whatsoever. She has great integrity.

Thus, in writing of *Robinson Crusoe* (and incidentally of Hardy and Proust) she describes the spirit of her own work:

> We have our own vision of the world; we have made it from our own experience and prejudices, and it is therefore bound up with our own vanities and loves. It is impossible not to feel injured and insulted if tricks are played and our private harmony is upset. Thus when *Jude the Obscure* appears or a new volume of Proust, the newspapers are flooded with protests. Major Gibbs of Cheltenham would put a bullet through his head tomorrow if life were as Hardy paints it; Miss Wiggs of Hampstead must protest that though Proust's art is wonderful, the real world, she thanks God,

has nothing in common with the distortions of a perverted French-
man. Both the gentleman and the lady are trying to control the
novelist's perspective so that it shall resemble and reinforce their
own. But the great writer—the Hardy or the Proust—goes on his
way regardless of the rights of private property; by the sweat of
his brow he brings order from chaos; he plants his tree there, and
his man here; he makes the figure of his deity remote or present
as he wills. In masterpieces—books, that is, where the vision is
clear and order has been achieved—he inflicts his own perspective
upon us so severely that as often as not we suffer agonies—our
vanity is injured because our own order is upset; we are afraid
because the old supports are being wrenched from us; and we are
bored—for what pleasure or amusement can be plucked from a
brand new idea? Yet from anger, fear, and boredom a rare and
lasting delight is sometimes born.

As we have seen, it is precisely this altered perspective which
is bestowed on us by Virginia Woolf's writing. She varies the
proportions, man: nature: society, to create new and striking
patterns, to redistribute the points of emphasis, to bring new
relations into view. Sometimes it is the solitary individual, like
Jacob Flanders, who stands out, over against society but clearly
in harmony with natural things; sometimes it is a social group,
Mrs Ramsay and her children, with a perfect relationship to
nature too, but colliding violently with refractory and ego-
centred individuals like Mr Ramsay and Charles Tansley. The
variations are manifold. And always they are related to the
great question: which pattern corresponds most closely to
reality? what is the good life?

In her critical writing her sympathy and admiration go out
most strongly to those novelists who achieve significant variations on the central pattern. She shows us Defoe 'keeping his
own sense of perspective', snubbing our desire for sunsets and
sublimities on the desert island. She shows us Sterne, dis-
appointing still more drastically our conventional value-hunger.
This is a great part of Sterne's fascination for Mrs Woolf. For
he not only revolutionised the form of the novel, and the style,
so that the very processes of thought became transcribed on to
paper: he also turned the hierarchy of themes upside down.

This change in the angle of vision was in itself a daring innova-
tion. Hitherto, the traveller had observed certain laws of proportion and perspective. The Cathedral had always been a vast
building in any book of travels and the man a little figure,

properly diminutive, by its side. But Sterne was quite capable of omitting the Cathedral altogether. A girl with a green satin purse might be much more important than Notre-Dame. For there is, he seems to hint, no universal scale of values. A girl may be more interesting than a cathedral; a dead donkey more instructive than a living philosopher. It is all a question of one's point of view.

Moreover Sterne transfers our interest, she tells us, from the outer to the inner; and this is an even more radical shift. He makes silences speak. 'In this preference for the windings of his own mind to the guide-book and its hammered high road, Sterne is singularly of our own age. In this interest in silence rather than in speech Sterne is the forerunner of the moderns.'

We must look a little more closely at this achievement, which was Mrs Woolf's as well as Sterne's, the transference of interest from the outer to the inner. For in exploring the inner world she made a disturbance of the scale of values there too. In *A Room of One's Own* she divides novelists into naturalists and contemplatives. In another essay, on the writings of E. M. Forster, she makes a different classification: the preachers and the pure artists. It is easy to see that Virginia Woolf is not a preacher, and that she is a pure artist. But how are we to place her in the first classification? Is she a naturalist or a contemplative? Something of both, I think. She observes new facts, and old facts in a new way; but she also combines them, through the contemplative act, into new and strange patterns. Eye and brain work admirably together. The outer is not only related to, it is absorbed into the inner life. And just as the outer order of man, nature, society was displaced and recombined, so too the inner world of passions, thoughts, feelings, intuitions, sensations, interests is shuffled about ruthlessly. The conventional novelist is content not to disturb the conventional order: for in so doing he would upset the stock responses to which his public has become accustomed. So his characters are shown as motivated by sexual love, hatred, social aspirations, patriotism, money, friendship, religion, art—somewhat in that order of importance, with love a very good first indeed. The unconventional novelist —and here she gives due praise to Gissing—modifies the common order of importance, and may introduce new terms into the series. He may even venture to introduce thought as a force.

With all his narrowness of outlook and meagreness of sensibility, Gissing is one of the extremely rare novelists who believe in the power of the mind, who make their people think. They are thus differently poised from the majority of fictitious men and women. The awful hierarchy of the passions is slightly displaced. Social snobbery does not exist; money is desired almost entirely to buy bread and butter; love itself takes a second place. But the brain works, and that alone is enough to give us a sense of freedom. For to think is to become complex; it is to overflow boundaries, to cease to be a "character", to merge one's private life in the life of politics or art or ideas, to have relationships based partly on them, and not on sexual desire alone. The impersonal side of life is given its due place in the scheme.

Again, she might be writing of herself. And for her, of course, there is a special reason, which she does not fail to point out again and again, why the emphasis in her novels should fall differently from of old. Most novelists are men; she is a woman. She sees life from a woman's point of view. She relies more on intuition than on reason. She is interested in the relations not only of men with men, or of men with women, but also of women with women. She is more fascinated by the life of things, such as snails and trees, than with the life of societies, such as churches and banks and schools. She doesn't 'fancy that what we call "life" and "reality" are somehow connected with ignorance and brutality', that realism means sordidness and vice. Action to her means less than meditation and pure *being*.

In a brilliant essay on 'Professions for Women' in the collection *The Death of the Moth* she gives us a most valuable flash of insight into the creative processes of the woman writer's mind. First she shows us how every novelist, whether man or woman, wants to be as unconscious as possible.

He has to induce in himself a state of perpetual lethargy. He wants life to proceed with the utmost quiet and regularity. He wants to see the same faces, to read the same books, to do the same things day after day, month after month, while he is writing, so that nothing may break the illusion in which he is living—so that nothing may disturb or disquiet the mysterious nosings about, feelings round, darts, dashes and sudden discoveries of that very shy and illusive spirit, the imagination. I suspect that this state is the same both for men and women.

Yes, that is probably true. Mr E. M. Forster confirms that creation is an activity which proceeds in a state of trance. The unconscious washes up with its tides over the sands of the conscious, takes control, draws utterly unexpected patterns, leaves deposits of treasure, then retreats. But there is a difference, Virginia Woolf goes on to tell us, in the working of the subconscious as a creative activity in men and in women. She describes her own experience.

> I want you to imagine me writing a novel in a state of trance.
> I want you to figure to yourselves a girl sitting with a pen in her hand, which for minutes, and indeed for hours, she never dips into the inkpot. The image that comes to my mind when I think of this girl is the image of a fisherman lying sunk in dreams on the verge of a deep lake with a rod held out over the water. She was letting her imagination sweep unchecked round every rock and cranny of the world that lies submerged in the depths of our unconscious being. Now came the experience, the experience that I believe to be far commoner with women writers than with men. The line raced through the girl's fingers. Her imagination had rushed away. It had sought the pools, the depths, the dark places where the largest fish slumber. And then there was a smash. There was an explosion. There was foam and confusion. The imagination had dashed itself against something hard. The girl was roused from her dream. She was indeed in a state of the most acute and difficult distress. To speak without figure she had thought of something, something about the body, about the passions which it was unfitting for her as a woman to say. Men, her reason told her, would be shocked. The consciousness of what men will say of a woman who speaks the truth about her passions had roused her from her artist's state of unconsciousness. She could write no more. The trance was over.

In the woman artist's mind, then, there is a censor: a fear of the conventional judgment of the other sex; and this impedes and restricts. Certainly in Virginia Woolf's work we find no extensive survey of the field of the passions; and here, clearly enough, she gives us the reason. So when she speaks of Emily Brontë and Charlotte Brontë as cramped and thwarted by their environment, her indignation is more than impersonal. She has felt the same chains herself.

Thus Virginia Woolf's avoidance of the theme of passionate love does not arise simply from a voluntary shifting of perspective. It comes also from the feeling that she must write frankly of sexual passion, or not at all. The first alternative was impossible when she began writing; and when she, and her generation, had achieved more freedom, she no longer wanted to write about such things. But there *is* a lack there, and a thwarting. There are certain realms of the unconscious which she might have explored, but didn't. It leaves a blank in her canvas.

Nevertheless, it is clear that she found her kingdom. 'All great writers', she tells us in an essay on Henry James, 'have an atmosphere in which they seem most at their ease and at their best; a mood of the great general mind which they interpret and indeed almost discover, so that we come to read them rather for that than for any story or character or scene of separate excellence.' What mood of the great general mind Virginia Woolf discovered is now sufficiently evident. It is a mood at once passive and creative. Passive, in that no overt action is taking place. Active, in that the solitary mind in its communion with things, with pure life and beauty, creates a world of significance: the moment of intuition is achieved, the flash of understanding in which time stands still and there is a perfect happiness.

Out of these separate and fleeting moments no general pattern can honestly be constructed. Nevertheless something remains to the reader, when he turns the last page of her writings, and looks into the red heart of the fire, or gets up and looks out of the window at the garden. There has been an intense re-creation of scenes, and incidents, and persons. There is the conviction of having been in contact with a most gifted and distinguished mind. And more than that. Gradually, without emphasis or preaching or argument, there has grown up a system of values, human values, to which he can give his own allegiance. Virginia Woolf, he finds, has taught him something, or has overwhelmingly strengthened beliefs already held. Like Malvolio, she thinks nobly of the soul of man. She is not to be overawed by size or prestige, by societies or codes of law. Life is sacred, and life alone. The great duty of the individual is to be himself, and to be honest with himself, and not to judge others. Tolerance is the supreme virtue. We must learn to let others alone; this is much more important than helping them, or thanking them. We can do that when they come to us for thanks and help. In other words, we must develop our sensibilities, our understandings: we must send out fine filaments of understanding in all directions, into the world of things as much as into the world of men. Indeed, it is by enlarging our contacts, our imaginative contacts, with things, that we shall come, in solitude, to understand ourselves better and our friends better. We must link up much more than we do with the non-human world.

This we can only bring about by practising non-attachment. First we have to get the ego out of the way, before we can see the divine uniqueness and beauty of things: and with the ego must go all the incrustations around it: possessiveness, greed, uncharitableness and the rest. These are the negative principles which bar our approach to reality. We need to see the world of things and of people with the clear unprejudiced vision of the child. Then all its colour and variety and movement will break upon us and we shall overflow with the happiness of it.

Yet it will not do to fly from the enigma of life, or close our eyes to the evil and suffering. The devotion to truth is as supreme a virtue in the intellectual sphere as tolerance is in the emotional sphere. We have to shun the temptation to make a perfect circle by missing out the bits of life that don't fit. There is a problem at the heart of the universe, which we cannot solve. We cannot find a universal harmony. But we can, from time to time, come into a world where that problem seems to have solved itself in ways we do not understand. These are the moments of vision, which don't last, but are as real while they are in being as are the impacts of evil and suffering. Perhaps, who knows, more real? For they do seem to hold within them *more*, a greater variety of kinds of experience, than do the apprehensions of evil. They hold the laughter of children, and the cleanness of sand, and the joy of friendship, and love, and poetry and music. Moreover, they are creative, where the pang of evil is destructive. They make us want to complete the circle, to take the step forward, the step of faith which Virginia Woolf could not take; which Eleanor, at the end of *The Years*, takes for her.

There must be another life, she thought, sinking back into her chair, exasperated. Not in dreams; but here and now, in this room, with living people. She felt as if she were standing on the edge of a precipice with her hair blown back; she was about to grasp something that just evaded her. There must be another life, here and now, she repeated. This is too short, too broken. We know nothing, even about ourselves. We're only just beginning, she thought, to understand, here and there. She hollowed her hands in her lap, just as Rose had hollowed hers round her ears. She held her hands hollowed; she felt that she wanted to enclose the present moment; to make it stay; to fill it fuller and fuller, with the past, the present and the future, until it shone, whole, bright, deep with understanding.

INDEX

253

INDEX

254

INDEX